THE BRAND NEW
OLD HOUSE
CATALOGUE

Main entrance, Mary McCleod Bethune House, Washington, D.C., as restored and adapted for reuse by Wm. Ward Bucher, architect.

Other Titles in the Old House Books Series

available now

The Old House Book of Living Rooms and Parlors
The Old House Book of Bedrooms

forthcoming

The Old House Book of Outdoor Living Spaces
The Old House Book of Halls and Stairways
The Old House Book of Kitchens and Dining Rooms

THE BRAND NEW OLD HOUSE CATALOGUE

Compiled by Lawrence Grow

WARNER BOOKS

A Warner Communications Company

Designed by Carl Berkowitz

Warner Books, Inc.
75 Rockefeller Plaza
New York, N.Y. 10019

A Warner Communications Company

Printed in the United States of America

First Printing: August 1980

10 9 8 7 6 5 4 3 2 1

Library of Congress Cataloging in Publication Data

GROW, LAWRENCE.

THE BRAND NEW OLD HOUSE CATALOGUE.

1. HISTORIC BUILDINGS—UNITED STATES—CONSERVATION
AND RESTORATION—CATALOGS.   I. TITLE.
TH 3411.G76   1980   728.3'028'8   80-36900
ISBN 0-446-51214-1 (hardcover)
ISBN 0-446-97557-5 (pbk. U.S.A.)
ISBN 0-446-97778-0 (Canada)

Contents

Foreword

The assembly of a book of this sort is an extremely complex operation. From hundreds of sources, the names of craftsmen, manufacturers, suppliers, distributors, artists, dealers in old materials, and consultants and architects are meticulously gathered. Curators of historic houses and museums make many recommendations; other useful suggestions come from contractors and from people active in preservation societies and associated with various private and public agencies. Although several cross-country trips were made to visit with some of the craftsmen and manufacturers, considerable time was also spent investigating the reproduction-materials market in Great Britain, a source for many remarkably fine objects compatible with the traditional trappings of the North American scene. All of this searching is just a beginning.

As important as the search is the evaluation of products and services. Approximately 25 percent of these are selected for write-ups, with another 25 percent listed at the end of each chapter. Fifty percent are rejected completely. In the evaluation process, several considerations are paramount. Someone who renders a service must be available on a regular basis and must possess the credentials required to do a proper job; manufacturers and craftsmen must prove that the objects they can supply are designed and executed in a stylistically proper or documented manner and are made of materials which are both durable and fitting. As best as we can, we also try to determine whether products and supplies are sold and delivered in an efficient and honest manner.

After all materials and information are properly evaluated, the task of compiling the write-ups in a useful manner gets underway. Since we want the book to be as fresh and up-to-date as possible, it is necessary to rush to print as quickly as we can. Lists can be assembled almost instantly, but the writing of textual material requires careful and thoughtful consideration. Advice on how and when to use various products or services is interwoven with the individual write-ups. Additional lists of suppliers are included for each category covered in the various chapters.

Each *Old House Catalogue* is an entirely new book —word for word. New sources are included on nearly every page, and products or services from a source previously acknowledged are new as well. Entirely new items from such important suppliers as San Francisco Victoriana, F. Schumacher, Decorator's Supply, and Period Furniture Hardware, for instance, are featured in *The Brand New Old House Catalogue*. At the same time, however, we are summing up in every chapter—either in the text itself or in the list of additional suppliers at the end of each chapter—those objects or services previously featured. One book thus builds on another in a way that we think is most useful to the ever growing old-house market.

The assembling and writing of *The Brand New Old House Catalogue* has been an effort involving the skills of many people. This writer is particularly indebted to Alexandra Artley, who provided British material from her special observation post in London, and to the staff and members of The Main Street Press back home in the New Jersey countryside who helped to solicit, evaluate, and organize the vast amount of information which arrived almost daily. Supplementary illustrative materials used throughout the book come from a variety of sources, the most important of which is the Historic American Buildings Survey of the National Architectural and Engineering Record, Washington, D.C. Al Chambers and Carter Christianson of the HABS staff and Mary Ison of the Library of Congress' Prints and Photographs Division are owed special thanks for providing most of these photographs.

The assistance of friends and associates in the restoration field who have shared their knowledge so freely is greatly appreciated. Some of these are craftsmen or professionals who have offered their own evaluations of particular products, and, in a number of cases, recommended the work of competitors. The preservation/restoration world is still a friendly one inhabited by individuals who enjoy their work and who labor for more than profit. Long may this spirit prevail.

Introduction

Patience, I learned as a teenager in the local pizza parlor, is *a virtue;* at least that is what an incongruous old-fashioned motto in that plastic emporium proclaimed. In more splendid surroundings, I have since learned that patience is *a necessity*—especially when the work involved concerns the preservation and restoration of period houses. The reasons are simple and become crystal-clear when undertaking any serious project: (1) time—there just aren't enough hours in a day; and (2) money—if one is to use quality materials, and it is foolish not to, the cost prohibits what I would call "the grand San Simeon gesture"; today not even millionaires can always afford to tie up their capital in hundreds of square feet of parquet flooring, ceramic tiling, or 100%-silk fabric.

Whether you are attempting just the basic structural work of preserving a building or stepping further into the fray by restoring its exterior and interior, you are—by default—trying to do the impossible. You are going against the grain. There is nothing efficient in the exercise of restoration, and there are no ready mixes to depend on. Friends may suggest shortcuts; manufacturers of so-called period materials often promise instant fixes which turn out to be far from satisfactory. Salesmen in hardware stores and lumberyards are usually hopeless when it comes to recommending, if not stocking, products which suit a period house. Certain woods, you will have been told, are impossible to find. Even solid-brass curtain rods seem to have disappeared from the inventory of the average hardware store. Don't even

attempt to find shutter dogs—iron shutter hardware—that will stand up in a windstorm. Here and there, however, the tide is turning—away from the quick and easy. But, by and large, once you have entered the world of preservation and restoration, you have left the world of the sane, the rational. The best possible advice for one contemplating a restoration project is that offered recently by Dona Guimaraes in a humorous and incisive *New York Times* article: "Leave well enough alone." But, as she adds, "I wish I could remember that one." No one can —no one, that is, who has been bitten by the bug to save a wreck of a lovely old house. Again, as Dona

9

Guimaraes has recounted, "One would think that after two wreck renovations, that on the third house I would have learned my lesson and settled for a new one. Some women have children; I have houses."

So you're hooked. But you're not alone. It was the realization six years ago that there are many thousands of people with the same interests and problems that led me and my publishing colleagues to launch *The Old House Catalogue* series of books. And it has been our continuing hope that the books would satisfy the needs of many dedicated people in the preservation field and appeal, as well, to a more general audience, an audience of old-house lovers who are just beginning to explore the world of home restoration. Consequently, products and services of various levels of complexity and cost are included throughout the book. Each completely new catalogue—issued every other year—bends in a slightly different direction. We have learned over the past few years that the market for both original and reproduction materials has grown more sophisticated, more specialized, and also more devious. These days there are few major manufacturers or suppliers of building materials who do not offer some form of "antique" product. The kitsch market has exploded, and probably not even a major recession will curb the flow of "wood-like," "brass-like," "stone-like" trash. Manufacturers who are honest, of course, always attach that ubiquitous suffix—"like." Unfortunately, barnwood and a few other products that I could mention contain just enough of the real thing to qualify them as natural—but too little to make them less than odious.

This brings us to the other popular code word of our times—"authentic." I have always been intrigued by the term "an authentic reproduction." "Faithful," I would like to suggest, would be a better adjective. "Documented," a term used by some fabric and wallpaper manufacturers, is an even better way to classify a reproduction. But an "authentic" imitation? Impossible.

Everyone, of course, would like to find an original —perhaps the fireplace mantel that was thrown out in 1928, picture railings that were disposed of years ago when it suddenly seemed much easier to just pound a nail in the wall. It is becoming more and more difficult and expensive to track down the true antique from the Colonial period or the 19th century. Those who are now seeking to restore homes of the early 20th century have a much easier job on their hands. Except in a few urban centers, period building materials from at least World War I through the

1930s are not commonly collectible. If not available in the municipal dumps of our large cities and towns, they are certainly retrievable in salvage yards.

The great heyday of the restoration scavenger was the 1950s and '60s, when whole parts of cities were ripped down in the name of progress. Stained-glass panels were available almost everywhere; today, a large proportion of the existing stock is imported from England. An increasing amount of period material will in fact come from overseas. England also exports antique tiles, mantels, and even complete house frames. The most recent American cities to be tapped for antique materials—St. Louis, Buffalo, Cincinnati, Los Angeles, Memphis—are quickly being mined to the point of exhaustion.

The search for original materials is further compli-

cated by the new vogue for "architectural antiques." Smart shops will now sell a plaster column or wood cornice or terra-cotta ornament for purely decorative purposes, as an accent in an otherwise incongruous, but trendy, setting. Prices are very high for these nostalgic fragments, and are consequently pushing up the prices of truly functional architectural elements which belong in period homes and not on coffee tables. Perhaps it is better that such fragments are treasured rather than smashed to bits, but it is a shame to view their exploitation, their use on such an inappropriate level. The reduction of past craftsmanship to whatnot-status is yet a new step in the debasement of history. We've gotten used to butter-churn lamps and coffee-mill planters, but must we have architrave paperweights?

What's left, then? A good deal—if you have the

patience. You must look first in your own backyard —and look again and again. If you're lucky, you may find that the original owners of your house were puritanically stingy. Perhaps they never threw anything out—at least not any farther than the garage or barn. Perhaps you'll find molding in a barn loft or corner blocks in the attic. Perhaps there'll be Victorian wainscoting under 1930s kitchen tile or porcelain doorknobs in a cigar box hidden in a closet. But, with the exception of a few pieces, it is not easy at first to spot the old materials. That is why I advise looking and looking once again. Old boards were often used for new purposes—as siding in a horse stall; old sash may be serving as a covering for a makeshift cold frame; slats of shutters may hang in one place in the manner of a skeleton, and the frames in another. If

one wants to learn about preservation and restoration, it would be best to talk with experienced carpenters and builders to learn how houses are built. Once you do know something about how old houses were put together, the detective work of tracking down original materials becomes easier, but no less exciting. Knowledge of this sort, of course, also helps in the evaluation of reproductions.

If the backyard and the immediate neighborhood of your old house turn up nothing, then do not give up entirely on the wreckers of our civilization. They will not disappoint you forever. Buildings, unfortunately, will continue to come down whether they are worthy of the wrecker's ball or not, and the resulting debris will often contain spare parts of use to the home restorer. You might even be able to convince a demolition team that a mantel or window sash might

be worth removing before the *coup de grâce.* Then there are the "improvers," that odd tribe as attracted to dropped acoustic ceilings as moths to light. They cosmeticize a building, rendering it totally without character. If any building in your area is being so "improved," get over to the dumpster right away, and don't be afraid of being mistaken for a bag lady. In this fight, anything goes. Door and window hardware is often thrown out with abandon, as is God-knows what else of architectural value.

One last bit of advice in regard to original materials is to consult with such knowledgeable people in the field as curators, historical society officials, even builders or contractors who may have heard of sources in storage or about to become available. Unless you are planning a major purchase such as a whole room end, a mantel, or a stairway, the search for original materials is best conducted on the local or regional level. In the first place, you are more than likely to be searching for pieces which have at least a regional flavor or style. Don't necessarily believe that the beveled-glass transom or raised-panel door is unique to your house. The very same model may have been used in other houses built by the same builder or by one of his colleagues. This is especially true with late-Victorian houses in which the use of assembly-line commercial building products far outweighed those individually crafted. What appears so distinctive to our eyes today may have been commonplace in the past.

Most home restorers limit their search for original materials to those which are most durable, those which are most likely to survive the wear and tear of time. It is rare to find papers and textiles, for instance, which have survived for more than 40 to 50 years in any sort of decent shape. These can be replaced, but the cost is extremely high. For the average home restoration project, such reparation is a prohibitive exercise and not a necessary one. Wallpaper, of course, was changed with abandon during the 19th century, and was often cheaper to use than paint. The truly rare papers were those made by hand in the United States or Europe and which decorated the ultra-sophisticated homes of distinguished families— distinguished either for their wealth or their political renown. The story of textiles is quite similar to that of papers. Until the advent of the power loom in the early 19th century, elaborate patterned materials were not commonly available; a large amount of the fabric used for window hangings, bed hangings, and upholstery was produced in the home or by nearby craftsmen. In any large quantity, fine imported textiles from France, England, and the Far East were obtainable only by the wealthy.

Of all reproduction materials used in home restoration projects, fabrics and papers are among the easiest to obtain and to utilize. Unfortunately, they are not always as well made as they should be. But the story here is no different from that told elsewhere in the reproduction field. When a manufacturer is asked why a certain pattern or finish is not available or is not of the quality expected, the answer is the same: there just aren't enough buyers to justify the production of truly faithful reproductions. In many instances this excuse is now a rather tired one. Ten years ago I listened to a publisher explain that a book on historic preservation entitled *Lost America* would never sell in sufficient quantities to make its publication worthwhile. After it, and its companion volume, had each sold in excess of 20,000 copies, the story changed. Those of us interested in restoration are, ironically, always a little ahead of the times. And it is up to us to prove to those who are investing their money in making goods for the restoration market that, yes, there is a desire "out here" for quality materials of documented value.

The easiest papers and fabrics to obtain are those of a very simple design. They do not call for more than two or three colors or colorways; for the majority of American interiors these are quite sufficient if printed at all well. Most are available in your ordinary paint and paper stores and in fabric outlets. Some, such as the Sturbridge papers, are reasonably accurate renditions of classical designs. Since "Colonial" motifs have dominated the period décor field for years, it is not quite so easy to find patterns which are appropriate for 19th- or early-20th-century interiors. In recent years, William Morris designs have achieved a new popularity; it is to be hoped that others will follow. Especially needed are those Victorian patterns which are simple in composition and color scheme.

The home restorer should not overlook the foreign market for fabrics and papers. This may sound absurd at first, but British manufacturers are encouraging this practice. It is not so terribly difficult to transport or to have shipped such relatively lightweight materials. Nor are they very likely to be damaged in transit. The days of carting whole rooms or parts of them across the Atlantic are nearly at an end, but piece goods are something else. *The Brand New Old House Catalogue* carries special information on various sorts of goods available from England. The value-added tax (VAT) will be payable if an order—

either carried directly from the store by you or shipped by mail—is below a certain amount. The decision is made by each individual store or manufacturer.

It can pay to make a buying trip to London—even with the greatly inflated cost of goods and of lodging. Some of the most ordinary English papers and fabrics —ordinary by English standards—are appropriate for extra-ordinary American interiors. The British have never quite given up on the past; they remain incorrigibly old-fashioned, and thus there is a time-lag there which is of considerable interest to the historically-conscious American buyer. Organdy, satin, velvet, even silk may be available in a pattern that is suitable for your needs and at a price far below that paid in the States. Historically-faithful printed cottons and chintzes can be found almost everywhere you turn. You may wonder whether it is appropriate to use English materials in an American house. At least in terms of papers and fabrics, there should be no problem in most homes. Imports continued throughout the 19th century from the UK and the Continent, and American manufacturers most often copied the lead of their English counterparts.

How materials are manufactured should be of greater concern to the home owner than their place of origin. Papers are often vinyl-backed or finished with a so-called stain repellent as are many fabrics. You may not want this. The backing can cause problems in hanging; the finishes can give a paper or fabric a slick appearance only appropriate for chintzes or satin. There are some who claim that stain-repellent finishes actually hinder the cleaning of materials. Natural fibers, they say, become clogged with the chemical and cannot be dry cleaned or cleansed properly. Unless your old house is occupied by an army of sticky-fingered children, you may wish to leave your fabrics and papers unadulterated.

Natural fabrics, of course, are the best that one can buy. They are likely to last much longer than synthetics, and will—to the experienced eye—present a much better appearance. Anything which is natural costs more these days, and you may have to settle for a blend. Don't expect, however, to throw even such seminatural materials into the "delicate" wash cycle. They will have to be cleaned by hand at home or by a professional.

Owners of late-Victorian homes are often interested in other types of wall covering materials. One of these is Lincrusta-Walton, manufactured here and abroad until the 1930s. It is a heavily-embossed paper which imitates leather or plaster and was used widely in place of wood wainscoting in hallways. Burlap was also used—both below and above a dado —and can be readily purchased today; Lincrusta-Walton has, however, disappeared from view. There are several imitations available on the market today which successfully achieve the same result. The best are available from England.

Floor coverings are traditionally understood today as being woven. A great deal of recent research, however, has indicated that the materials used underfoot in North American in the past were a great deal more diversified. Consequently, workshops in various areas of the country have begun to produce such items as canvas floorcloths for use in 18th-century and early-19th-century interiors. Their popularity has spread rapidly, and we are now in danger of being flooded with patterns which are inappropriate. Amish quilt designs, for instance, are being employed, and, while handsome, they are not in the slightest way authentic as patterns for floor covering. This pinpoints a problem also encountered with papers and fabrics—the use of attractive traditional designs that derive from one form and, historically, at least, are not appropriate for another. Eventually, of course, these designs are further adulterated by being stamped on everything from dishes to dishrags. In time, they simply become a bore and fade from fashion. New documentary designs take their place in popularity and are in turn perverted by the kitsch purveyors.

Other types of floor covering sought by the restorer are Wilton and Axminster carpets as well as Brussels. Needlepoint rugs have faded in popularity. Orientals are still used in many Colonial-period homes and, in some cases, are out of place if the intention is period authenticity. Indeed, straw might be a more fitting finish. The owners of early 19th-century homes have particular difficulty in finding reproductions of early carpeting patterns, some of which may have been laid wall to wall. Scalamandré was one of the earliest American firms to reproduce such designs; the prices, however, are very high. So, too, are they at Stark. The tide, however, is turning. A number of American museums and historical societies have been ordering custom-made carpeting of the Wilton and Axminster variety for period rooms. Once the initial work is done in "programming" the loom (and this is an exceedingly complex and costly process), prices will come down fairly rapidly. Keep your eyes open for interesting carpeting that you see in various museums, and inquire about its source.

The ubiquitous braided oval still holds on in popularity. The difficulty today is to find one that is made of natural material and in colors that are fitting. You may find that the standard commercial types are completely unacceptable. If so, there are a number of craftsmen and small workshops that produce braided and rag rugs from natural fibers and who use natural dyes.

Later 19th-century rugs and carpeting are not terribly difficult to locate. The wall-to-wall carpeting that was popular earlier in the 19th century fell into disuse and was replaced, for the most part, by large area rugs or carpets. These are of the familiar Brussels type found in all rug emporiums and department stores. Some feature Chinese designs and others Middle-Eastern patterns. True orientals, of course, came into widespread use as floor coverings in the second half of the 19th century and, if affordable, can be used in practically any home that was obviously at one time a prosperous one. Orientals do look a bit out of place, however, in a modest workingman's cottage or row house.

The most important flooring material is, naturally, wood. Original wide-plank boards of pine can still be found fairly easily; the reproductions—if not specially made—are common and often repellent. Simulated pegs add nothing; thickness is sometimes insufficient. Originals may be of yellow pine, a much harder material than today's common pine. If you are going to replace boards, try to find the yellow— even though it is more costly. It is being recycled now from old industrial buildings.

The vogue for stenciling—on floors and walls— has practically become a mania. It is now "in" to have a stenciled border around windows, doors, and cornice, whether appropriate or not. There is no doubt that such surfaces were sometimes covered in various ways—stenciled, spattered, painted in solid colors— from the 18th century to the mid-19th century, and even later in less settled areas of the country. Patterns for do-it-yourself decoration are found in almost all decorating magazines from time to time and can be bought from special suppliers. What is right for a Federal room, however, may not be at all suitable for a Victorian town house.

Hardwood flooring is found in many 19th- and early-20th-century American homes. Happily, it hardly resembles the #2 oak commonly used today. With luck, antique floors will need only cleaning and not replacement or even patching. If they do need intensive work, however, then you probably will have to consult a supplier of specialty woods, of which there are many across the country. As long as wood-working remains one of the popular American hobbies, supplies of fine hardwoods will remain available.

For generations paint has been used as a quick way to cover up, to achieve a different mood, to generally "clean up" an interior. We know a good deal about the colors used in Colonial times and are beginning to discover the color values of our more recent ancestors. There are no commercially-available Victorian paint lines—not even in San Francisco. (The first such selection of Victorian colors is in preparation by Sherwin-Williams.) Colonial colors, however, are legion—Martin-Senour's "Williamsburg" line, Turco's "Sturbridge," Finnaren & Haley's "Historic Philadelphia," Devoe's "Historical Charleston," and on and on. Some of these shades or combinations of them have become too well known, in fact. The Victorian houses of San Francisco, the famous "painted ladies," are a relief when you are used to the dowdy matrons of Williamsburg, but in both cases, too much of one thing—shocking pink or mustard yellow—can become tedious. Experiment with paint and come up with your own colors, making full use of the tinting shades. Make certain, however, that at least your exterior paints are oil-based. Latex products often end up in great flaky ribbons of paint and do not have a muted finish which is pleasant to the eye.

It probably goes without saying that siding—except for natural shingling or clapboarding—is completely out of the question for the old house. Aluminum, vinyl, or fiberglass appeal to two needs today: insulation and freedom from painting. In the latter case, unfortunately, the artificial materials look awful and are more than likely to cause the original siding underneath to rot away for lack of air.

Other artificial products which you may be tempted to use are made of polyurethane. Any number of professional restorers have asked that these be removed from *The Old House Catalogue* series, but we continue to include them. In addition to decorative moldings, niches, shells, door and window casings, etc., there are many other polyurethane products, and their number will probably increase. I can understand the objections to these replacements for the real things: they are not as well defined as wood or plaster; they lack the necessary weight, and each decoration so produced is one less crafted by an artisan. The polyurethane substitutes, however, can be recommended as decorative fillers. Because of their lightness and malleability, they can be fitted into place with considerable ease.

One of the more professional and well-developed areas of the home restoration market is that devoted to lighting. We've come a long way from the days when anything resembling a light bulb had to be tucked away into a recess or an inappropriate fixture. Today nearly every kind of period fixture is available in reproduction form—from simple iron candlestands to gas-electric combinations. The important thing to check is the design and construction of the fixture. Is it plated or solid? Is the key on the gas wall bracket merely decorative or does it actually turn? Period fixtures have become so popular that standards have fallen. There are some wild combinations on the market, as witness the Victorian gasolier with swag chain, a form that unites Kennedy-era Holiday Inn design with that of the turn of the century. Cheap stained-glass lamps of the so-called Tiffany style are a dime a dozen. If lead or zinc is used at all, it is a sliver of material that barely holds the panels together. The glass itself is not of the subtle type associated with the best Victorian work, but of a flashy, garish tone. Avoid these horrors even if you're tempted to believe that the pony-tailed entrepreneur is really, as he pretends to be, a craftsman.

If your house dates from the second half of the 19th century, try at first to find original fixtures. There are a number of antique lighting dealers, and not all the fixtures have ended up in steakhouses or period barrooms. If it is possible and economical for you to use gas, fine, but, if not, old fixtures can be easily converted for electricity.

Colonial-period fixtures have been available in excellent reproductions for many years—sconces, chandeliers, lanterns, taperjacks, you name it. Electric candles are made which simulate a wax taper in almost every respect except for the flame. Personally, I have an adversion to the flicker-type and am even unsettled by mirrored wall sconces that reflect a steady, low glow. I'd rather use candles if possible in what were, after all, candleholders, and, for daily use, an old kerosene or oil lamp base with an electric adapter. Kerosene lamps are increasingly popular in this time of energy conservation, and the Aladdin model is one of the safest and most useful.

In choosing lighting fixtures, you will probably find that specialty dealers will offer you the widest selection and the best possible quality. The initial prices will be somewhat high, but the investment is among the best you can make for an old house. Attractive, sturdy fixtures are most likely to remain in place if you sell such a home, and they add measurably to its resale value. Properly made—and the UL code is followed almost universally by knowledgeable craftsmen—they will last as long as the house itself.

So, too, will fine hardware. You may be fortunate in having found a house that has not been unduly tampered with. On the other hand, it is more than likely that you will find that hinges, doorknobs, locks, latches, etc., are missing here and there or have been replaced with something inappropriate. Unless you are looking for wooden box locks or a clock jack for the kitchen fireplace, you should be able to find either original or reproduction materials without too much trouble. Again, as with lighting, the main problem is that of quality. You want to make certain that what you get is as solid as possible. If one of several large suppliers does not have what you want, then you may need to turn to a blacksmith who can custom-meet your needs. Fortunately, the art of blacksmithing has known a renaissance in the past ten years, and nearly every area of the country has its own resident smithy who can turn out cranes, locks, hooks, as well as lighting fixtures. Until recently the owner of a Victorian home has had to depend on the salvage market for hardware supplies. Now even such a traditional "Colonial"-style manufacturer as Ball and Ball supplies the sort of heavy brass decorative pieces indispensable for a well-turned-out Victorian door or cabinet.

The search for original and reproduction old-house materials is guided by three major considerations—time, money, and effort. The urge is always to "improve" things just as quickly as possible with the least possible effort and cost. The temptation to seize on what is readily available and easily worked into place is very difficult to resist if the price is right. But patience has its rewards. There are too many purveyors of old items and manufacturers of new who are all-too-happy to gratify one's desire for neatness, order, and accomplishment instantly. The question of whether an item is appropriate in style and form should be answered first, but this is by no means the only matter of importance. How durable is the object? How much maintenance will it require? Is it something integral to the expression of a period style or merely a passing fancy to be consigned to the attic or a garage sale ten years hence? The answers to these questions cannot be fully given in *The Brand New Old House Catalogue.* Each house has its own particular problems and needs. The process of finding, evaluating, and using a wide variety of materials, however, can be made a much less frustrating exercise with the use of this book. The process of restoring a room or a complete house should be an invigorating and satisfying project. We're still learning, sweating, and, yes, even smiling, after ten years of tackling the legacy of the past, its problems and its pleasures.

A Visual Chronology of Historic Architectural Styles

Recognition of particular period architectural styles can aid the home restorer and decorator in making important stylistic decisions. The terms "Colonial" and "Victorian" are useful in a general way, but they convey little sense of a particular time when a house achieved its stylistic character. Not every house in North America, of course, can be categorized in a neat, scholarly manner; the majority of old buildings are probably what is termed "vernacular" or display a mingling of period styles. Nearly all such buildings, however, partake of some of the elements of one or more well-defined styles. The following "models" are by no means perfect themselves, but each makes a conscious stylistic statement of historical interest and value.

In dating various period styles, the author is indebted to John J.-G. Blumenson, whose small volume *Identifying American Architecture* is a model of useful scholarship. The reader will find much material in this book which helps to fill in the outlines presented below and on the following pages.

Pueblo / Spanish and *Spanish Colonial*
1598-1848   1600-1840

Private residence, Santa Fe, New Mexico, early 1700s

16

Early New England Colonial
1620-1700

Thomas Clemence House, Johnston, Rhode Island, c. 1680

Early New England Georgian Colonial
1700-1750

Private residence, Westport, Massachusetts, 1710, 1720

Early and Late Middle Atlantic Georgian Colonial
1700-1800

Joseph Collins House, West Chester vicinity, Pennsylvania, 1727, 1760

Late Georgian Colonial (common to New England, Middle Atlantic, and Southern states)
1750-1800

"Cessford," Eastville, Virginia, mid-1700s

Federal
1780-1820

Colonel John Black House, Ellsworth, Maine, 1824-27

Greek Revival
1820-1860

"Rattle and Snap," Columbia vicinity, Tennessee, 1845

Gothic Revival
1830-1860

"Roseland," The Bowen House, Woodstock, Connecticut, mid-19th century

19

Italian Villa
1830-1880

Mills-Stebbins House, Springfield, Massachusetts, 1849-51

Italianate
1840-1880

Private residence, Evanston, Illinois, 1860s, 1872

Renaissance Revival
1840-1890

India House, New York City, 1850s

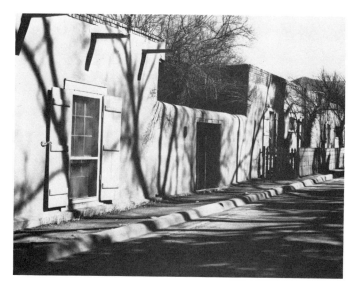

Territorial
1846-1912

El Zaguan, Santa Fe, New Mexico, 1840s, 1860s

Second Empire or Mansard
1860-1890

Private residence, San Francisco, California, 1871, 1895

Colonial Revival
1870-1920

Private residence, Little Rock, Arkansas, 1897-99

Queen Anne and *Eastlake*
1880-1900

Jeremiah Nunan House, Jacksonville, Oregon, 1891-92

Shingle
1880-1900

"Glenmont," West Orange, New Jersey, 1880

Spanish Colonial Revival and *Mission*
1890-1940

Private residence, Chico, California, 1928

Prairie
1890-1920

Frank Lloyd Wright House and Studio, Oak Park, Illinois, 1889, 1895

Bungalow
1890-1940

Private residence, Houston, Texas, 1929

English Tudor
1880-1940

F.H. Stuart House, Akron, Ohio, 1926

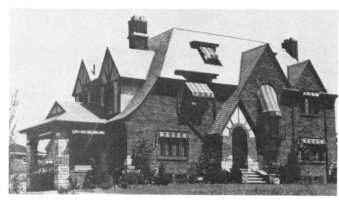

Pueblo
1905-1940

Private residence, Santa Fe, New Mexico, 1920s

Moderne
1930-1945

Kowalski House, Mt. Kisco, New York, 1934

Most of the illustrations have been drawn from the archives of the Historic American Buildings Survey, Heritage Conservation and Recreation Service, Washington, D.C.

THE BRAND NEW
OLD HOUSE
CATALOGUE

Wirick-Simmons House, Monticello, Florida, 1830s, as photographed in
1962 by Jack E. Boucher for the Historic American Buildings Survey.

1 Structural Products & Services

More space is devoted to products and services relating to structural needs than to any other section of *The Brand New Old House Catalogue* for one very simple reason—preservation must take precedence over restoration. In the rush to decorate a house, to endow it with period charm, there is often a tendency to forget the more important task of keeping things together. Although much that the old-house owner may require to prevent a building from collapsing around him can be found at the local lumberyard or hardware store, there are special sorts of things that must come from remote sources. In preserving a house for its future use, replacement parts cannot be chosen haphazardly. The window sash found in an 1820 Federal town house, for instance, is likely to contain a minimum of six lights or panes of glass. If such sash has deteriorated badly and must be replaced, one-piece modern plate-glass panels would be much cheaper to have made. They would also destroy the architectural character of the house from both inside and out.

Window sash, doors, columns, building materials such as brick and clapboarding, flooring, beams, roofing materials—these are the basic structural elements which not only help to hold a house together but provide the fundamental ground for its style. Few old houses have survived without some alteration, but most retain enough of the original plan and its execution that it is possible to determine how a structure *should* look. Working toward that goal, one can then proceed to shore up what is fundamental or replace those parts which are irretrievable with something that is compatible with the whole.

A considerable amount of attention is given to the services of preservation/restoration consultants in the following pages. They are experts in adapting old buildings for new uses. With historical knowledge and technical expertise, they can work the kinds of subtle, but fitting, changes which can add years of useful life to an aging building. Assistance of this sort, however, is not needed on a majority of projects. Most of us cannot afford the services of such experts and have to proceed slowly on our own, hoping that what we are doing makes some sense. It is good to know, however, that help can be summoned on even a small detail when and if needed.

Architectural antiques dealers and suppliers of old-house materials are superb sources for used or reproduction replacement parts. The number of suppliers increases each year as the pace of rehabilitation quickens and the cost of new construction continues to skyrocket. Decorative embellishments, rather than basic materials, are often stressed by such traders, but the general level of offerings and of craftsmanship is high. These suppliers are experts, of course, in providing the period stylistic embellishments such as cornice moldings, drip caps, stained-glass windows, finials, and pediments, which make a house a distinctive home. At the same time, however, they probably possess the skills and knowledge required to execute reproduction parts which will

25

fool even an architectural historian.

A large number of the architectural-materials suppliers and craftsmen are young people. They have been attracted to the field because it offers them an opportunity to work with honest, quality materials and to develop individual skills which will last them a lifetime. The young stonecutters now at work on the Cathedral of St. John the Divine in New York City are building something great, and they know it. The work of cutting away at solid rock is rendered no less difficult by the possession of this knowledge, but pride in workmanship and participation in a cause more compelling than the self are considered more important. So it is in preservation, especially in those phases of it which concern the fundamentals of building.

Restoration Consultants and Contractors

Since the early 1960s rebuilding of old homes along authentic period lines has become an important aspect of the construction business in North America. Whole urban neighborhoods have been rehabilitated in the past twenty years, and there is no sign that the pace of work is slowing down. When new construction comes to a virtual halt, as it has in 1980, rehabilitation and restoration activity usually increases. Rebuilding a private residence or restoring some aspect of it may not be an inexpensive proposition, but it usually does not involve the sort of mortgage financing called for in new construction. Restoration, however, often requires the kind of expertise which cannot be summoned up easily. Restoration consultants and contractors can bring to a project the skills, knowledge, and persistence which the home owner cannot often supply.

Sources listed first are those which are new to this volume. These are followed by firms and individuals previously, but no less enthusiastically, recommended.

Atwood & Tremblay Associates

This is a general contracting firm with a special interest in preserving 18th-century properties. Old northeastern homes are located, dismantled, and re-erected throughout the United States. The firm is prepared to supply either old materials or to fabricate new ones wherever needed. With a crew skilled in carpentry, plumbing and electrical work, masonry, and iron work, the contractor can be expected to achieve a proper level of adaptation which respects the historical record but allows for modern living convenience.

Atwood & Tremblay Associates, Inc.
Timber Swamp Road
Hampton, NH 03842
(603) 926-8625

Babcock Barn Homes

Homes created from old barns have been part of the contemporary architectural portfolio since the 1950s. At first barns were converted for use as studios and guest houses and grad-

Dutch Type Barn

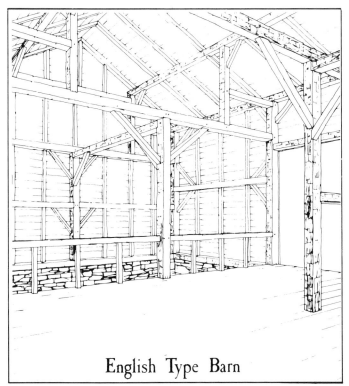

English Type Barn

ually assumed fuller domestic use. Unlike many of the so-called barn homes available today, designs which are only *inspired* by traditional forms, Richard Babcock's barns are the real thing. One of the pioneers in saving and recycling such structures in the East, he continues to search out both Dutch and English types as illustrated here. Dismantling such structures can be a tricky matter, but Babcock's familiarity with the history of building types makes the job easier and that of reassembling more thoughtful and imaginative.

Printed literature available.

Babcock Barn Homes
P.O. Box 484
Williamstown, MA 01267
(413) 458-3334
(413) 738-5639

Wm. Ward Bucher, Architect

The multifaceted character of today's preservation consultant is exemplified by the Bucher group which provides architectural design, restoration research, period landscape design, feasibility studies, construction management, and museum exhibit design. Adaptive reuse of old structures, particularly in urban areas, is one area of special interest and expertise. The firm's report on commercial reuse of existing buildings in Washington's DuPont Circle area (the Connecticut Avenue-P Street Project) clearly outlines the difficult economic, social, aesthetic, and environmental problems which have to be addressed in any changing neighborhood. This report is available for $3. The urban scene is not the sole focus of the firm's work. Shown are a country house in Lebanon Township, Hunterdon Coun-

ty, New Jersey, which required interior renovation, and drawings of various porch elements which had to be replaced.

Wm. Ward Bucher, Architect
1638 R Street, N.W.
Washington, DC 20009
(202) 387-0061

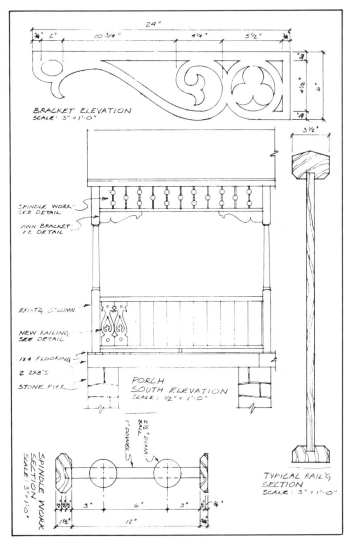

R. H. Davis, Inc.

Those who appreciate good wood and fine carpentry will understand Richard Davis's love of the Colonial and 19th-century New England house. He has constructed a replica of a frame schoolhouse at the Hancock, Massachusetts, Shaker Village and completed various restoration projects for the community. His services are available throughout New England.

Brochure available, $2.

R. H. Davis, Inc.
Antrim, NH 03440
(603) 588-6885

Clovis Heimsath Associates

Interest in the whole range of historic preservation and restoration—architecture, the decorative arts, and environmental quality—has led Clovis Heimsath, F.A.I.A., to undertake many different kinds of projects in urban, small town, and rural areas. He is the author of *Pioneer Texas Buildings*, one example of which is shown under restoration here. The Fayetteville Workshop, a group of artists working in traditional craft areas, was founded under his aegis and continues to supply useful materials for various projects.

Clovis Heimsath Associates
On the Square
Fayetteville, TX 78940
(713) 378-2712
(Houston) (713) 522-0777

Allen Charles Hill, A.I.A.

New Englanders considering major restoration of their own homes or of churches, office buildings, stores, or historic

buildings might be well advised to contact an experienced preservation architect such as Allen Charles Hill. He can not only do the preliminary studies necessary for successfully launching such projects, but can provide suitable design and manage its execution. In his own words: "We bring to our work a commitment to the preservation and continued use of old buildings and places and devote intensive personal attention to meeting our clients' needs." This is as it should be.

Allen Charles Hill, A.I.A.,
Historical Preservation and Architecture
25 Englewood Road
Winchester, MA 01890
(617) 729-0748

The Acquisition & Restoration Corp.

By the end of 1980 nearly 200 restoration or renovation projects will have been completed in this Indianapolis-based firm's 14-year history. These are buildings found throughout the United States. The work includes consultation, general contracting, and interior design.

The Acquisition & Restoration Corp.
1226 Broadway
Indianapolis, IN 46202
(317) 632-1461

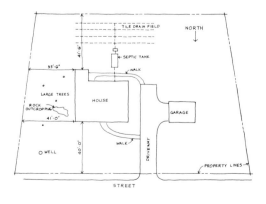

Project: _____   **Site Plan**   **Northeast American Heritage Co.** **1**
Date: _____   **Example**
Notes:

INSTRUCTIONS FOR DRAWING SITE PLAN

1. Obtain site plan, plot plan or survey from personal records, registry of deeds, local building department, assessor's office or other source.
2. If the above document only shows property lines and does not show your house, measure perpendicularly from the property lines to the corners of the house and draw in the house once you have completed drawing your first floor plan. If you cannot locate property lines, you can have a surveyor do this.
3. Indicate locations of utility lines, (water, gas, electricity, storm sewer, sanitary sewer), septic systems, wells, outbuildings (garages, sheds), driveways, sidewalks, retaining walls and major natural features of the site.
4. It is very important to indicate on the site plan which compass direction is north.
5. If buildings on adjoining properties are relatively close, show their locations as accurately as possible.
6. Note that the printed site plan form is gridded in ¼ inch squares. Use one square per 5 feet to obtain scale of 1 inch equaling 20 feet, or establish some other scale to show all pertinent data at as large a scale as possible.

Northeast American Heritage Co.

Someone has the right idea. David M. Hart, A.I.A., and his associates in Boston provide the old house owner with custom design services by mail. It all begins with the owner completing the forms in a "Custom DesignPak" (cost, $7) which can be ordered from the firm. One page from this, the "Site Plan Example," is illustrated here. Once the material is returned to the firm—with measurements of rooms, rough plan of property, description of proposed changes, floor plans, and photographs—the owner can request various services. These might include something as routine but useful as an "evaluation of your restoration plans and a written report on them" (for a fee of approximately $125) or more elaborate schematic plans and preliminary construction cost estimates and outline specifications along with a written report (for a fee of approximately $325). If full architectural services are desired, then what has developed as a relationship through the mail will require a more direct and personal approach by both parties.

Northeast American Heritage Co.
77 Washington Street North, Suite 535
Boston, MA 02114
(617) 227-2932

The same firm, but under the name of David McLaren Hart & Associates, A.I.A., is ready to provide custom restoration of homes and commercial buildings from the earliest Colonial style to much more recent period interpretations such as the bungalow or Colonial Revival dwelling. The team consists of four architects, a building conservator, architectural historian, and a laboratory technician who performs historic paint and mortar analysis and metal identification.

David McLaren Hart & Associates, A.I.A.
(Same address and telephone number as above.)

Mark F. Pfaller Associates

The restoration or rehabilitation of historic structures, mainly public buildings such as churches, theaters, and other institutional facilities, is a specialty of this architectural firm. Mark F. Pfaller Associates can provide such services of particular interest to home owners as historic furnishings plans, research and documentation of structures to assure proper restoration techniques, and advice on the financial aspects of restoration as they apply to buildings which have achieved state or National Register status.

Mark F. Pfaller Associates, Inc.
3112 W. Highland Blvd.
Milwaukee, WI 53208
(414) 344-5350

The Preservation Partnership

Experience and expertise are shared by all the principal members of this consulting team headed by Maximilian L. Ferro,

A.I.A., R.I.B.A. When one considers that the group has been entrusted with the restoration of America's oldest surviving house, the Fairbanks House (1636) in Dedham, Massachusetts, then there is little to fear in its stewardship of almost any project. Like other restoration firms, it offers a wide variety of services of use to private individuals as well as groups or publicly-funded organizations.

The Preservation Partnership
74 W. Central Street
Natick, MA 01760
(617) 237-3735

Richard L. Sanderson

A contractor, Richard L. Sanderson can bring his firm's abilities to bear on almost any aspect of a restoration project. In addition, he is prepared to undertake new construction along traditional lines, and to provide reproduction materials.

Richard L. Sanderson
210 Michigan Avenue
Sturgis, MI 49091
(616) 651-4097

J. Gordon Turnbull, A.I.A.

A handsome mixture of contemporary and traditional designs has been executed and supervised through the building stage by this innovative team of architects. The principal in the firm is the former architect of The Foundation for San Francisco's Architectural Heritage. An addition to an old structure is harmoniously conceived and executed after the existing building is carefully studied. Illustrated is an elevation of the Sidney Unobskey residence in San Francisco which overlooks the Bay and which was restored by the Turnbull group.

Brochure available.

J. Gordon Turnbull, A.I.A.
Architectural/Preservation/Planning
15 Vandewater Street
San Francisco, CA 94133
(415) 788-3954

Halstead S. Welles Associates

Design of period gardens is by no means outside the perimeters of restoration. Since most plantings do not survive more than several generations, preservation is often out of the question. One of the firms which has specialized in Victorian town-house gardens—both backyard and front—is Halstead S. Welles Associates. The firm's work has been confined largely to New York City, but the Tom Thumb Nursery, which it owns, is located in Nyack, New York. Here may be found the special kinds of trees and shrubs required for city plantings as well as other unusual stock. It is open to the public Tuesdays through Sundays.

Halstead S. Welles & Associates
287 E. Houston Street
New York, NY 10002
(212) 777-5440

Tom Thumb Nursery
South Blvd.
Nyack, NY 10960
(914) EL8-3269

Included in the following listings are restoration consulting firms that have been recommended in previous editions. It is a pleasure to recommend them again and to include additional information on their work.

Townsend Anderson

This craftsman is a house joiner in the best New England tradition, ready and able to put together the pieces which define the best heavy-timber braced-frame construction. He has recently formed a partnership with Gary Bressor and Richmond Restorations of Richmond, Vermont, and they have begun a project involving the reconstruction of seven Vermont houses. They'll also be reclaiming the farmlands which are an integral part of the overall project. Shown is the "Robert Bundy House" as found in Bethel, Vermont, and as it is being reconstructed in Richmond.

Brochure available, $1.

Townsend H. Anderson
R. D. 1, Box 44D
Moretown, VT 05660
(802) 244-8843

Arch Associates/Stephen Guerrant

Home inspection services are among those emphasized by this Chicago-area restoration specialist and architect. Arch Associates provides all the other customary services. It will also help with interior design and furnishing that is, in its own words, "directed toward historical compatability with architectural form."

Arch Associates/Stephen Guerrant
874 Greenbay Road
Winnetka, IL 60093
(312) 446-7810

A. W. Baker Restorations, Inc.

Anne Baker is skilled as a consultant and contractor. She has proved her ability to interpret the historical past in both a realistic and imaginative manner over and over again. Illustrated is one such challenge—the joining together of two houses to make one. The first and second photographs show the elements which came together in the third photograph after much preliminary research of a documentary, structural, and archaeological sort; disassembly of both buildings; and their reassembly. The client discovered the two buildings (he was searching for only one) and insisted that they be brought to-

gether. In Anne Baker's own words:

"Careful dismantling and architectural investigation revealed that both structures were excellent examples of 17th-century Rhode Island 'stone-enders.' The hip roof section of the two-story house [photograph #1] was an 18th-century addition, the remaining area all 17th century, although the chimney had been replaced by a brick stack.

The Cape, #2, . . . had been a two-story house and ell originally. The first story had been removed 150 years ago. . . , the house lowered, and the area next to the ell squared out, creating a center chimney Cape. Consequently, a great deal of the original fabric had been destroyed, including the chimney. However, we were able to recycle the timbers from the 18th-century section of house #1 into the needs of #2.

The re-erection of these two structures became the real challenge—how to put them together as one structure without losing the architectural integrity of either."

Seriously interested in old house restoration? Call Anne Baker.

Brochure, résumé, and fee schedule available upon request.

A. W. Baker Restorations, Inc.
670 Drift Road
Westport, MA 02790
(617) 636-8765

Historic Boulevard Services

William and Alys Lavicka have undertaken more than $350,000 worth of renovation construction. They combine both design and contracting services in the manner of the carpenter/builder of the past and are very sensitive to the need for fine materials and even finer craftsmanship in every aspect of a house's restoration.

Historic Boulevard Services
1520 W. Jackson Blvd.
Chicago, IL 60607
(312) 829-5562

Howell Construction

Custom housebuilding of the best sort is by no means alien to the field of restoration. Howell devotes the same care and attention to its old house projects as it does to those built anew.

Howell Construction
2700 12th Avenue S.
Nashville, TN 37204
(615) 269-5659

Preservation Associates

This firm continues to offer full restoration and custom-made items to match the original fabric of a building. The two principals, Douglass C. Reed and Paula Stoner, are knowledgeable and understanding of old house needs. He is the author of three booklets—*From Tree to Beam, America's Mortise and Tenon,* and *Log Cabin Mythology*—which can be ordered directly from the firm at $1.60 each, postage paid. Preservation Associates will also build authentic reproduction log houses.

Brochure available.

Preservation Associates
P.O. Box 202
Sharpsburg, MD 21782
(301) 432-5466

Preservation Resource Group, Inc.

This Virginia-based educational and consulting firm is also a useful source of technical books, including many listed in the bibliography of this volume. It is also a handy place from which to order tools and instruments useful for restoration work. For further information on one such tool, a profile gauge called "Form-A-Gage," see the tool listings in Chapter 3.

Preservation Resource Group
5619 Southampton Drive
Springfield, VA 22151
(703) 323-1407

Rambusch

The Rambusch Co. celebrated its 80th birthday last year, and, by that time, this legendary firm had completed over 18,000 major projects. The work of at least the most recent years could probably not be done by any other company, for Rambusch consists of eight shops: a stained glass studio, art metal shop, mural and sculpture studio, painting and decorating studio, liturgical design service, general contracting department, restoration services department, and a lighting division. With over 80 employees, it can take on such major restorations as the Ballantine House in Newark, New Jersey, and the redoing of Boscobel in Garrison, New York. Exterior restoration can be done by other firms, but, for the true landmark interior rich with decorative architectural materials, Rambusch should be consulted.

Brochure available.

The Rambusch Company
40 W. 13th Street
New York, NY 10011
(212) 675-0400

Restorations Unlimited

This firm specializes in the renewal of old kitchens, primarily those of Victorian vintage. Restoration work in this most functional area of the house, as many consultants have learned, requires a delicate balance between historical and present-day needs. Not even the most antiquated housewife is likely to

want to put up with a hand pump, icebox, or coal stove. A monitor-top refrigerator might have added "charm" to the kitchen illustrated here, but little else. It was better that the kitchen of the 1903 Swab House was supplied with attractive cabinets, an embossed steel ceiling, ceiling fan, and up-to-date appliances. The handsome coal stove can still be used, but no one has to depend on it every day. Restorations Unlimited is a dealer for Rich Craft Custom Kitchens and features its special cabinets.

Restorations Unlimited, Inc.
24 W. Main Street
Elizabethville, PA 17023
(717) 362-3477

San Francisco Victoriana

Various restoration materials available from this best known of West Coast firms is featured in almost every section of *The Brand New Old House Catalogue.* There has been no slowdown in production or reduction in the quality of services offered over the past two years. All operations, however, have been centralized in one location which formerly served as the company's warehouse.

San Francisco Victoriana
2245 Palou Avenue
San Francisco, CA 94124
(415) 864-5477

The Valentas

You may have to wait in line for assistance from this family of talented craftsmen. The pace is still frantic and the amount of time limited in which to undertake restoration work. The Valentas will, however, be glad to do what they can via the mail (or UPS), consulting on particular problems with woods and finishes that can be diagnosed with the use of samples.

The Valentas
2105 S. Austin Blvd.
Cicero, IL 60650
(312) 652-7485

Other Restoration Services

Historical documentation and interpretation can be performed by almost all of the consultants and contractors recommended previously. There are specialists, however who are expert in doing the often necessary work of compiling a building's curriculum vitae prior to the start of any restoration work.

T. Robins Brown

Professional services on a contractual basis are provided to various public and private organizations and to individual home owners by T. Robins Brown. These are basically of a historical nature and may involve study of building materials and of how a building or group of buildings evolved in form, and information on those who built and have lived in the building. This consultant can also initiate and complete the often onerous task of completing forms required for placing a building on the various registers of historic places.

T. Robins Brown
12 First Avenue
Nyack, NY 10960
(914) 358-5229

Ellen Beasley

A preservation planning consultant, Ellen Beasley is well-known for her work on projects in Tennessee and Texas; she has also worked with the National Trust for Historic Preservation on some of its properties. Thoroughly versed in the history of domestic architecture and period interior design, she can provide both the documentation necessary for a restoration plan and the technical know-how required to put it into action successfully.

Ellen Beasley
P.O. Box 1145
Galveston, TX 77553
(713) 762-9852

One of the best preservation tools of all is an attractive portrait of your house or one that you and others are trying to save. While architects and consultants can often produce miracles with the bureaucrats who make so many of the decisions concerning our neighborhoods and their future, a picture can be worth more than a thousand words, especially if the artist is...

Joan Baren

She has kindly given us permission to reproduce this pen and ink drawing of the Matthew Topping House. Her evocative drawings of historic American homes, farms, and neighborhoods are available on commission. She will work on location or from suitable photographs. She always finds the distinctive in the structure, the character which renders it more than a personality-less construct from the past.

Brochure available.

Joan Baren
Sag Harbor, NY 11963
(516) 725-0372

Reproduction Period Homes

The rediscovery since World War II of the clean, honest lines of early American architecture has been marked by the diffusion of thousands of ready-made house designs or plans. The majority of such designs leave much to be desired. Regional differences were great in the 17th and 18th centuries, and it is often difficult to determine whether a particular modern plan derives from Massachusetts (Sturbridge), the Middle Atlantic states, or Virginia (Williamsburg). Late Georgian high-style elements are often applied to a simple clapboard house with casement windows dating from the 1600s. Brick laid with an inappropriate mortar is often juxtaposed with cedar shakes and both are combined with fake stone facing to form what can only be described as an abortive mess. Most of the modern designs are drawn with the use of assembly-line synthetic materials in mind. Unfortunately, use of such substitutes is a waste if the appearance of an authentic period house is the only aim.

If you wish to start from scratch and to build a new home that meets minimal historical standards, it would be best to consult a knowledgeable custom builder. Some of the restoration specialists such as Townsend Anderson and Preservation Associates can help you in this respect. The skills of the housewright and joiner have not been completely lost. Old skills have been relearned in workshops across North America; new materials can be handled and used in a way that is honest and convincing. And there are ready-made plans which can be adapted to your particular needs.

Birch Hill Builders

Eugenie Wallas was part of the original Housesmith group which reintroduced the public to timber framing. This form is well illustrated in the two photographs. Birch Hill builds complete houses in the York, Maine, area and can ship a custom frame to a builder anywhere in the United States. Native white pine is used in the traditionally joined frame. These can be pur-

chased either rough sawn or hand planed; studs, windows, doors, sheathing, etc., are not shipped. Birch Hill also offers *The Timber Framing Book* ($11.95 plus $1 postage) by Stewart Elliott and Eugenie Wallas, but this should be ordered from Housesmiths Press, P.O. Box 157, Kittery Point, ME 03905.

Brochure with list of available plans, photos, and description of services, $4.

Birch Hill Builders
P.O. Box 416
York, ME 03909
(207) 363-2814

Entwood Construction Fraternity

The principals of Entwood have a clear understanding of the essentials of post and beam framing and a deep appreciation of fine materials. Eastern white pine and northern red spruce are used for the timbers of the frame, and the same materials enclose the frame from inside to out. Cedar clapboards and shingles are used for outside walls and the roof, respectively. Entwood will build throughout the United States and the Caribbean. All frames are individually built. Various levels of service are available—from building of a frame to be finished by the buyer or his contractor to a totally finished house. The firm is also skilled at reproducing historic structures.

Brochure available, $3.

Entwood Construction Fraternity, Inc.
R.R. 1
Marshfield, VT 05658
(802) 472-5043

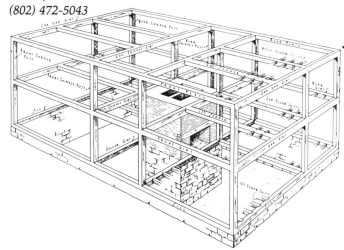

Sun Designs

Gazebos and summerhouses are among the plans offered by this innovative firm. Illustrated is what is termed the "Edgewater" design from the company's *Gazebo Study Plan Book* ($4.95 plus $1.97 for 1st-class mail or $1.20 for 3rd-class). Individual blueprint drawings for the construction of such at-

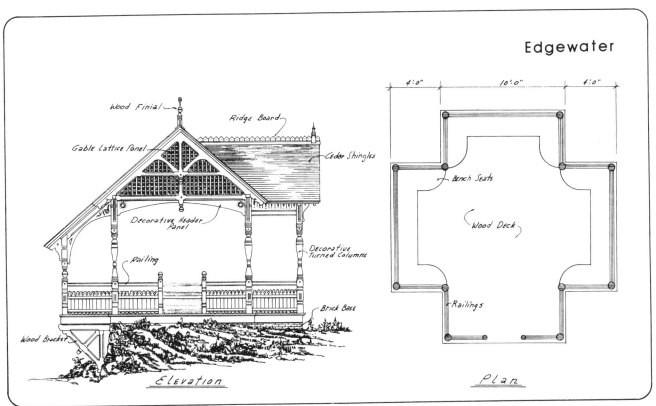

Edgewater

Wood Finial
Ridge Board
Gable Lattice Panel
Cedar Shingles
Decorative Header Panel
Railing
Decorative Turned Columns
Brick Base
Wood Bracket

Bench Seats
Wood Deck
Railings

4'0"   10'0"   4'0"

Elevation

Plan

tractive outbuildings are available at various prices, along with a list of necessary materials. Materials specified are common to most lumberyards and hardware stores. Sun Designs also has plans to issue two new books this year: *New Faces*, showing homes before and after the use of matching fascia, railings, shutters, and canopies; and a second book on covered bridges, foot bridges, cupolas, and a variety of small specialty buildings. Construction plans will be available for all the new designs.

Sun Designs
Rexstrom, Inc.
P.O. Box 157
Delafield, WI 53018
(414) 567-4255

THE SARAH ALBRIGHT HOUSE
(See next page.)

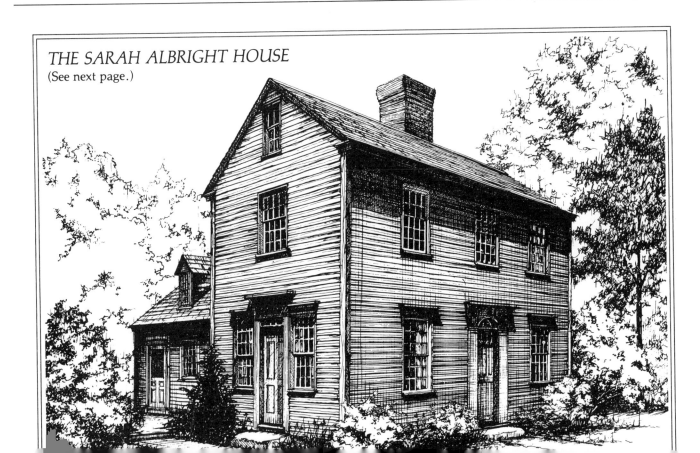

The first two Old House Catalogues *featured several other producers of traditional house frames or finished reproduction homes.*

The House Carpenters

This firm is among the best. Illustrated is "The Sarah Albright House." The frames are built of Massachusetts red oak and white pine, and are joined in the mortise-and-tenon manner and dovetailed. White oak pegs are used as fasteners. A wide range of reproduction architectural materials can be furnished by the company.

The House Carpenters
N. Leverett Road
Montague, MA 01351
(413) 367-2673

David Howard, Inc.

David Howard and his partner have built more than 125 frames in the past five years and have delivered them to twenty different states. They've also completed numerous houses. Now they are launching a new venture. In association with R. Durtnell & Sons, Ltd., Westerham, Kent, England, they are dismantling antique English frames for reassembly in the United States. Ten barns and three houses are already available, and all date back to either the 1400s or 1500s and are built completely of oak.

Booklet available, $4.

David Howard, Inc.
P.O. Box 295
Alstead, NH 03602
(603) 835-6356

Glass

Proper glass can be as important to the appearance of a period house as paint, moldings, or other trimmings. The differences between new plate glass and that used in the past are not readily noticeable by most people, but these can be considerable. Many homes have lost their old windows, transoms, or other glass panels. To replace them with modern plates of glass, however insulated they may be by double or triple glazing, can despoil a façade. This is especially true if the glass being replaced is stained, etched, or engraved.

Old window glass is not easy to obtain. A number of the restoration suppliers and consultants included in this chapter have a supply on hand from time to time. Reproduction panes can be obtained from a number of the glass workshops across the country and from Blenko Glass.

Blenko Glass

All sheets have some bubbles and a texture like early American window glass. Stock sheets are approximately 18" x 23" untrimmed. The glass is priced at $4.54 per square foot.

Blenko Glass Company, Inc.
Milton, WV 25541
(304) 743-9081

Etched, textured, and engraved glass is somewhat easier to obtain. A number of firms in North America kept going in the 20th century with commissions for churches and public institutions. With the resurgence of interest in things "Victorian," these old companies have been joined by many enterprises run by the young in heart and body who find glassmaking an exciting and profitable craft.

Electric Glass

Beveled windows are this company's specialty. Illustrated is one of its many designs, "Arabesque," which measures 24" x 36". Custom panels can be made to almost any design and shape. Other designs of particular interest to old-house owners, especially those who live in late-19th and early-20th-century homes, are "Simplicity" and "Nouveau." Prices range from $429 to $717, with shipping and crating extra.

Catalogue available, $2.

Electric Glass Co.
1 E. Mellen Street
Hampton, VA 23663
(804) 722-6200

Ice Nine Glass Designs

Acid-etched designs are offered by this Minnesota firm. Many are appropriate for door glass in late-Victorian houses. The panels are frosty in appearance and offer the semi-privacy first considered desirable when large sheets of plate glass became available. One such design is illustrated here. The firm also offers border patterns well suited for sidelights, transoms, and door panels. Discretion is advised since not all the designs offered are suitable for serious old-house enthusiasts.

Catalogue available, $2.

Ice Nine Glass Design
6128 Oldson Memorial Hwy.
Golden Valley, MN 55422
(612) 546-7222

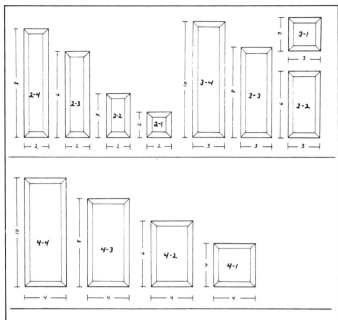

Master's Stained & Etched Glass Studio

Custom work—beveled doors and leaded, beveled, stained (painted), and etched windows—makes up the business of this firm. Special attention is given to deeply-etched designs on glass.

Master's Stained & Etched Glass Studio
729 W. 16th Street, B-1
Costa Mesa, CA 92627
(714) 548-4951

J. Ring Stained Glass Studio

The standards are very high at this Minneapolis studio; the majority of the work done is for other stained-glass studios, architects, designers, and government agencies concerned with restoration. Hand-beveled and engraved glass is produced along with stained glass. Glass painting, glass bending and forming, and mirror silvering and resilvering are among the other skills practiced. The studio is particularly interested in commissions to reproduce high-quality pieces—lamp panels, Victorian and Art Nouveau windows, bevels up to 1¾" wide for leaded windows, door panels, and mirrors. Illustrated are standard bevels made from ¼" float plate glass with a full ½" bevel at a steep 20% angle.

Catalogues and price lists.

J. Ring Stained Glass, Inc.
2125 E. Hennepin
Minneapolis, MN 55414
(612) 379-1444

Sunburst Stained Glass

This small studio, located in the historic southern Indiana town of New Harmony, will provide stained-glass and beveled-glass design, fabrication, repair, and restoration. Recent commissions have included the Old Post Office and Custom House, Evansville, Indiana, and Holy Angels Catholic Church in New Harmony. Sunburst will travel for on-site work when appropriate.

Sunburst Stained Glass Co.
P.O. Box 5
New Harmony, IN 47631
(812) 682-4065

Many of the sources recommended in both The Old House Catalogue *and* The Second Old House Catalogue *remain useful in the glass field.*

Castle Burlingame

This is a source for early window glass.

Castle Burlingame

R.D. 1, Box 352
Basking Ridge, NJ 07920
(201) 647-3885

Cherry Creek Enterprises

The company custom-produces extraordinarily brilliant hand-beveled glass as well as wheel-engraved designs on bevels. These designs incorporate flora and fauna in naturalistic patterns. There are also less expensive machine-beveled, straight-line glass windows which will more than adequately serve the needs of many home owners.

Catalogue available.

Cherry Creek Enterprises, Inc.
937 Santa Fe Drive
Denver, CO 80204
(303) 892-1819

Stained glass has become almost as popular today as it was 100 years ago. A great deal of the antique material found in homes then, however, is now being used in trendy steak houses. There just isn't enough of the real material left to fill all the needs of the enthusiasts. When that happens, bad copies rush in to fill the void. Fortunately there are craftsmen who have learned the skills of the past, who know what colors are correct, how lead must be applied, what designs are appropriate, etc. It is unlikely that any one of them is another Tiffany, but there are reproductions and new works which display an uncommon artistic touch. These craftsmen can also repair old glass which can sometimes be unearthed in out-of-the-way places. Some of the architectural antiques suppliers try to keep a stock of such windows on hand. You will find that a majority of these antiques are now coming from Great Britain.

Architectural Emphasis

This San Francisco firm has developed a line of stained-glass sidelights and accent panels which are extremely simple in composition. They are not the highly-colored beauties prized by collectors, but rather standard designs which, in fact, may be more in keeping with the average late-Victorian or post-Victorian house than more florid compositions. These have been developed for the use of today's real estate developer and contractor, and their availability to the general public is uncertain. If you're interested, it is worth an inquiry. The panels can be triple glazed (sealed between two pieces of tempered glass), thus avoiding one of the common problems encountered with the use of stained glass—its tendency to leak heat. Architectural Emphasis is also a good source for hand-beveled panels.

Literature, $2, refundable with first purchase.

Architectural Emphasis, Inc.
1750 Montgomery Street
San Francisco, CA 94111
(415) 362-0832

William Armstrong and Associates

Repair and restoration of fine stained glass is a specialty of this firm. It will also design and build original windows. Armstrong is one of the few craftsmen who mentions the restoration of skylights in his literature, a service that some home owners may find useful.

Brochure available.

William Armstrong and Associates
20 Dalton Street
Newburyport, MA 01950
(617) 465-5264

Sandra Brauer

This talented artist understands the subtle processes required to achieve fine stained glass and to restore the old. She has exhibited her own designs in the New York area and illustrated is one of her traditional pieces. She has developed the skill of stabilizing old windows. The primary problem often encountered is what is known as "buckling." Glass shifts out of the lead channel, lead breaks away from the reinforcing bars, and putty dries out; this combined with natural warpage or shrinkage of the sash results in the buckling action.

Literature available.

Sandra Brauer/Stained Glass
364-B Atlantic Avenue
Brooklyn, NY 11217
(212) 855-0656

Manor Art Glass Studio

Rosalind Brenner Koeppel is another talented artist. She has created new window designs for many homes and restaurants. Her traditional work ranges from late Victorian to Déco, and all work is undertaken on a commission basis.

Manor Art Glass Studio
20 Ridge Road
Douglaston, NY 11363
(212) 631-8029

Meredith Stained Glass Studio

A full range of services are supplied by this firm—from new custom work to repair and restoration. Installation of pieces can also be handled. There is a special interest here in Art Nouveau glass.

Meredith Stained Glass Studio
231 Mill Street, N.E.
Vienna, VA 22180
(703) 281-4334

Mimram Stained Glass Studio

Why not go to the source of some of the best stained-glass work—England? Mike Davis runs the stained-glass studio at Digswell House and is an associate of the British Society of Master Glass Painters. The studio makes a wide range of decorative glass from full stained-glass windows down to small panels using English, French, and West German antique (blown sheet), English Streaky Cathedral (a rolled glass developed by Messrs. Hartly Wood of Sunderland), as well as clear, opalescent, or patterned rolled glass.

Much of the work is glazed in the traditional way, using lead calm; some is copper foiled in the Tiffany method. The glass may be decorated in a number of ways. Line or tone can be painted on with oxides of iron or copper, which are fired on in a kiln for permanence. This method has not changed greatly since its earliest use in the 11th century. The stain, from which the generic name "stained glass" may have derived, was discovered in the 14th century. It consists of compounds of silver, or sometimes antimony, and when applied to the reverse of the glass, gives a wash of yellow. Antique glass is either a solid color, called "pot metal," or blown with a thin layer of stronger color on one surface, the "flash." This flashed glass can be acid-etched, i.e., the thin skin of color can be stripped away with hydrofluoric acid to reveal the glass beneath.

Mimram Stained Glass Studio
Digswell House, Monks Rise
Welwyn Garden City, Herts.
England
Tel. Welwyn Garden 26169

Pompei Studio

Period reproductions of rather basic leaded stained-glass

panels for use as windows, transoms, fanlights, sidelights, door panels, and mantel mirrors are standard work for this studio. Illustrated are a few of the designs available.

Catalogue available, $1.

Pompei Studio for Stained Glass Art
455 High Street
Medford, MA 02155
(617) 395-8867

Studio Stained Glass

Custom windows and Tiffany-style shades are the specialty of this Indiana firm. It will also undertake antique window and shade repair and restoration.

Studio Stained Glass
117 S. Main Street
Kokomo, IN 46901
(317) 452-2438

Walton Stained Glass

Illustrated is one of the beveled window designs produced by

Walton, a firm that also features stained-glass work and sandblasted mirrors.

Walton Stained Glass
209 Railway
Campbell, CA 95008
(408) 866-0533

Virtu

The artists in this fine stained-glass studio are continuing to produce extremely original new work which reflects and builds upon the art achieved by turn-of-the-century craftsmen. Work of this sort, although not strictly traditional or authentic, should be given a place in period homes of the late-Victorian and early-modern periods.

Virtu
P.O. Box 192
Southfield, MI 48037
(313) 357-1250

Accessories

Both artists and do-it-yourself home restorers working with glass may find it convenient to consult one of the suppliers of quality materials and tools.

S. A. Bendheim Co.

This firm offers a wide range of stained-glass materials including French, German, and English glass of various finishes, colors, and forms. Bendheim makes available bull's-eye glass, handspun and pressed rondells, and handspun crown bullions —among other unusual items.

Catalogue 111-A available.

S. A. Bendheim Co., Inc.
122 Hudson Street
New York, NY 10013
(212) 226-6370

Whittemore-Durgin

All the supplies needed by glass artists can be found in this firm's catalogue or in four self-service stores located in Rockland, Massachusetts, Bergenfield, New Jersey, East Lyme, Connecticut, and Peoria, Illinois. The home owner might be particularly interested in the glass termed "Antique" in the trade but which is new material. It is almost as transparent as window glass and has numerous imperfections such as reams, seeds, bubbles, striations, etc. It is recommended for hanging ornaments, but might, although thin, be used as a replacement for old glass panes. As the catalogue notes, color #4311, "Light Amethyst," is also known in the Boston area as "Beacon Hill."

"Many of the windows in Colonial houses on Beacon Hill have glass which has discolored through the action of the sunlight upon them over the years. #4311 closely resembles this natural discoloration." Sheet antique glass is made in random-sized sheets, and orders must be for even pounds.

Catalogue available.

Whittemore-Durgin Glass Co.
Box 2065
Hanover, MA 02339
(617) 871-1743

Architectural Antiques

Architectural antiques were once known as salvage, junk, or trash. These are the decorative and functional elements from a doomed building—doors, windows, beams, flooring, plaster ornaments, brackets, etc.—which were hauled off to the dump or allowed to rot in situ. Presumably the ruins of both ancient civilizations and a 1930s hot dog stand would be considered "antique"—so far have we come in reappraising the debris of the past. However ridiculous and bizarre, the situation today is better than it has been in years. It is good to see a premium applied to what was previously discarded with so little thought. The old-time home restorer may find it difficult to visit an architectural antiques boutique where corbels are displayed with the care formerly given only to Old Masters, but such shops are here to stay and will probably proliferate. Unless the "antique" is a recent one, the dump is an unlikely source for useful and attractive junk. Better to scout out your needs in the warehouses, antique shops, and stores scattered across the country.

Architectural Heritage of Cheltenham

North American suppliers of architectural antiques often turn to English sources. Why, then, shouldn't you? Sample items from this English firm's January, 1980, broadside are: "suite of 4 Continental walnut doors with acanthus decoration and heart-shaped bevelled glass panels;" "three wrought iron radiator covers;" "period oak floorboards—various widths—good condition;" "several terra cotta urns etc.;" "a number of Georgian cast and wrought iron balconies of varying patterns and sizes."

A quarterly descriptive list of items in stock is available from the company. Shipping of items from the United Kingdom need not be a prohibitive exercise if you are willing to wait for a combined shipment by sea. Photographs and detailed descriptions of items that interest you are, of course, a must unless you are planning to be traveling in England and can stop in this attractive area close to the Cotswolds.

Architectural Heritage of Cheltenham
The Manor, Swindow Village
Cheltenham, Gloucestershire

England
Tel. Chelt. (0242) 45589, 26567

Architectural Salvage Co. of Santa Barbara

At the other side of the world is this used-house-parts firm that specializes in doors, windows, and fixtures. Owners of Spanish Colonial or Mission style homes may find this a good source for 200-year-old Mexican doors. Stained and etched glass is another specialty.

Architectural Salvage Co. of Santa Barbara
726 Anacapa
Santa Barbara, CA 93101
(805) 965-2446

Art Directions

The showroom of this nationally-known company contains 20,000 square-feet of merchandise—antique bars, doors, windows, lighting fixtures, paneling, molding, urns, brackets, and on and on. Joined to the showroom is a workshop where re-pairs and restoration work are performed.

Brochures available, gratis; catalogues, $5.

Art Directions
6120 Delmar Blvd.
St. Louis, MO 63112
(314) 863-1895

Artifacts Inc.

Home restorers in the southeastern and Middle Atlantic states may find this a good source for such items as mantels, newel posts, pedestal sinks, old hardware, columns, doors, brackets and spindles. Illustrated is one of the approximately 1,000 items which are currently in stock—a primitively carved capital with Ionic volutes.

Photographs available on request.

Artifacts Inc.
702 Mt. Vernon Avenue
Alexandria, VA 22301
(703) 548-6555

The Bank

This firm claims to be the largest in the South, and, considering the architectural glories of the area in which it is located, there is a need to be well prepared to meet restoration needs. In addition to the usual doors, mantels, shutters, and stained and beveled glass, there are whole front porches and staircases. Re-pairs can be performed as well, and there is a nearby stripping service.

The Bank, Architectural Antiques
1824 Felicity Street
New Orleans, LA 70113
(504) 523-6055

Paul M. Broomfield

This gentleman specializes in northeastern American building materials, and like other dealers has an ever-changing stock. Among the more interesting finds are a complete fireplace assembly of cut granite stones with a crane, a complete country store, an antique office safe, and a 200-year-old blacksmith shop with forge. More to the point for most domestic needs are Sandwich-glass knobs, white-pine mantels, staircases, hard-pine floorboards, paneled doors, and window sash with hand-made panes of glass.

Paul M. Broomfield
Carolina, RI 02812
(401) 364-7233

Irreplaceable Artifacts

This aptly-named enterprise is run by Evan Blum who cannot resist taking on the saving of monumental objects from doomed landmark buildings. Most objects are purely ornamental and date from 1860-1935. The materials are of the finest sort—good stained glass, marble and terra cotta, mahogany and cherry. The shop is open by appointment only.

Irreplaceable Artifacts
526 E. 80th Street
New York, NY 10021
(212) 288-7397

Levy's Gasolier Antiques

Lighting fixtures of the gas age and early electric period are a permanent item in the Levy inventory. Victorian hardware and marble mantels of the sort illustrated here are also featured.

Levy's Gasolier Antiques
Box 627
Washington, DC 20044
(202) 232-1985, Sundays and evenings except Friday

Joe Ley Antiques

We've not visited this emporium, but we'd like to. There seems to be a lot of everything—hundreds of sets of brass locks, hinges, letter slots, door bells, knockers; chandeliers of every sort; more than 2,000 antique doors; a large inventory of Victorian woodwork. Too bad Joe Ley didn't start collecting fifty years ago when he could have found ten times what is available today.

Brochure available.

Joe Ley Antiques
620 E. Market Street
Louisville, KY 40202
(502) 583-4014

The London Architectural Salvage & Supply Co.

Illustrated are several of the thousands of items sold by this English firm during the past year. Duplicates of each are still available; a cast-iron floor grating, c. 1870 (around £10); pair of Marylebone copper street lanterns, c. 1880 (£ 200 each); and

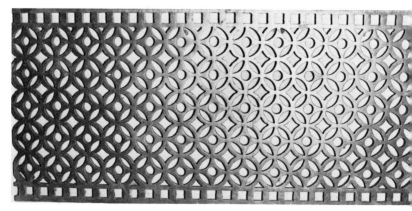

an exterior six-panel door, 19th century, stripped and refurbished (around £ 60). Many ordinary items are kept in stock—shutters, many with original hardware; handrails; casement windows; Victorian cast-iron fireplace inserts—and prices are reasonable.

Bulletin available; photographs upon request.

The London Architectural Salvage & Supply Co. Ltd.
Mark Street
London EC2 A4ER
England
(01) 739-0448

Old House Supplies

Early Pennsylvania architectural artifacts are the specialty of this Lancaster County firm. Pine doors, 18th-century red-clay shingles, old window glass, square fireplace hearth bricks, interior shutters, flooring and siding, hinges, etc., are available from time to time. The business is located in a restored and working inn, the 1725 Witmer's Tavern.

Old House Supplies
Pandora's Antiques
2014 Old Philadelphia Pike
Lancaster, PA 17602
(717) 299-5305

Olde Theatre Architectural Salvage Co.

Proprietor Pat Shaughnessy is shown here standing amid her plentiful stock of stained-glass windows and paneled doors. The carved ornament she is holding appears to be a decorative bracket or piece of an elaborate capital. Shown is only one section of the store devoted to every possible sort of object.

Brochure available.

Olde Theatre Architectural Salvage Co.
1309 Westport Road
Kansas City, MO 64111
(816) 931-0987

Rejuvenation House Parts Co.

Used and new fittings for old houses are carried by this retailer. Doors, hardware, siding, molding, and lighting fixtures are among the old staples. A new line of reproduction solid-brass Victorian lighting fixtures is being launched this year.

Catalogue available.

Rejuvenation House Parts Co.
4543 N. Albina Avenue
Portland, OR 97217
(503) 282-3019

The suppliers described previously by no means exhaust the sources of architectural antiques. The reader is urged to consult the listings at the end of the chapter for firms described in previous Catalogues, *and to consider the following new information supplied by some of them.*

Architectural Antiques/L'Architecture Ancienne

This is Canada's largest supplier of details and fittings, including all the standard categories. Reproduction stained-glass panels are also produced by in-house craftsmen. Specific requests can be answered with a photo.

Architectural Antiques/L'Architecture Ancienne
410 St. Pierre
Montreal, Quebec H2Y 2M2
Canada
(514) 849-3344

The Architectural Antique Warehouse

Proprietor David Doucher formerly operated The Cellar, and his new establishment continues to supply everything from complete Victorian verandahs to the smallest pieces of hardware.

The Architectural Antique Warehouse
17 Bentley Avenue
Ottawa, Ontario
Canada
(613) 224-5530

The Renovation Source

This firm is a one-stop market for antique materials, reproduction items made by various manufacturers, and new woodwork—moldings, turnings, etc., which can be replicated by Robert and Kathy Raffel's craftsmen. Such items as newel posts, cornice brackets, and turned spindles are especially well-stocked.

The Renovation Source, Inc.
3512-14 N. Southport
Chicago, IL 60657
(312) 327-1250

The Wrecking Bar

Not to be confused with the Dallas establishment of the same name, The Wrecking Bar of Atlanta offers 18,000 square-feet of antique materials. The vast majority of them are of the decorative sort popular in restaurants and shops, but there are always objects of practical use and aesthetic appeal for the home.

Brochure upon request.

The Wrecking Bar of Atlanta, Inc.
292 Moreland Avenue, N.E.
Atlanta, GA 30307
(404) 525-0468

House Inspection Services

There is probably nothing more important before the purchase of an old house than its inspection by an expert. Even the most professional of home restorers will agree that a "second opinion" is a good investment. Buying a house—new or old—is always an emotional experience and one's judgment is not always what it should be. The intangibles are often what attract a buyer, especially if the building is old enough to possess some charm. Most restoration consultants and architects can provide inspection services and a report which may come in handy when negotiating with the seller or broker. It is also advisable to speak with local service people—the fuel company, a carpenter, plumber, electrician, and if in the country, pump and septic systems technicians—who may have kept things in working order over the years and are privy to secrets the seller may prefer to keep hidden. There are many people located throughout the country who specialize in home inspection. One of these is—

Howard Lieberman, P.E.

If you live in the New York area and are considering the purchase of an old house, you might want to contact Mr. Lieberman. He will be able to tell you the whole story from its structural, mechanical, and electrical angles.

Howard Lieberman, P.E.
Home Buyers Inspection Service
277 White Plains Road
Eastchester, NY 10709
(914) SP9-3773

Guardian National House Inspection, Inc.

Previously recommended in earlier Catalogues, Guardian National House Inspection, Inc., covers New York, New Jersey, Connecticut, Rhode Island, and Massachusetts. A copy of the firm's very thorough inspection report form can be obtained for $1.

Guardian National House Inspection, Inc.
Box 115
Orleans, MA 02653
(617) 255-6609

Other suppliers of home inspection services are listed at the end of the chapter.

Brick

Although America is built primarily of wood, its most abundant building material, some of the most significant homes, especially those in urban areas, have been built of brick since the 17th century. Ordinances passed in many Colonial towns and cities required the building of fireproof brick and masonry structures. Brick, however, was also used in prosperous country homes, most significantly in the South and Middle Atlantic areas. The patterned brickwork houses of south Jersey, for instance, are some of the most unusual and distinguished examples of American domestic architecture. Wherever quality clay or shale could be easily extracted from the earth, brickmaking became a tradition. Just how much brick was brought to the New World as ballast on ships remains a matter of pure conjecture.

Today the home owner seeking a small amount of antique brick for repair or restoration work is best advised to consult with a contractor or building supplier in his area. Some of the restoration supply houses stock such material, but its transport any distance may be a problem. Until fairly recently, there was a plentiful supply of old machine-made brick that had been used in mid- to late-19th-century buildings as demolition activity far outpaced that of restoration. If one inquires around, stocks of this period material can be found. Handmade brick of an earlier time will require more digging. Outbuildings in rural areas which have been left to crumble are one source; so, too, are early industrial buildings which have been allowed to deteriorate to the point that not even the best-intentioned preservationist can figure out how to recycle them for new uses.

For antique brick to be of any use, of course, it must have retained its basic shape and strength. Much of that made in a field kiln or even more sophisticated ovens during the 18th and 19th centuries was not of the highest quality and has crumbled badly. No amount of pointing can make it right. For this important reason, and secondarily for convenience, use of new "antique" brick may be the solution. Fortunately, there are suppliers of such materials who understand the differences in size, texture, and shape which mark bricks made in one time and place from another.

Glen-Gery "1776"

If laid with a proper mortar, this company's new bricks suitably reproduce the look of the old. The "1776 series" approximates in size molded Colonial brick, and, in the words of the manufacturer, still "enjoys all the durability of the entire Glen-Gery line." Included in the line are the following forms—a molded, standard size measuring 3⅝" wide x 2¼" high x 8" long in a true brick-red color; "Vermont Blend," in the same standard size but of a lighter and more varied mixture of color; two facing bricks, "Old White" and a regular brick shade, the former in both standard and oversize, the latter only in standard; and two oversize bricks, "Lexington" in an almost solid brick shade, and "Concord White." The oversize is 4" wide x 2¾" high x 8½" long.

Glen-Gery's "1776" line is carried by distributors throughout the country.

Brochure available.

Glen-Gery Corp.
P.O. Box 280, Rte. 61
Shoemakersville, PA 19555
(215) 562-3076

Old Carolina Brick

The handmade bricks produced by Old Carolina have been strongly recommended in earlier catalogues. They have a warmth and texture which will fool an expert looking for the true antique. The company offers several other products and services of special interest to the restorer. It will custom match handmade brick to existing old brick as closely as possible if a representative sample of the old is sent to them. The sample

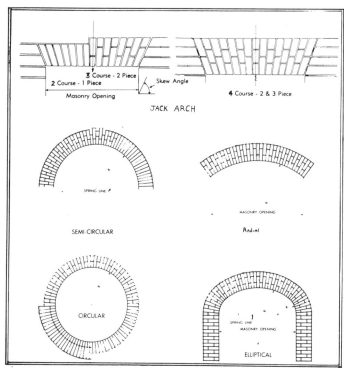

periods. While terra-cotta tiles and chimney pots are still produced in North America, we are not aware that any company here is prepared to produce new material to match the old. One firm in Britain, however, will undertake such work.

Hathernware

This firm is part of the Shawn-Hathernware Group of companies which have been making architectural terra cotta for nearly 100 years. It also pioneered in introducing glazed faience for buildings. Most importantly, it still has the craftsmen to produce such largely hand-modeled and molded materials. To replace deteriorated terra cotta is a monumental task and may involve several preliminary steps, including at least dimensional sketches and perhaps the taking of plaster molds, neither of which Hathernware is likely to be able to execute on the site. A sample of the existing material is a must whether business is done directly in England or through inquiry from the States, and a match will be prepared for approval. Putting the new material in place will have to be contracted for separately as the company does not undertake site work—either here or in Britain—but they will advise on this part of the operation.

Hathernware Ltd.
Loughborough
Leicestershire LE12 5EW
England
Tel. 0509-842273

will be returned with a price quotation for the approximate quantity desired. Old Carolina also makes available such special shapes as 8″ x 8″ Dutch pavers, split pavers, and jack arches. As noted on the drawing shown here, "These arches are all of the basic types that are generally used. We will make them to fit any opening and in any style if we have the dimensions of masonry opening, skew angle, height of arch, thickness of mortar joint, etc." Each arch will be assembled and properly crated for shipment.

Brochure available, $1.

Old Carolina Brick Co.
Majolica Road
Salisbury, NC 28144
(704) 636-8850

Columns and Pilasters

The replacement of exterior columns of a structural sort can be an extremely costly and precarious project. It is perhaps fortunate that the façades of most North American Greek Revival, ante-bellum, and Colonial Revival homes are not finished with marble, but, rather, with wood columns. The pilasters which protrude only slightly from the façade and usually match the columns were also made largely from wood. Marble was saved for more lofty purposes—banks, churches, schools. Plaster and composition can be employed perfectly well within the interior of a home, but wood or iron—properly treated—has the durability needed for the outdoors. If wood columns are what are required, then look no farther than A. F. Schwerd.

A. F. Schwerd

This firm has been in business since 1860 and properly claims that Schwerd has been "the standard of quality" since that time. Northern white pine is used for all exterior columns and pilasters, and these are constructed by gluing together wood staves. "The result when the staves are glued together," the company reports, "is a shaft which has the proper taper and entasis built-in. The finished column is *equally heavy* at any

Stone and Terra Cotta

Stone is still widely quarried in North America. Our supplies of such traditional materials as brownstone, various sandstones, granite, bluestone, and marble are by no means unlimited, but they are sufficient for restoration work. Fieldstone is also available, but is not quite as commonly found as the cut variety. If there are not quarries or stone dealers in your area who can advise on supplies of various sorts, contact a mason who you know has worked with the material you want.

Terra cotta is a much more elusive commodity these days. Widely used for the decoration of commercial buildings in the late-19th and early-20th centuries, it also appears as decorative motifs on grand homes of the Beaux Arts and Colonial Revival

point in its length; the lathe turning operation removes only the roughness of the lumber."

Aluminum ventilated plinths and turned member bases are recommended for all exterior columns 8", 10", 12", 14" and 18" in diameter. Columns in the Tuscan, Greek and Roman Doric, and Ionic Orders and various other forms—square and octagonal—are available with ornamental capitals, including the Roman Corinthian; composite; Scamozzi; Temple of Winds; Greek, Roman, and Modern Ionic; and Roman Doric. It is hard to believe, but, yes, these are all "standard" works at Schwerd. Custom work, of course, can also be undertaken.

Catalogues available.

A. F. Schwerd Manufacturing Co.
3215 McClure Avenue
Pittsburgh, PA 15212
(412) 766-6322

Roofing Materials

A good roofing material is indispensable for any old house, and its application must be carefully done. A leaking roof can cause no end of structural problems which may be extremely expensive to correct. When one considers just how many square feet of a building's exterior may be covered with roofing material, its importance is better understood. Although much of it is often out of sight, it cannot be out of mind. This is especially true in the majority of North American regions where a roof is traditionally inclined to ward off the elements. Only in arid regions, such as the Southwest, where rainfall is slight and snow rare, are roofs traditionally flat. Many modern builders have learned to their regret that flat roofs collect rather than shed the elements. Why they couldn't figure this out in advance is puzzling.

The materials traditionally used on houses—slate, wood, metal, and asphalt shingles; coated iron or "tin"; and ceramic tiling—are still available today. Sources of them have actually increased in recent years despite their increased cost. Slate, for instance, is acknowledged to be the most impermeable and best of roofing materials. It is available in various shades and thicknesses, and, if properly laid, can last for many, many years. Ceramic tiling is similarly durable, and is much to be preferred to cement and steel imitations. Both slate and ceramics, however, are costly materials to purchase and to apply. Properly treated cedar shingles are considerably cheaper and may be appropriate for many homes; shakes are not. Asphalt shingles may last for 15 to 20 years without giving trouble; fiberglass shingles will give better wear and are available in more appropriate finishes. The traditional tin roof of galvanized sheets of steel or ungalvanized sheets of wrought iron coated with tin or zinc cannot be duplicated very easily. Rather, the home owner probably will have to turn to other galvanized-steel substitutes or to terne metal (also known as

"roofer's tin" and most often used today for flashing and valley work) which is made of a combination of tin and lead laid over steel.

Berridge Manufacturing

Many of the quality products produced by this metal roofing firm are appropriate for modern buildings. Imitations of Spanish tiles and Victorian wood shingles should be used with caution on old buildings. The "mansard" frames used on so many commercial buildings today resemble big hats on little people and are about as fetching in appearance as bottle caps. Berridge's "Galvalume" (galvanized steel) tee-panels can be used unfinished to age and weather naturally. This may be a suitable substitute for galvanized-metal roofing of the type used in the past for both rural homes and outbuildings.

Catalogue available.

Berridge Manufacturing Co.
1720 Maury Street
Houston, TX 77026
(713) 223-4971

Conklin Tin Plate and Metal

Metal shingles are offered by this firm, founded in 1874. Metal, like slate, may last a lifetime or more. Shingles are made in galvanized steel, 16 oz. copper, .025 aluminum microzinc, and terne. Terne may be your best bet. Better yet, inquire about the galvanized sheets which will approximate the kind of roofing material so often used in the past.

Brochure available.

Conklin Tin Plate and Metal Co.
P.O. Box 2662
Atlanta, GA 30301
(404) 688-4510

Follansbee Steel

Terne metal sheets may be supplied by this nationally-known company with district offices in almost all major commercial centers. Paint will take well to the material's surface of steel coated with a lead-tin alloy.

Brochure available.

Follansbee Steel Corp.
Follansbee, WV 26037
(304) 527-1260

Ludowici-Celadon

It is difficult to conceive of a more handsome traditional roofing material than vitrified clay tile. No firm knows more about the manufacture and use of such products than Ludowici-Celadon. It has produced the material used in many fine restorations. The variety of forms is considerable; some are appropriate for Spanish Colonial and Mission houses of both early and revival stages; others may find a congenial place perched atop French Norman-style country houses, imitation Cotswold cottages and Tudor Revival mansions, and Colonial Revival residences. There are 24 standard colors to choose from.

Flyers available.

Ludowici-Celadon Company
201 N. Talman Avenue
Chicago, IL 60612
(312) 722-7700

Shakertown

Large commercial manufacturers are becoming more and more aware of the popularity of period building materials. Shakertown is to be commended for leading the way with its new "Fancy Cuts" line of red-cedar shingles. The patterns available are diagonal, octagonal, hexagonal, arrow, half-cove, fishscale, diamond, square, and round. Used on the exterior (*not* inside, please), they are an economical alternative to handmade shingles. All measure approximately 4¹⁵⁄₁₆" wide and 18" long and are sold by the carton, each one of which contains 96 shingles.

Pattern sheet and free sample available.

Shakertown Corp.
Box 400
Winlock, WA 98956
(206) 785-3501

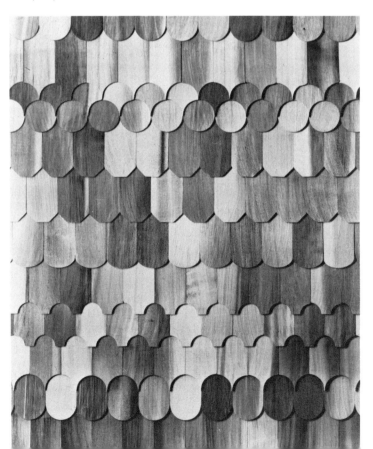

Beams

Nothing says "Colonial" more forcefully to most people than open-beamed ceilings. Unhappily, the "look" has become a cliché. And what may appear to be wood may be nothing more than styrofoam or some other synthetic material. While beams of this sort will never whet the appetite of termites, neither will they earn the approbation of thoughtful antiquarians. Fake beams look awful, and there is no reason to use them. Old beams there are aplenty, and if the right size or style can't be found somehow, there are always timbers around which can be shaped to fit. Many restoration suppliers can help.

A few other reminders are in order. Remember that beams were often plastered over at a very early date and perhaps should not be uncovered at all; the "rustic" look popular today was not in the least admired in the 1700s or 1800s. The heavy "stressed" appearance given to so much considered "early American" in the 20th century may also be misleading. If beams were left exposed at all, they were sometimes chamfered or beaded. The beautiful beams or vigas found in some early Southwestern homes were peeled logs worthy of display.

John A. Wigen

This contractor, like many others, has a ready supply of hand-hewn barn beams, as well as wide pine flooring, old doors, and siding. His prices are reasonable, and trucking can be arranged a fair distance.

John A. Wigen/Contractor
R.D. #1
Cobleskill, NY 12043
(518) 234-7946

Kensington Historical Company

This firm's structural inventory regularly includes hand-hewn beams of spruce, Eastern white pine, white oak, and chestnut. These are the simplest of supplies they make available, their forte being original 18th-century components and custom millwork.

Kensington Historical Company
Box 87
East Kingston, NH 03827
(603) 778-0686

Paneling/Flooring/Clapboarding

In writing of clapboarding, paneling, and flooring, consideration is being given only to standard wood products. Other materials and forms are presented and discussed in Chapters 2 and 5. Antique lumber can be found in most areas of North America, but one must be sure that it is appropriate for use in and around the house. The type of planks used for barn siding may be much too rough and weathered for your needs. What was considered sufficient to provide shelter for cows and horses is still not recommended for human beings. As far as new lumber is concerned, the situation may be somewhat better at the local lumberyard today than in recent years. With the dip in new home construction, there may be a willingness expressed on the part of the proprietors to help you find the woods and sizes you need.

Colonial Restoration Materials

Wide pine boards and paneling are the specialties of Dale Carlisle. The boards range from 15″ to 22″ in width and from 8′ to 16′ in length. They are cut a full inch thick, rather than ¾″. Planing can be performed if requested. Pine clapboards are also available.

Colonial Restoration Materials
Route 123
Stoddard, NH 30464
(603) 446-3937

Mountain Lumber

This Virginia firm styles itself a dealer in "rare and special woods." Mountain Lumber supplied much of the 18th-century

flooring used in the restoration of the Rotunda at the University of Virginia. Hardwoods of exceptional beauty such as wormy chestnut and heart pine are available for paneling or flooring. Most of the material is more than 100 years old. All heart-pine and chestnut tongue-and-groove paneling is available in random widths ranging from 4″ to 12″, and in random lengths. Other woods offered are pecan, walnut, butternut, and oak.

Mountain Lumber Co.
1327 Carlton Avenue
Charlottesville, VA 22901
(804) 295-1922

Standard Roofings

This building-products supplier is representative of those who have become aware of the growing popular market for materials suitable for old houses and new homes built in period styles. It buys directly from the mills Western red cedar, Atlantic white cedar, and New England pine siding in both horizontal and vertical boards, thereby lowering the cost to you.

Standard Roofings, Inc.
670 S. Clinton Street
Trenton, NJ 08611
(609) 599-2548

Stairways

Complete stairways, such fundamental components as treads and stringers, and decorative elements like railings, spindles, and newel posts are among the stock items carried by many restoration supply houses. Either they or consultants in the field should be able to direct you to a source for antique materials. Stairways can be as simple as the tightwinders or closet stairs found in many Colonial houses or as complicated as the gracefully-formed grand staircase of a high-style Southern mansion which seems almost to float in air. The only kinds of staircases fabricated today by commercial firms which may interest the old-house owner are the spirals. The remaining models compatible in a period interior should be custom-built.

Stairways Inc.

One model—the all-wood spiral stairway—could be used in a converted barn home or in a small house where space is at a premium. The standard model is built around a laminated 6″, thirteen-sided solid pine column; the treads are of red oak. The manufacturer stresses that this is *not* a kit, but a fully assembled stairway which only requires surface finishing and installation.

Brochures available.

Stairways Inc.
4323-A Pinemont
Houston, TX 77018
(713) 680-3110

Steptoe & Wife Antiques

Since the publication of the first *Old House Catalogue*, the Steptoe cast-iron sprial staircase, featured in those pages, has become more and more popular. Illustrated is the reproduction of a 19th-century cast-iron model. For further details, and information on distributors, contact,

Steptoe & Wife Antiques, Ltd.
3626 Victoria Park Avenue
Willowdale, Ontario M2H 3B2
Canada

Doors

Perhaps nothing better expresses the character of a house than its main entrance. More attention has been lavished on doors and entryways in books and magazine articles than on any other architectural element. An inappropriate doorway can destroy an otherwise stylistically interesting building. The use of stamped aluminum and mass-produced wooden screen-
and-storm combination doors with cutsey-pie "Colonial" motifs will render any distinguished entryway ridiculous. In the interior of the house, doors should be made of solid materials, and in a style congenial to the age of the structure. This may mean board and batten, raised-paneled, carved, glass-paneled, or any one of a hundred variations and combinations.

Doors are among the least difficult antique components to find. Even junkyards often stack them up for prospective buyers. Restoration suppliers may have hundreds of models from which to choose, including French, sliding, simple pine slabs with four or six panels, heavy carved mahogany and oak monsters, and perhaps even whole front-door assemblies. If these sources fail you, then you might want to try one of the manufacturers of new doors or a craftsman who will custom make any model desired.

Architectural Emphasis

This San Francisco supplier features five basic models, as illustrated here, which are appropriate for late-Victorian and early-20th-century homes. The materials that can be used are pine, redwood, mahogany, or oak. All include cap molding on the front side as standard, and there is an extra charge for repeating the work on the reverse. Custom models can also be produced.

Brochure available.

Architectural Emphasis, Inc.
1750 Montgomery Street
San Francisco, CA 94111
(415) 362-0832

2002

1010

2003

505

1002

Maurer & Shepherd

Interior pine doors $^{15}/_{16}$" thick and 1¾" thick exterior doors are one of the specialties of this Connecticut firm. Elaborate pedimented entryways of the Georgian-Colonial period are also reproduced upon request.

Maurer & Shepherd, Joyners
122 Naubuc Avenue
Glastonburg, CT 06033
(203) 633-2383

Nord

This is one of the largest of home product manufacturers and supplies a wide array of wood items. Only exterior doors, however, are made of solid wood, those for the interior having weatherbond panels. There are several vaguely Colonial models available and a few that might be fitting in Spanish Colonial Revival homes.

Brochures available.

E. A. Nord Sales Co.
P.O. Box 1187
Everett, WA 98206
(206) 259-9292

Silverton Victorian Mill Works

Victorian period front doors and all the appurtenances—stops, surface caps, trim, casings—are produced on a custom basis. Illustrated is one of the firm's designs. Oak, redwood, and pine are used for all millwork.

Catalogue available, $2.

Silverton Victorian Mill Works
Box 523
Silverton, CO 81433
(303) 387-5716

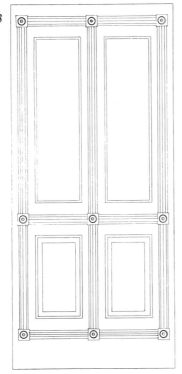

Norman Vandal

Mr. Vandal is a jack-of-all-trades—cabinetmaker, housewright, and restoration consultant. Illustrated is one of his designs for a pilastered entrance with entablature used in the restoration of a late-18th-century house. Some of his cabinetmaking skill is on display in Chapter 9.

Norman Vandal
P.O. Box 67
Roxbury, VT 05669
(802) 485-8380

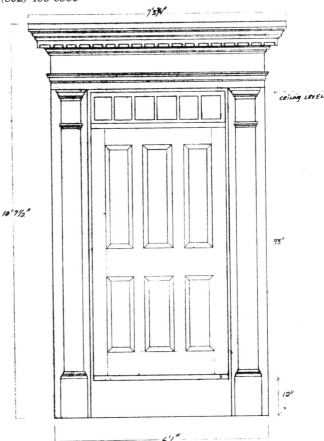

The Woodstone Co.

Insulated wooden doors made in chilly New England make sense, and Woodstone supplies them. This is a custom millwork shop that keeps a good supply of domestic and imported lumber on hand for high quality work.

The Woodstone Co.
Westminster, VT 05158
(802) 722-4784

We have previously featured the doors made by Spanish Pueblo Doors and are glad to do so again. These are exterior doors, 1¾" thick, made of either Ponderosa pine or Philippine mahogany. These can be made heavier (up to 3") or lighter (1¼") if desired. As the company explains, standard designs are less

Windows/Shutters/Shades

If windows are the eyes of the house, then they must be as beautiful as possible. Most North American houses are blessed with an abundance of light-filled openings, and they provide a focus for much interior and exterior decoration. Casement windows are a rarity, most of them having disappeared after the advent of the English double-hung sash form in the early 1700s. When we are pulling and tugging at our old wooden sash, however, we often wish that there was an easy casement to flip open. And now with energy costs zooming, we wonder from time to time just how much heat we are losing each winter night because of ill-fitting sash. Don't ask us to change them over for modern double- or triple-glazed lightweights of aluminum. It is not necessary, however, to freeze in style. Old window sash can be rebuilt, fitted with new hardware, reglazed if necessary, and protected in cold weather by easily-installed storm windows. If you find that it is impossible to make do with the old, however reconditioned and protected, don't feel that you have to go with modern plate glass.

Charles Bellinger/Architectural Components

Eastern white pine is used in all of Bellinger's wood products, including the 12-over-12 sash hung in a plank window frame with a molded pediment. Mortise and tenon joints, held secure

expensive, but all are custom milled. Illustrated is a variation on their style No. 115.

Spanish Pueblo Doors
P.O. Box 2517, Wagon Road
Sante Fe, NM 87501
(505) 471-0811

with square pegs rather than glue, are employed in each piece of millwork. Other types can be custom made.

Brochure, 50¢.

Charles Bellinger/Architectural Components
P.O. Box 246
Leverett, MA 01054
(413) 549-1094

Simon Newby

An English craftsman of uncommon ability, Newby has settled in the United States. Typical of his work is the raised wainscoting, and 9-over-6 sash with a sliding raised panel shutter illustrated here, all of which are made of Eastern white pine and grain painted. Like Bellinger's, all construction is mortised, tenoned, and wood pinned in the traditional manner. Each joined window sash is made to fit window frames of the 18th-century type. Custom-made reproduction 17th-century casements with diamond light with leaded bars are also available. Several non-standard forms can be made up: double-hung casement frame with mullion, fixed sash, etc. Transom lights are also made to order.

Simon Newby
Shop at 670 Drift Road
Westport, MA 02790
(617) 636-5010

Quaker City Manufacturing

The "Window Fixer" is Quaker City's answer to broken sash cords and weights or spring counterbalances. Its window channels can be installed by the home do-it-yourself expert, thereby saving old windows and money on the fuel bill. The channels are heavy-duty aluminum and stainless steel and will also end sticking and rattling problems. They will fit 85% of all wood sash, and are stocked at lumberyards and home centers across the United States.

Quaker City Manufacturing Co.
701 Chester Pike
Sharon Hill, PA 19079
(215) 586-4770

Preservation Resource Center

Preservation Resource Center has been recommended several times as providing the very best reproduction window sash and shutters. We can only repeat our words once more. The group is particularly responsive to the needs of old-house owners. Recently it began to offer storm sash since: "Many old houses, otherwise efficient, suffer large heat losses through and around the windows. Preservation Resource Center can provide properly fitting storm sash to help you improve upon this situation without sacrificing authenticity." Storm sash is available for Colonial and Victorian-period homes.

PRC is also beginning to produce a new line of standard sash—prefabricated and available in a number of sizes at considerably lower cost than the custom sash which was previously the firm's only offering.

Brochure available, $2.

Preservation Resource Center
Lake Shore Road
Essex, NY 12936
(518) 963-7305

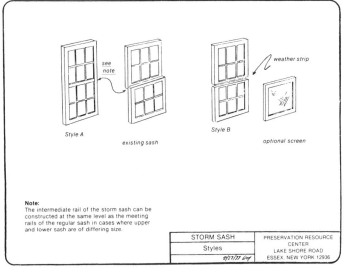

Norton Blumenthal

Blumenthal's wood Venetian blinds are well-known in the New York area and deserve a national reputation. The slats are of pine and are 2" wide. There are 50 tape colors in stock, and installation brackets are supplied. The blinds are available up to 14' wide and to any height.

Norton Blumenthal, Inc.
979 Third Avenue
New York, NY 10022
(212) 752-2535

Holland Shade Co.

This leading manufacturer produces a similar Venetian shade and offers as well custom-crafted shutters for interior use. Yet another product useful for old-house owners is energy saving shades. Ten to one, Holland claims, is the average ratio of energy waste of window areas as opposed to other wall surfaces. An investment in special insulated shades may save you much money in the future.

Holland Shade Co. Inc.

306 E. 61st Street
New York, NY 10021
(212) 644-1700

Tin Ceilings

Tin ceilings have become such an "in" thing in urban areas that a reaction is beginning to set in. But, no, let's be thankful that there is a trendy substitute for dropped acoustical panels, and let bygones stay with us in the form of pressed-tin ceilings. Ceilings finished in other ways—fancy plasterwork, painted, papered, gilded, etc.—are covered in other sections of this book.

Ceilings, Walls & More

Tin ceilings were hardly a stylish, aristocratic sort of thing in their Victorian heyday. It should not shock the purists, then, to learn that classic metal patterns are now available in lightweight, high impact polymer and vinyl materials. These are easy to install and are quite well executed in design. Three basic patterns are available now, and surely more will be forthcoming. A sample kit, with literature and price list, is available. One for $3.50 includes quarter-size samples; the other for $5.50 contains full-size panels.

Ceilings, Walls & More
P.O. Box 494
124 Walnut Street
Jefferson, TX 75657

W. F. Norman

Norman is back! W.F.'s "Hi-Art" steel ceilings are considered artful again, and his 1909 catalogue has been reissued. Of the 139 ceiling components shown in that edition, 124 can still be produced today. The story of the rediscovery of the Norman legacy is too good not to be repeated:

"Out in a warehouse at the rear of the Norman half-block plant in downtown Nevada are scores of the original plaster-of-Paris patterns from which the dies for processing the steel ceilings, walls, wainscoting, etc., were made almost a century ago. Some of the patterns have been damaged by the passage of time and a fire years ago, but most of them are intact and reveal the tremendous artistry that went into their creation. Many of the 700 to 900 pound cast-iron dies have been preserved, too, though some were siphoned off by scrap drives during World War II.

"There are dies for everything: ceiling center plates, outside and inside corner plates, border plates, cornice and frieze plates, mold plates, inside and outside mitres, girder finishes, side walls, and wainscoting. And there are the drop hammers that use the various dies to convert a piece of sheet metal into

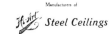
Greek, Colonial, Rococo, Empire, Gothic, and Oriental designs—even Masonic symbols for ceilings, walls, or ornaments for the temples of that brotherhood. The drop hammers, being more of an instrument of art than mere machine, produce stampings no two of which are precisely alike and, thus, are works of art in themselves.

"And they're all being used once again."

Need more be said? The 1909 catalogue goes for $3 and is worth every penny, as are the ceilings.

W. F. Norman Corp.
P.O. Box 323
214-32 N. Cedar Street
Nevada, MO 64772
(417) 667-5552

Hi-Art East

This firm serves as the Eastern U.S.A. distributor for the metal ceiling products manufactured by Norman.

Hi-Art East
6 N. Rhodes Center N.W.
Atlanta, GA 30309
(404) 876-4740

While celebrating the rebirth of Norman, we should not forget two veterans of the metal ceiling fraternity who have managed to stay alive for many years and whose own rediscoveries were celebrated in these pages some time ago. These are the Barney Brainum-Shanker Steel Co., of Glendale, Queens, New York, and the AA-Abbingdon Ceiling Co. of Brooklyn. Their addresses will be found in the List of Suppliers.

Other Suppliers of Structural Materials & Services

Consult List of Suppliers for addresses.

Restoration Consultants and Contractors

American Building Restoration
Robert W. Belcher
John Conti
Richard Henry Eiselt
The 18th-Century Co.
Wilbert Hasbrouck
International Consultants
Kensington Hitorical Co.
Old Town Restorations
Restorations Ltd.
John A. Wigen Restorations

Reproduction Period Homes

Donald E. Davis, Inc.
David Howard, Inc.

Glass

Artifacts, Inc.
A Tourch of Glass
Ball and Ball
Century Glass, Inc.
The 18th-Century Co.
Gargoyles, Ltd.
Bernard E. Gruenke
The Judson Studios
J. & R. Lamb Studios
Penco Studios
Renovator's Supply
Rococo Designs
Paul Thomas Studio
Unique Art Glass Co.
United House Wrecking
The Wrecking Bar (Atlanta)
The Wrecking Bar (Dallas)

Architectural Antiques

A. W. Baker
Early New England Restorations
Gargoyles, Ltd.
Great American Salvage
Materials Unlimited
Pat's Antiques
Greg Spiess
United House Wrecking
Urban Archaeology
Westlake Architectural Antiques
The Wrecking Bar (Dallas)

House Inspection Services

Arch Associates
A. W. Baker
David McLarn Hart Associates
Allen Charles Hill
Old House Inspection Co.
Preservation Associates

Brick

Artifacts, Inc.

View of sprial staircase, Shaker Centre Family Trustees' Office, Pleasant Hill, Kentucky, as photographed in 1963 by Jack E. Boucher for the Historic American Buildings Survey.

Diamond K. Co., Inc.

Columns and Pilasters

Decorators Supply
Walter E. Phelps
Dennis Paul Robillard
Saldarini & Pucci

Roofing Materials

Artifacts, Inc.
Bestwood Industries, Ltd.
Dana-Deck, Inc.
Hendricks Tile Mfg. Co.
Koppers Co., Forest Products Div.
San Francisco Victoriana

Beams

Robert W. Belcher
Broad-Axe Beam Co.
Diamond K. Co., Inc.
Kensington Historical Co.
Mountain Lumber Co.
Period Pine

Paneling/Clapboarding/Flooring

Townsend Anderson
Architectural Paneling, Inc.
Dale Carlisle
Craftsman Lumber Co.
Diamond K. Co., Inc.
Driwood Wood Moulding and Millwork Co.
The 18th-Century Co.
French and Ball
Carlo Germana
Kensington Historical Co.
Maurer & Shepherd
Old World Moulding and Finishing, Inc.
Period Pine
Potlatch Corp.
San Francisco Victoriana
Simpson Timber Co.

Stairways

Driwood Wood Moulding and Millwork Co.
Mexico House
York Spiral Stair

Doors

Allwood Door
Townsend Anderson
Artifacts, Inc.
Charles Bellinger
Castle Burlingame
The 18th-Century Co.
Elegant Entries
French and Ball
Gargoyles, Ltd.
Michael's Fine Colonial Products
Thomas Moser
Simon Newby
Walter E. Phelps
Preservation Resource Center
San Francisco Victoriana
United House Wrecking
The Wrecking Bar (Atlanta)
The Wrecking Bar (Dallas)

Windows/Shutters/Shades

Air-Flow Window Systems
Blaine Window Hardware
Grilk Interiors
Perkowitz Window Fashions
Pinecrest, Inc.

Tin Ceilings

Kenneth Lynch & Sons

Stone and Terra Cotta

Hendricks Tile Mfg. Co.
Structural Slate
Vermont Marble

Ornamental detail, Mary McCleod Bethune House, Washington, D.C., as
restored and adapted for reuse by Wm. Ward Bucher, architect.

2 Woodwork, Plaster Work & Other Fittings

The framework of a house, a structure stripped of its layers of architectural materials, is a rather nondescript affair. Not until its form has been filled out—sash and doors installed, stairways completed, casings and moldings put in place—does any real sense of style emerge. Many houses built today, however, lack the kind of finishing which makes a house a stylish home. An old house is usually very different, and the kinds of architectural elements employed to give it a decided character in years past are again today of crucial importance in restoration work.

Finding craftsmen who can reproduce various architectural elements is one of the largest problems facing the old-house owner. Woodwork, for instance, can be rather simple in form, but it is also likely to have been used to define nearly every structural element in a room, from shoe molding or baseboard to cornice. There are suppliers of somewhat standard moldings and casings that can satisfy the needs of many restorers; their products are likely to be machine-made. This is not necessarily a drawback; a large proportion of the woodwork used in mid- to late-Victorian houses, for example, was turned out in almost assembly-line fashion. The kind of moldings and casings found in earlier houses, however, may have been hand-planed, and their general profile is not one that can be simply machine-tooled. Included in this chapter is material on craftsmen who will undertake custom work that requires a personal touch.

The type and form of decorative elements which appear in any room should be studied with care. Most likely, it will be discovered that the woodwork may be of one piece—that is to say that the motifs used in moldings are of the same style and profile. This may apply to moldings used to define wall panels, those employed around windows and doors, and perhaps even that found in a chair rail or fireplace mantel. The same sort of moldings may even be used in several rooms—usually the principal ones such as dining room, parlor or living room, and perhaps the master bedroom. What may differ is the type of wood used, with fine hardwood being specified for the "best" rooms and such soft woods as pine and cypress used elsewhere.

Plasterwork is a more complicated matter. Decorative plastered walls and ceilings are a rarity. These rare cases occur in some of the most historic North American homes of the Colonial period that feature rooms with beautifully plastered pilasters, cornices, and wall panels; work of an equally elaborate sort was also executed in the homes of the very wealthy during the last decades of the 19th century through the 1920s. Much more commonly encountered are plaster ornaments—ceiling medallions and corner designs, wall brackets and corbels. Replacement or repair of such elements is not an inexpensive proposition, but, as the following pages illustrate, this is by no means an impossible feat. Some home owners may find that polymer substitutes for plaster will do just fine; others will insist on the real thing.

A word on composition moldings and ornaments is in order. This material has been used for years and may be no less authentic a medium than plaster or wood. The strength of composition—if properly made—can be as great as that of solid materials, and it is used in such interior objects as columns and elaborate mantels. Cast in molds in somewhat the same way as plaster, composition has a malleability which is desirable in decorative work.

Metal may also be useful in cornices, especially those of a complicated sort. Stamped out in one piece, such metal ornaments are easier to install. The appropriateness of metal consists not in its composition, but in the fineness of the stamping. Metals of various sorts have been used in homes since the early 19th century, although their primary use has been in commercial and institutional structures. For exterior use—in cornices, crestings, finials, grilles, and frieze windows—there is no better material.

In bringing an old house back to life or in recrea-ting a period room or dwelling, nothing is quite as important as the architectural elements used inside and out. Even a workingman's cottage is likely to have been blessed with some minor form of decoration—a fretwork railing, a turned newel post, oak wainscoting. To lose any of the elements is a pity; not to replace them is inexcusable if authentic detail is your goal. Over the past few years we have watched one of the landmarks of the Greek Revival style in our vicinity lose its cast-iron roof cresting, something which could be replicated in iron, or cost prohibiting, in an epoxy-impregnated material or polymer. How much has been allowed to crumble away inside is not known, but such neglect is yet another instance of how often in the New World we want to block out reminders of the old.

Custom Millwork

Although most localities that abound in old houses will undoubtedly have one or two local craftsmen conversant with the traditional arts of old-house carpentry, there are times when a carpenter's poor reputation, the impossibility of getting local labor to honor scheduled appointments, or just the simple desire to get an important restoration job done right *will suggest employing the services of firms specializing in the manufacture of custom millwork.*

Robillard

Dennis Paul Robillard, Inc., is a service-oriented organization that will manufacture wood moldings, carvings, millwork-sawn ornaments, columns, balusters—or virtually anything made out of wood. The wooden articles can be made from a sample set or from a line drawing or workable standards. The company will ship anywhere, and installation, in some cases, can be arranged.

Brochure available, $1.

Dennis Paul Robillard, Inc.
Front Street
South Bewick, ME 03908
(207) 384-9541

Maurer & Shepherd

Work that Maurer & Shepherd, Joyners, has done includes doors and entryways, carved rosettes and other details, swan necks, pediments, moldings, raised panel walls, wainscoting, shutters, clapboards, mantels, wide-pine and oak flooring, and much additional architectural woodwork. The firm, like that of Charles Bellinger, hand planes all face surfaces, interior and exterior, and uses mortise-and-tenon joints held together with square pegs.

Literature available.

Maurer & Shepherd, Joyners
122 Naubuc Avenue
Glastonbury, CT 06033
(203) 633-2383

Charles Bellinger

Working from measured drawings or from actual pieces,

EARLY 18ᵗ CENTURY DOORWAY

Charles Bellinger of Architectural Components produces a line of interior and exterior doors, small-pane window sashes, plank window frames, and a variety of moldings patterned after Connecticut Valley architecture of the 18th and early 19th centuries. He also undertakes a variety of custom orders including paneled fireplace walls, custom entrances (one pictured here), interior and exterior shutters, and fanlight sash. His hand-planed wide-board wainscoting is supplied either beaded or with a featheredge.

Brochure available, 50¢.

Charles Bellinger
Architectural Components
P.O. Box 246
Leverett, MA 01054
(413) 549-1094

Walter E. Phelps

Since he is not limited to a few stock Colonial patterns and can easily produce any type of antique architectural woodwork from the 17th through the 20th centuries, Walter E. Phelps will be happy to quote prices on crown moldings, base moldings, door casings, mantels, paneled doors, batten doors, stair rails, balusters, newel posts, columns, all types of sash work, corner cupboards, entryways, and much more. He will copy any piece of woodwork from a sample or measured drawing and guarantee the authenticity and accuracy of the finished work without compromise.

No catalogue available, but will respond to inquiries.

Walter E. Phelps
Box 76
Williamsville, VT 05362
(802) 348-6346

Veneers and Inlays

Veneers can offer the old-house restorer unlimited and unrealized opportunities. Covering the surfaces of cheaper woods with veneer only 1/28-inch thick costs far less than buying corresponding solid wood. Furthermore, many of the world's finest and most exotic woods are available only in veneer form. Since the rich color and grain of veneers is more uniform than solid woods because of the way in which they are cut from the log, they finish better than other woods.

Albert Constantine and Son

Constantine offers what it calls "the world's largest selection of fine veneers," almost 80 varieties in all, including such rarities as African zebrawood, Japanese tamo, Brazilian tulipwood, and Hawaiian koa, all available in lengths of 36″ and widths of

4″ to 12″. For use in large projects (doors, paneling), Monarch veneers in 15 varieties are available for surfaces 7′ and longer. (No woodworker, incidentally, should be without Constantine's catalogue, a garden of earthly delights for any do-it-yourselfer.)

Catalogue available.

Albert Constantine and Son, Inc.
2050 Eastchester Road
Bronx, NY 10461
(212) 792-1600

Homecraft Veneer

In its understated way, Homecraft Veneer outdoes "the world's largest selection of fine veneers" by offering 130 different varieties in widths from 4″ to 18″ and in 3′ lengths. Upon request, lengths up to 8′ (random widths) can usually be supplied.

Literature available.

Homecraft Veneer
901 West Way
Latrobe, PA 15650
(412) 537-8435

Wood Moldings and Ornamentation

Nothing is more basic to the stylistic finishing of an old house than woodwork. Moldings have a practical purpose, to hide the places where structural elements have been joined. Their complexity, however, will differ from dwelling to dwelling. Carpentry work of the sort done in an early Colonial New England home, for instance, would not have involved the application of intricate moldings of the type used in the Georgian Colonial period. Similarly, the woodwork found in Federal, Greek Revival, and Italianate houses is often relatively flat— two-dimensional in comparison to that adorning Second Empire or Queen Anne dwellings of later in the 19th century.

Moldings and other forms of ornamentation may also be applied for purely decorative reasons. With greater availability of machine-made wood products in the mid- to late 1800s, the average home owner could afford to indulge in such fanciful devices as spandrels, brackets, grilles, and medallions. Many of the architectural critics of the time felt that fretwork ornamentation of this type was being used to an excess. And by the turn of the century, there was clear evidence that popular taste was moving in the direction of simpler forms not unlike those common a century earlier.

The outline created by a molding is known as a profile. Some of the simpler forms may be available today in the average

lumberyard or home center. The use of chair rails, in country or Colonial-style interiors, for instance, is popular once again, and these straightforward pieces can be fabricated with little skill. Generally, however, the kinds of moldings and combinations thereof found in the period house have to be special ordered or custom made. Moldings of a similar type are likely to have been used in at least the principal rooms of a house, but there is always the odd form—in the kitchen or bathroom, perhaps—which defies standardization.

Such decorative forms as corner blocks, brackets, fancy fretwork panels, spindles, elaborate posts, drops, and rails are frequently even more difficult to find. A skilled carpenter can make them all, but, lacking such a craftsman in your area, you may wish to call upon the services of a specialist or supplier for whom fancy woodwork is the standard and not the exception.

Atwood & Tremblay

This firm regularly supplies both antique and new millwork for use in various restoration projects throughout the United States. Virtually any architectural piece can be duplicated detail for detail.

Atwood & Tremblay Associates, Inc.
Timber Swamp Road
Hampton, NH 03842
(603) 926-8625

Cumberland Woodcraft

The demand for Victorian millwork was first met on the West Coast by such innovative suppliers as San Francisco Vic-

toriana. Now the wave of interest in high-Victorian styles is moving to the East, and Cumberland is prepared to meet the needs. Illustrated is a new line of designs for exterior and interior use. All products are made from premium-grade, solid, kiln-dried hardwoods. Oak and poplar are generally used, but such woods as walnut, cherry, or maple can be specified. As illustrated in the second photograph, Cumberland will also supply turnings and posts. Also available are exterior corbels with appropriate pendant drops, and balusters and rails.

Full-color catalogue and price list available, $3.

Cumberland Woodcraft Co., Inc.
Walnut Bottom Road, R.D. 5
Box 452
Carlisle, PA 17013
(717) 243-0063

Haas Wood & Ivory Works

Cabinetwork and wood turning of every description is the special strength of this well-known San Francisco shop, founded in 1887. Illustrated are some of the 16 turning styles which are part of the standard repertoire of these craftsmen.

Haas Wood & Ivory Works
64 Clementina Street
San Francisco, CA 94105
(415) 421-8273

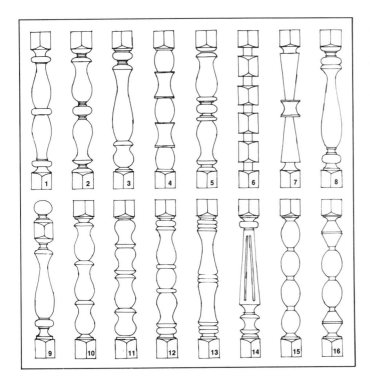

All the previously-mentioned woodwork suppliers are new to this book. We would be remiss, however, if we did not include products from some of the sources previously chronicled. In each case, product lines have been increased in the past two years.

Bendix Mouldings

A wide variety of moldings and ornaments, many of them traditional in design, are available in carved, embossed, or plain forms. Moldings are sold in random lengths from 3 to 15 feet, with the majority falling in the 6 to 10-foot category; beaded moldings are produced in lengths of 2½ and 3 feet. The carved moldings require the use of fine hardwoods; embossed moldings can be produced with the same materials or with such softer woods as pine and obeche.

Catalogue available, $1.

Bendix Mouldings, Inc.
235 Pegasus Avenue
Northvale, NJ 07647
(201) 767-8888

Vintage Wood Works

Gingerbread of the sort once used by country carpenter/builders is available again. Illustrated is just a sampling of the fanciful, scrolled designs which are cut from pine. As with some other suppliers of moldings and ornamentation, the pieces are shop-sanded and shipped ready for finishing as the buyer wishes—paint, stain, or clear sealer.

Brochure available, $1.

Vintage Wood Works
Rte. 2, Box 68
Quinlan, TX 75474
(214) 356-3667

Hallelujah Redwood Products

We've long admired the redwood moldings, brackets, corbels, appliqué blocks, and porch rails produced by this small firm. Redwood is a superb wood, and its use in hundreds of thousands of period homes in the Far West is a well-established fact. Hallelujah will produce its standard offerings in other woods as well, and will undertake custom work. Illustrated are two of the porch rail designs.

Brochure available, $1.

Hallelujah Redwood Products
39500 Comptche Road
Mendocino, CA 95460
(707) 937-4410

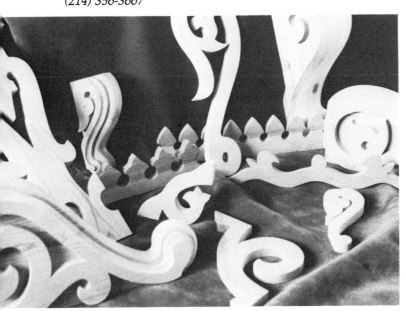

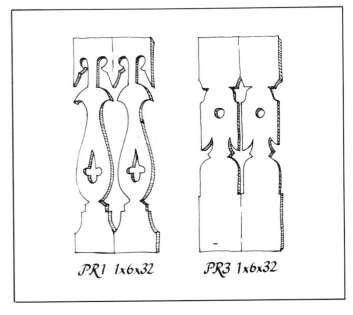

PR1 1x6x32   *PR3 1x6x32*

Old World Moulding & Finishing

Panel, crown, and trim moldings are the special forte of Old World. All are produced in random lengths from 8 to 16 feet of kiln-dried poplar, but it would be possible to have other woods used on a custom basis. These moldings are machine-produced —as are most available today—but they are remarkably faithful to traditional pieces.

Catalogue available, $1.

Old World Moulding & Finishing Co., Inc.
115 Allen Blvd.
Farmingdale, NY 11735
(516) 293-1789

Preservation Resource Center

PRC is one of the few firms that we will allow the use of the term "authentic." The word has been abused by so many companies whose products merely simulate the "look" of a period object, that warning flashers immediately light up when we see the term in print. PRC makes available both stock and custom moldings and is refreshingly honest about the virtues of both: "For the average restoration, we recommend the Standard Grade as any small flaws will be more than offset by the much lower price. For those ordering the unfinished molding, we provide instructions on how to simplify hand sanding through construction of a contour sanding block." Moldings can be made in any wood desired; basswood is a regular stock item in the hardwood category. Thirty inches (three lengths) is the minimum order that will be accepted; lengths are available up to 90". A 4" sample can be sent for $2.

Brochure available, $2.

Preservation Resource Center
Lake Shore Road
Essex, NY 12936
(518) 963-7305

San Francisco Victoriana

The experience gained from many home restoration projects and the knowledge acquired from the study of building manuals, suppliers' catalogues, and house plan books is very evident in the reproductions made by this pioneering firm. Shown are two post cap designs which emerged from the research and work done over the years. Newel posts, handrails, balusters, and shoe rails and fillers as well as a selection of moldings are made from clear redwood. San Francisco Victoriana also carries the Cumberland line of ornamental oak designs.

Literature available upon request.

San Francisco Victoriana
2245 Palou Avenue
San Francisco, CA 94124
(415) MI8-0313

Door and Window Casings

Casings are assemblies of moldings or one wide molding which "cases" in an interior door or window. These frames or cases are sometimes made up of only beaded boards; others are "built-up" with the addition of a second profile such as a bolection or more gently curved molding. The windows and doors in some houses, of course, have no visible casings or frames since the supporting members, with the exception of a sill, have been plastered over and hidden from view. This is found most commonly in English Colonial houses, particularly those built of stone, and in adobe and Spanish Colonial Revival structures which derive their form from the commingling of Indian and Spanish Colonial building traditions. The vast majority of North American homes, however, do display examples of architectural millwork in window and door treatments. Various edging designs became very popular in the second half of the 19th century and were produced by machine. Machines are again at work duplicating these forms; more sculpted casings are also being hand-planed in yet an older tradition.

Driwood Moulding Co.

Assembly casings of various types are available from this best known of millworks. Most are suitable for high-style Colonial and early-19th-century interiors, although a few might be appropriate for late-19th-century dwellings of heroic dimensions. Kiln-dried poplar is used for all work and is left unsanded for painting. The manufacturer will be glad to quote on the use of such other woods as mahogany, oak, walnut, cherry, etc.

Catalogue available, $3.

Driwood Moulding Co.
P. O. Box 1729
Florence, SC 29503
(803) 669-2478

Preservation Associates

This is one of many small enterprises that provide restoration supplies, consulting services, and custom-made millwork. Hand-planed moldings and trim are among the items that can be reproduced in the same manner that they were originally made. Such moldings can be used in a casing assembly.

Brochure available.

Preservation Associates
P.O. Box 202
Sharpsburg, MD 21782
(301) 432-5466

San Francisco Victoriana

The types of casing offered by Victoriana, here classified and illustrated as types A, B, and C, are suitable not only for many San Francisco homes but for those of the late-19th century which are found in many parts of North America. Yet further types of profiles are illustrated in the firm's exceptionally useful architectural moldings catalogue. Used with proper baseblocks, headblocks, corner blocks, and hoods, the casings will serve admirably in a remarkable number of Second Empire (Mansard), Shingle, Queen Anne, or Eastlake houses. Parts such as these—machine produced in the past and again today —were perhaps more commonly used than we might think. All are produced in clear dry redwood and are available in 6- to 12-foot random lengths; blocks, of course, are sold per piece.

Catalogue of architectural moldings available, $4.

San Francisco Victoriana
2245 Palou Avenue
San Francisco, CA 94124
(415) MI8-0313

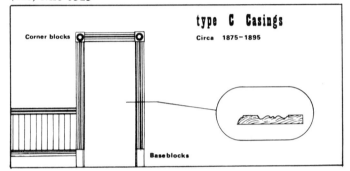

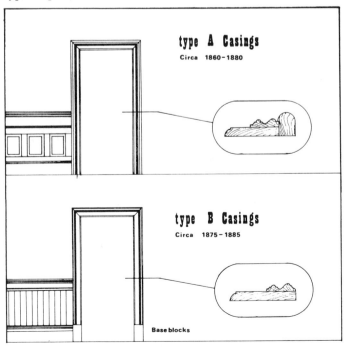

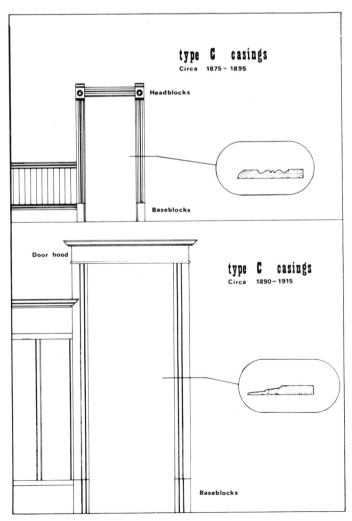

Silverton Victorian Mill Works

The door and window casing profiles offered by this firm are not quite as elaborate as those featured by Victoriana, but they are no less useful for many interiors of the late Victorian period. All the profiles are either one- or two-piece, there being only four of the latter. These are illustrated here, and along with the others are available in kiln-dried oak, redwood, or pine. Lengths will vary from 5 to 12 feet unless otherwise specified. Silverton is also well equipped to supply the other elements—blocks in particular—needed to complete a full casing assembly.

Catalogue available, $2.

Silverton Victorian Mill Works
Box 523
Silverton, CO 81433
(303) 387-5716

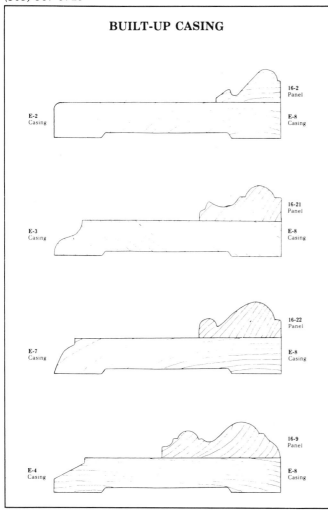

BUILT-UP CASING

Among the most widely-admired features of a period room are *fine paneling and built-in examples of the cabinetmaker's art. In the Colonial-period house, a paneled fireplace room end may stand out as the most impressive of architectural achievements. The earliest of these antique wall units often consist of nothing more than beaded boards or sheathing, with an opening for a door or two, and perhaps a closet or cupboard, but without a mantel or even a shelf. The true masterpieces are of a later date, from the 1720-1800 Georgian period when a room end was often defined in the classical manner with an ornate cornice, panels with moldings, a paneled dado, a chair rail, pilasters, and a mantel with a tabernacle or cupboard above.*

In the 19th century classical motifs were gradually replaced with those of French and Italian inspiration. Wood wainscoting reached higher and higher up the wall, and cornices and friezes dipped lower from the ceiling. Picture and plate rails defined the remaining area.

Whereas pine had been used widely in Colonial room ends, fancier hardwoods came into popularity in the early 1800s and continued to be employed for the best work. Such softer woods as cypress and redwood continued to find use in middle-class homes in the South and West, respectively, but, when affordable, oak, mahogany, cherry, and walnut were selected for the dining room, parlor, and perhaps the master bedroom.

All such work can be duplicated today by master craftsmen. Repairs can be made with the same woods in a manner that almost defies detection by talented carpenters and cabinetmakers. And, perhaps most importantly, the kinds of standardized paneling found in the period home—of whatever era—can be provided on either a custom or, in many cases, a stock basis.

R. H. Davis

Davis undertakes custom millwork of Colonial design. Panel work is one of the specialties at his shop. It can be executed in a manner so that the home owner can himself install the various elements.

Brochure available, $2.

R. H. Davis, Inc.
Antrim, NH 03440
(603) 588-6885

Mountain Lumber

Custom kitchens using heart pine and paneled walls of the same fine wood are two of the offerings of the Mountain Lumber craftsmen. The price for a basic wall is $7 to $12 per square foot, exclusive of cabinet work, and it is designed with flat or raised panels let into molded or square-edge stiles and rails. The same wall can be made of hardwood, painted poplar, or basswood. These wall sections, of course, must be custom fit.

Mountain Lumber Co.
1327 Carlton Avenue

Wood Paneling, Wainscoting, Baseboards, Room Ends, Cabinets, Cupboards

Charlottesville, VA 22901
(804) 295-1922

Simon Newby

Interior wall finishing is available in many forms including 17th-century shadow-molded wainscot and 18th-century raised paneling. Chimney breasts are also made to order.

Simon Newby
670 Drift Road
Westport, MA 02790
(617) 636-5010

Period Pine

The people at Period Pine can not only locate beautiful antique Southern yellow heart pine for you, but can assist with the design and execution of handsome paneling, an example of which is seen here. Raised panels, fireplace mantel, and fireplace molding with the same crossetted corner design as the main door frame come together in a harmonious manner. Heart pine is also used in the window trim, raised panel pocket doors, ceiling beams, and cornice.

Period Pine
P.O. Box 77052
Atlanta, GA 30357
(404) 876-4740

The Woodstone Co.

Cabinets and paneling are custom made from hundreds of pat-

terns in stock. Planing to 26" wide can be executed.

The Woodstone Co.
Westminster, VT
(802) 722-4784

Two of the firms previously recommended enthusiastically in *The Old House Catalogue* are the Kensington Historical Company and Maurer & Shepherd, Joyners. For their addresses, consult the List of Suppliers. Both specialize in custom millwork in the 18th-century manner. Kensington also stocks a supply of antique raised-panel room ends, chimney breasts, complete fireplace walls, and panel segments. Horizontal and vertical sheathing, featheredge or beaded, may also be found here.

Composition and Wood Fiber Moldings and Ornaments

Composition and fibrous materials have been used for ornamental work for several centuries. They are an appropriate medium for lightweight, but well-defined, decoration. Today, unfortunately, the term "composition" conjures up a vision of flimsy kitchen cabinets and shoddy pieces of furniture. Composition board—hardly a kissing cousin of the composition products here recommended—is a fairly recent development.

Decorators Supply

This is the firm of firms. When we visited the plant, interior designers were busily at work in the showrooms choosing elements which could be used in houses, shops, and offices from coast to coast. There have to be several hundred thousand different patterns, models, and forms to choose from. If you can't find what you want from this selection, the company will custom produce exactly what you are looking for. In addition to composition and wood fiber carvings, Decorators also produces cast ornamental plaster items.

Wood fiber carvings catalogue, $1; woodwork-furniture ornaments, $13 (309 illustrated pages).

The Decorators Supply Corp.
3610-12 S. Morgan Street
Chicago, IL 60609
(312) 847-6300

Saldarini & Pucci

Saldarini & Pucci style themselves "architectural sculptors," and for good reason: their composition ornaments for woodwork, fiberglass castings for exterior restorations (in lieu of plaster, iron, stone, etc.), and plaster ornaments are first rate. Scrolls, wreaths, cornices, rosettes, garlands, etc., are made of composition, and while the selection is not as extensive as that offered by Decorators Supply, it is more than adequate for most home owners.

Saldarini & Pucci, Inc.
156 Crosby Street
New York, NY 10012
(212) 673-4390

The Lily Collection

The assemblage of ornamental motifs available from this firm is by no means as extensive as that of Decorators Supply, but it may be just as useful. There are more than 3,000 objects for interior and exterior application. Illustrated is one of the more whimsical.

Catalogue of architectural ornaments available, $10 (157 pages).

The Lily Collection
1313 N. Main
Ann Arbor, MI 48104
(313) 668-6324 or 769-4225

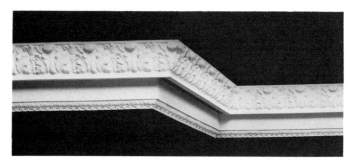

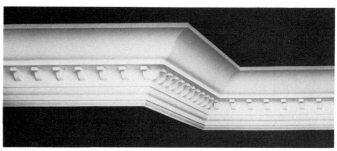

Focal Point

This firm has been featured in each edition of this book, and each time we are glad to acknowledge that more progress has been made in the technology required for the use of polymers. It is a particularly resilient material, but it must be handled with care. A special mastic is required for the filling of joints, and countersunk finishing nails are recommended for placement at either side of joints and studs. The installation of these moldings is, however, a great deal easier than those of multiple members in plaster or wood. Illustrated are two designs, first the Candler cornice, an exact replica of a plaster molding found in one of Atlanta's first skyscrapers; and second, a modillion cornice molding.

Catalogue available.

Focal Point, Inc.
2005 Marietta Road, N.W.
Atlanta, GA 30318
(404) 351-0820

A second manufacturer of polymer architectural materials, Fypon, Inc., was also featured in other editions and is still recommended. For this firm's address, consult the List of Suppliers.

Polymer Moldings and Ornaments

The use of modern polymers is about as badly understood as that of composition. It was inevitable that a formula would be found that allows traditional architectural millwork, usually produced in plaster or wood, to be molded from plastics. The feel of the material is similar to pine. Certain architectural elements are still quite economically produced in plaster or wood; we're thinking especially of centerpieces, medallions, rosettes, panel moldings, and rails of various sorts. Complicated moldings of the kind used for a cornice, however, are expensive to manufacture—even by machine—and to install. So why not consider polymers?

Plaster Moldings and Ornamentation

The plasterer's art is the most demanding and often the most accomplished of the various traditional building arts. Plastered walls and ceilings are now the exception rather than the rule, various fibrous substitutes having taken their place. Plaster moldings and other types of ornamental objects have also fallen by the wayside in the 20th century. Production of plaster-of-Paris and fibrous-plaster items, however, continues in a small way to this day and, indeed, may be enjoying a renaissance.

Giannetti's Studio

Ornamental plaster ceiling medallions are one specialty of this Washington-area firm. It is also involved in the preservation and restoration of old plasterwork and will supply casts suitable for exterior ornaments in epoxy reinforced with fiberglass.

Catalogue available, $2.

Giannetti's Studio
3806 38th Street
Brentwood, MD 20722
(301) 927-0033

Jack Guinan

Ceiling centerpieces, corners, and moldings are available in standard designs which are appropriate for a wide variety of interiors. Illustrated are some of the corners and moldings. Guinan will also produce custom castings to your design, a service which is especially appreciated when plasterwork has to be replaced in an authentic manner. Guinan is also a certified installer of products from Felber Studios, a source listed later in this section.

Catalogue available, $1.

Jack Guinan
Box 215
Barnesville, PA 18214
(717) 467-2809

San Francisco Victoriana

Victoriana's remarkable collection of plaster brackets and centerpieces is visually exciting and historically sound. All are produced by hand with casting plaster and are very reasonably priced. The models illustrated are, in order of appearance, "Midwinter Fair," "Elizabeth," and "California Street." The designs are taken from actual examples of brackets or centerpieces in use during the late 19th century in the San Francisco area. This does not mean, however, that they might not be appropriate as well for other regional types of homes. Nevertheless, some caution in this regard is in order. The use of centerpieces in American domestic interiors dates back to the 18th century, and designs appropriate for the 1860-1900 period may not be at all fitting for the rooms of an earlier house, whatever its location. Also illustrated are two bracket designs: "Italianate," at left; and "Page Street," at right.

Catalogue of ornamental plaster available, $5.

San Francisco Victoriana
2245 Palou Avenue
San Francisco, CA 94124
(415) MI8-0313

CEILING CORNERS & MOULDINGS

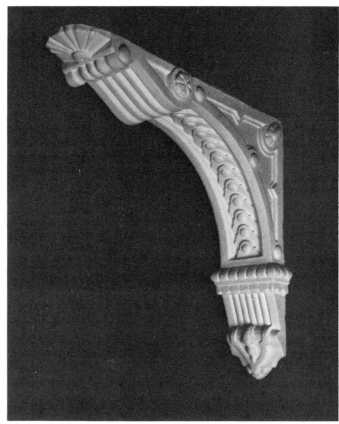

T. & O. Plaster Castings

Fibrous plaster, plaster laid upon a backing of canvas stretched over wood, has been used for many generations, especially for ceilings and complicated moldings. This English firm produces a wide variety of ornamental work—corbels, cornice moldings, friezes, wall and ceiling moldings, corner pieces, niches, centerpieces, wall plaques, pilasters, pedestals, statues, and door casing assemblies. These are for interior use since fibrous plaster is not recommended outside. Shipment of such materials to North America could be a problem, but if properly crated, they should survive the overseas voyage as well. Prices are quite reasonable, and the designs are most appropriate for interiors in the Georgian or Federal style.

Brochures available.

T. & O. Plaster Castings
80 Victoria Road
Romford, Essex
England
Tel. Romford 45619

Plasterwork Ceilings

Ornamental ceiling designs and fully-plastered ceilings are luxuries today. The cost of new materials and their installation is extremely high, but this was also the case 100 or 200 years ago when many plasterers were at work. Plaster in slabs, often of the fibrous sort, has made the affixing of whole ceilings a great deal easier. The application of small motifs need not be anywhere as costly or time-consuming a process as putting up a whole ceiling. Elaborate plastered ceilings are not frequently found in North American homes, but, where they are present, they should be protected and preserved.

Felber Studios

Period ceilings have made Felber's reputation. Designs from this firm have been published in previous editions of this book. Jack Guinan, whose work is discussed earlier in the chapter, works with Felber materials as does Tayssir Sleiman whose write-up follows. Felber has over 8,000 models in stock which, in its words, reflect "all of the basic architectural period styles." Of this vast number of designs, ceiling patterns are relatively few in number, but do reflect such period styles as Gothic Revival, Beaux Arts, and Tudor Revival.

Catalogue available, $2.

Felber Studios
110 Ardmore Avenue
P.O. Box 551
Ardmore, PA 19003
(215) MI2-4710

Tayssir Sleiman

Tayssir Sleiman is one of the craftsmen who work with Felber materials. He will also custom design ceilings of any period and execute the restoration of the antique.

Tayssir Sleiman
423 Horsham Road
Horsham, PA 19044
(215) 672-2607

Ornamental Metalwork

The type of metalwork used in period homes is usually found on the exterior. Gates, railings, fences, and grilles may define outdoor spaces and offer security as well. Stamped metal ceilings (covered in Chapter 1) and moldings, however, have been used inside since the 19th century. Metalworkers who produce cast, wrought, and stamped materials of this sort exclusively are few in number, but blacksmiths can provide assistance.

Student Craft Industries, Berea College

Among the most successful and popular programs conducted at Berea is that devoted to wrought iron. Illustrated is a gate which is representative of the quality of work performed. All the items are custom made to fit the customer's particular needs.

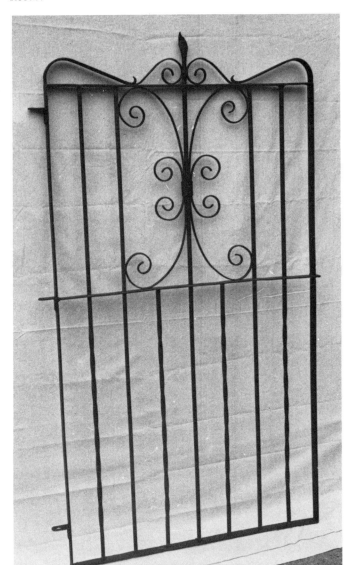

Catalogue available, 50¢.

Student Craft Industries
Berea College
Berea, KY 40404
(606) 986-9341, ext. 473

Bernardini Iron Works

Bernardini has been involved in the restoration of a number of antique fences, and it fabricates grille work for interior spaces and exterior windows. For Federal, Greek Revival, and Italianate homes with frieze windows, this could be the proper supplier. The company can also produce the type of grilles necessary for proper Spanish Colonial and Tudor Revival windows and doors.

Brochure available upon request.

Bernardini Iron Works, Inc.
418 Bryant Avenue
Bronx, NY 10474
(212) 589-8600 or (914) 699-5056

Tennessee Fabricating

Various types of grilles and grates can be cast in iron from traditional patterns which this firm keeps in stock. Illustrated are several which can be used for Victorian and Spanish and French Colonial buildings. This is also an excellent source of decorative architectural railings, crestings, and finials.

Catalogue of ornamental metal components, $2.50.

Tennessee Fabricating Co.
2336 Prospect Street
Memphis, TN 38106
(901) 948-3354

Kenneth Lynch & Sons

Always given attention in this book are the high-quality products from Kenneth Lynch & Sons. Of special note are the sheet metal ornaments—wreaths, garlands, moldings, scroll enrichments, crestings, miters, rosettes, etc.—which are executed with exceptional craftsmanship. Such cast-lead and stone objects as urns, garden seats, planters, and sundials are covered in Chapter 10, devoted to accessories.

Architectural sheet metal catalogue, $3.50.

Kenneth Lynch & Sons, Inc.
78 Danbury Road
Wilton, CT 06897
(203) 762-8363

Ceramic Ornaments

Tiles of various forms and finishes have been used in homes for centuries. In the New World they most often have decorated the fireplace hearth and mantel, and have been displayed in the kitchen and bathroom. Roof tiles are covered in Chapter 1. Floor tiles are discussed in Chapter 4.

Amsterdam Corp.

Very traditional Delft tiles are the stock in trade of this firm. Individual modular 5″ x 5″ tiles in blue (crackled and non-crackled), and polychrome (non-crackled) are featured. Tableaux are made up of 5″ x 5″ tiles and are polychrome (crackled). All the tiles are hand painted and exhibit such designs as birds, flowers, ships, etc.

Catalogue available, $1.50.

Amsterdam Corp.
950 Third Avenue
New York, NY 10022
(212) 644-1350

Barbara Vantrease Beall Studio

Custom hand-painted ceramic tiles with either traditional or modern designs are produced by this very talented artist. Murals are a specialty; plain tiles with special colors can also be ordered.

Barbara Vantrease Beall Studio
23727 Hawthorne Blvd.
Torrance, CA 90505
(213) 378-4410

Ironbridge Gorge

Maw & Co. at Jackfield, Ironbridge, was the largest manufacturer of decorative tiles in 19th-century Britain and by the 1890s included Edward VII, the Khedive of Egypt, and the Maharajah of Mysore among its many customers. After peaking during the Edwardian period, the demand for decorative tiles ceased after World War II, but Ironbridge Gorge Museum has commercially revived the manufacture of tiles, using Maw's original 19th-century molds. The tiles are molded in a 19th-century hand-operated press to reproduce the fine relief detail, and they are richly glazed and colored.

Tiles are produced in two sizes—approximately 6″ and 8″ square. Most are available in one of three colors—honey, coppice green, or delphinium. They are most appropriate for use in Victorian fireplace surrounds and hearths. Six-inch tiles are priced at £1.90; 8″ at £3.50.

Flyer available.

Ironbridge Gorge Trading Co., Ltd.
Coalport China Works Museum
Coalport, Telford TF8 7BR
England
Tel. Ironbridge (095 245) 3522

Plain & Fancy Accents

Hand-painted imported tiles are available through a number of North American outlets. These include tiles made in England, Holland, Denmark, Portugal, Mexico, and Turkey, and can approximate in design those brought from overseas in earlier years. Plain & Fancy has a particularly good selection.

Plain & Fancy Accents
714 E. Green Street
Pasadena, CA 91101
(213) 577-2830

Helen Williams/Rare Tiles

Helen Williams always has a stock of very handsome *antique* Delft tiles and faience. Illustrated are six 17th-century tiles featuring fish and allegorical sea animals. The sizes are approximately 5" x 5", and the earliest are painted in polychrome colors and in blue and white; in the 18th century the manganese color was added.

Literature available; a stamped self-addressed envelope is requested.

Helen Williams/Rare Tiles
12643 Hortense Street
North Hollywood, CA 91604
(213) 761-2756

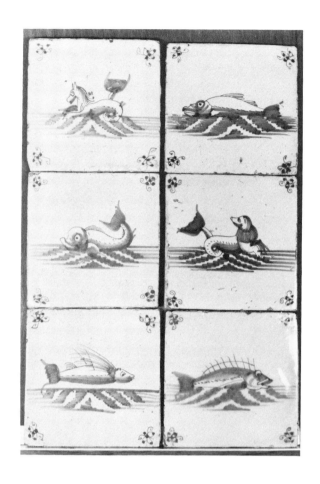

Other Suppliers of Woodwork, Plasterwork & Other Fittings

Consult List of Suppliers for addresses.

Custom Millwork

Amherst Woodworking and Supply
Douglas Campbell
R. H. Davis
French and Ball
Kensington Historical Co.
Michael's Fine Colonial Products
The Millworks
Simon Newby
Preservation Resource Center
San Francisco Victoriana
Silverton Victorian Mill Works

Veneers

Artistry in Veneers, Inc.
Dover Furniture Stripping
Gaston Wood Finishes, Inc.
Bob Morgan Woodworking Supplies
The Woodworkers' Store

Wood Moldings and Ornamentation

Colonial Moulding and Frame Co.
Driwood Moulding Co.
KB Moulding, Inc.
Klise Manufacturing Co.
Orlandini Studios
Renovator's Supply
Victorian Reproductions
The Woodworkers' Store

Door and Window Casings

French and Ball
Preservation Resource Center

Wood Paneling, Wainscoting, Baseboards, Room Ends, Cabinets, Cupboards

Douglas Campbell
Dale Carlisle
Castle Burlingame
Craftsman Lumber
Michael's Fine Colonial Products
San Francisco Victoriana
Silverton Victorian Mill Works

Plaster Moldings and Ornamentation

Architectural Ornaments
Decorators Supply
Felber Studios

Plaster Ceilings

Decorators Supply

Ornamental Metalwork

Guilfoy Cornice Works
House of Iron
Steve Kayne Hand-Forged Hardware
Newton Millham, Star Forge
Robinson Iron Corp.
Richard E. Sargent
Vulcan Iron Works

Ceramic Ornaments

Backlund Moravian Tile Works
Country Floors
William H. Jackson Co.

Instructor in ornamental ironwork, Student Craft Industries, Berea College,
Berea, Kentucky.

3 | *Hardware*

A visit to the neighborhood hardware store in the 1940s was an adventure. Hundreds upon hundreds of small boxes, carefully fitted into floor-to-ceiling wall cabinets, contained thousands of tiny surprises, more "what's-its" than we could begin to cope with. Brackets, screws, fasteners, grommets, bits, washers, nails, latches, weights—how did the salesman know what was what and where to find it? Not only was he able to put his hands on just the right thing, but he could even offer advice on its use. Then there were the tools hung in rows along the back walls, all shiny metals with sturdy oak handles, poles, etc. If I could have had one of each to grasp and try out, I would have been in hardware heaven. That was when I was a child, and now as an adult I can still only dream. The store is gone, replaced by a harshly-lit "home center" with more plastic than steel, acres of vinyl rather than open shelves neatly filled with cotton duck and canvas.

What I didn't know then and have only learned in recent years is that first-rate hardware is sold through the mail and that it may be produced not far away in what is an old-fashioned blacksmith's shop. While the commercial world has gone tootling along the synthetic path, a counterculture in—of all things—hardware has sprung alive. The catalogues of the best of the national purveyors of high-quality and unusual objects are featured throughout this chapter. So, too, are the handcrafted works of many talented young blacksmiths who have gone back to the hearth.

Hardware, you may say, is hardly worth such a fuss. A door latch or hinge is, indeed, a minor affair, but, for the lover of the old house, well-designed metals are of real consequence. A well-turned brass door knocker will catch the eye; fine pressed-glass knobs sparkle and handsomely embellish an interior door. The cast-bronze incised door and cabinet hinges of the late-Victorian era are charming reminders of a time when function followed form and not vice versa. Their delicate designs and sturdy construction reflect a commitment to craftsmanship that was more than a trade slogan.

Antique hardware can be found today in specialty shops. Old forms such as strap hinges and latches, however, are collector's items which are as likely to sit on a collector's shelf as they are to be used in a practical manner. Most of the hardware used today in old houses is of recent vintage, and much of it is every bit as good as the old. The reproduction industry really got underway in the 1930s and '40s when such master craftsmen as Donald Streeter and other antiquarians of an admirably stubborn bent refused to accept what was commercially available and produced their own wrought reproductions. Since that time the number of able workers has multiplied to the point where there is no reason to accept the flat, unconvincing copy of a so-called "Colonial" bean latch or a flashy stamped butterfly hinge.

Sometimes the advertisements of hardware makers make it appear that early Americans knew only such fine metals as bronze and brass. The appointments suggested by many commercial manufacturers for the average house of a Colonial style are far too grand for our taste and hardly conform to the historical record. If any metal is typically American it is iron—wrought until the mid-19th century, and cast thereafter. Finer metals were, of course, used throughout American history, but their utility was limited until what has been rightly termed the "Gilded Age" of the last several decades of the 1800s.

The entries in the following chapter suggest many of the ways in which hardware can be used in restoring the rooms of an old house, including the kitchen and bathrooms. There are also interesting references to sources and uses of furniture hardware. Nothing so mars the appearance of an antique chest or bureau as flimsy pulls or turned handles. As with the doors and windows of the period house, fine antique furniture deserves and can have better.

Architectural Hardware

At the beginning of the 19th century the term "hardware" meant chiefly mechanics' tools and builders' hardware, but it soon came to mean all small metal articles used in the construction of houses or for household purposes, tools of mechanics' trades, furnishing goods for kitchen and dining room service, tin plate, sheet iron, nails, screws, fence wire, etc. By the beginning of the 20th century it was not uncommon for a large hardware house to have in its catalogues nearly 100,000 kinds and sizes of articles. Given the quantity and variety of hardware hand made and mass produced in America, it's no wonder that most old houses still have original pieces intact. Guard and preserve these artifacts from the past, but, if you need to seek replacement parts, collect some of the excellent catalogues of reproduction pieces that follow. We haven't counted, but we think that you'll come close to the quantity available at the turn of the century.

Hinges

Long wrought-iron strap hinges with their decorative flared cusps were the most commonly used door-hanging hardware in Colonial America. They are widely available today from a variety of sources. Most blacksmiths mentioned on these pages

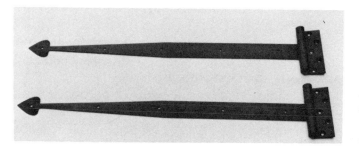

are willing to undertake custom work. Stock sizes can be ordered from a number of mail order outlets including The Renovator's Supply which has 14" and 18" pairs for $18.30 and $21.40, respectively.

Catalogue available, $2, refundable with purchase.

The Renovator's Supply
71 Northfield Road
Millers Falls, MA 01349
(413) 659-3542

Robert Bourdon, who specializes in custom forged-iron designs, tells us that his production, including hinges, is "limited to what one man can do in a small shop. Quality not quantity is the idea of my operation."

No catalogue, but will sketch to your specifications.

Robert Bourdon
Wolcott, VT 05680
(802) 472-6508

The true pintle strap hinge has a stationary end which is driven into the framing beam or fence post and supports the weight of the door or gate. The pintle is a bit more primitive than the plate hinge and does not always operate as smoothly, although many are still in service in the older rural areas. The hinges shown here were produced at Newton Millham's Star Forge.

Catalogue available, $1.

Newton Millham—Star Forge
672 Drift Road
Westport, MA 02790
(617) 636-5437

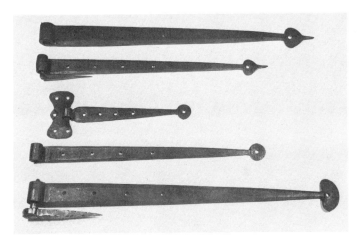

A blacksmith's creativity can be expressed in the kind of cusp designs he works into his hinges, as these by D. James Barnett attest.

Catalogue available, $1.

D. James Barnett, Blacksmith
710 W. Main Street
Plano, IL 60545
(312) 552-3675

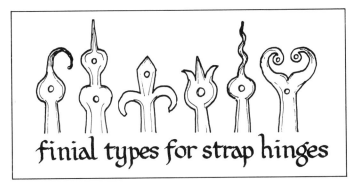

finial types for strap hinges

Door Knobs

Despite the frequency of their use, door knobs seem to survive from generation to generation in many old homes. In those instances where time and changing fashion have taken their toll, a number of suppliers can be counted on to have just about whatever is required for your 19th- or 20th-century house.

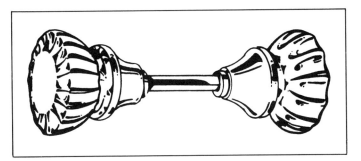

Heavy glass door knobs are common enough—until you go out and look for them. A pair of clear glass knobs with spindle, spacer washers, and set screws can be ordered from The Renovator's Supply for $3.95.

Catalogue available, $2, refundable with purchase.

The Renovator's Supply
71 Northfield Road
Millers Falls, MA 01349
(413) 659-3542

What better source for Victorian hardware than England? And what better place for door knobs than the London firm of Locks & Handles? One brass knob which doesn't seem to be readily available in this country has a long shank and a diameter of $1\frac{3}{8}$". Such an appointment would be well-suited to the interior of a period town house.

Brochure available.

Locks & Handles
8 Exhibition Road
London, SW7 2HF
England
(01) 584-6800

Baldwin has long been in the forefront of door hardware production. Its line of knobs includes brass, crystal, and porcelain, every one of which is a correct reproduction of its period predecessor.

Various brochures available, 50¢.

Baldwin Hardware Mfg. Corp.
841 Wyomissing Blvd.
Reading, PA 19603
(215) 777-7811

Door Knockers

During the 18th and 19th centuries, when visiting one's friends and neighbors was a more common event than it is today, a solid knock at the front door signified the start of a social ritual. The friendly knock may come less frequently now than it did then, but we can still find plenty of authentic and reproduction knockers in the marketplace. Be chary of the temptation to overwhelm, and select a piece that is suitable to the period of your house; the knocker should be a greeting and not a shout.

The classically-inspired Adam knocker—solid brass, of course —is just as fitting on the portal of a Belgravia town house in London as it is at the entrance to its early 19th-century equivalent—a Federal dwelling in Boston or Philadelphia. Such a knocker, at $7\frac{1}{2}$" in height, is offered for sale by Locks & Handles, a shop that has the largest selection of high-quality reproduction period door hardware in London.

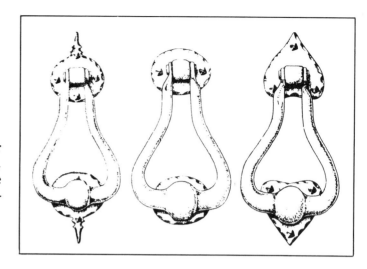

A door knocker in the form of a vigilant eagle seems a proper emblem to place on the door of an American home, provided, of course, that the motif is not repeated *ad nauseam* elsewhere in the house. Steve Kayne has cast this substantial and imposing piece of hardware in solid bronze.

Complete catalogues available, $3.

A knocker like this one from The Weather Vane is an excellent companion piece to iron strap hinges with heart-shaped cusps. If hearts are not a match, there are two other knockers with common cusp types from which to choose.

Complete catalogues available, $2.

Latches and Bolts

The simplicity of iron bolts and latches makes them—with one important exception—every bit as practical today as they were 200 years ago when such hardware was the primary means of securing most homes. For exterior applications a latch is inferior to a mortised lock with a modern tumbler that can be locked and unlocked from the outside. The more primitive slide bolt works fine, but can only be thrown from inside. There is no need to sacrifice security for authenticity.

The hardware now available to the consumer of restoration materials is comparable in quality to that of the 18th century, but is far exceeded in quantity and variety. Our predecessors could for the most part choose only from the work of local smiths. Today, we virtually have a whole world of styles at our fingertips.

A basic slide bolt like this one can be purchased from The Weather Vane in two sizes: a 4″ bolt with a 1¼″ x 3¼″ plate, and a 6″ version with a 1¾″ x 5¼″ plate.

Complete catalogues available, $2.

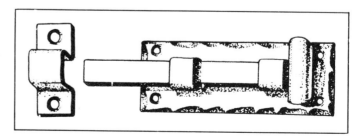

A closet bar latch is about as simple as a latch can get. Made of black wrought iron and supplied with matching square-head screws, this one from The Renovator's Supply is a lot of latch for $3.

Catalogue available, $2, refundable with purchase.

The Renovator's Supply
71 Northfield Road
Millers Falls, MA 01349
(413) 659-3542

The 9"-long Suffolk latch with triangular cusps is from the works of D. James Barnett, and is priced at $25.

Catalogue available, $1.

D. James Barnett, Blacksmith
710 W. Main Street
Plano, IL 60545
(312) 552-3675

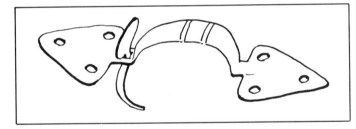

Had the now-trendy expression "state of the art" been in use in the middle of the 18th century, it probably could have been applied to Newton Millham's interpretaton of a latch from central Massachusetts. It measures 12½" x 4½" and has draw-filed cusps and beveled and molded edges. The grasp and part of the fancy back work are decorated with delicate punch designs. It sells for $130.

Catalogue available, $1.

Newton Millham—Star Forge
672 Drift Road
Westport, MA 02790
(617) 636-5437

As is his custom with all his work, Donald Streeter adheres rigidly to original practices in forging his spring latches. This type of door opener utilizes a knob to lift a spring-loaded latch into and out of the keeper attached to the doorframe. Streeter's least expensive latch is $90 and well worth it.

Complete catalogue available, $3; Norfolk latch brochure only, $1.

Donald Streeter
P.O. Box 237
Franklinville, NJ 08322
(609) 694-2428

Locks

Even the earliest colonial rim or box locks could be said to be precision instruments, each painstakingly constructed by a craftsman to serve flawlessly and unobtrusively for many years. Today's reproductions—Colonial through Victorian—are for the most part faithful to the originals although some have thoroughly modern internal mechanisms designed with security as important a factor as authenticity, neither of which comes cheap.

The Folger Adam Co.'s Williamsburg rim locks are arguably at the pinnacle of the authentic reproduction trade and, like the one pictured here, are cast from a brass formula which duplicates the mix used in the originals. The locks are fitted with brass knobs or drop handles, or a combination of the two. Cylinder flaps may be added to keyports to keep out cold and dirt. Some locks can be fitted with a modern cylinder operated by a small key.

Brochure available.

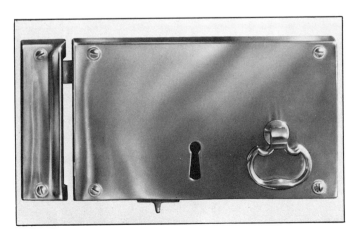

Folger Adam Co.
P.O. Box 688
700 Railroad Street
Joliet, IL 60434
(815) 723-3438

One of the most popular of all 19th-century locks can still be purchased through the Cumberland General Store. The reversible cast-iron lock has a tumbler, two bolts, and a button knobset in the face. The back plates and knobs are made of wrought steel. The set includes the necessary screws and can be bought for $38.83.

Catalogue available, $3.75.

Cumberland General Store
Rt. 3
Crossville, TN 38555
(615) 484-8481

For security with a touch of old-time feeling, you might want to look into a steel rim dead-bolt lock with a solid-maple cover. From the outside the lock is operated by a standard pin tumbler. It is sold in two sizes and each is unfinished so you can stain or paint it to match your door.

Brochure available.

Colonial Lock Company
172 Main Street
Terryville, CT 06786
(203) 584-0311

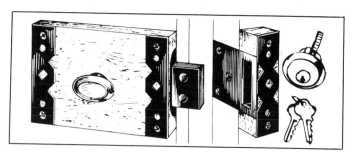

Nails and Screws

Considering the 70% improvement in holding power of wrought head cut nails over standard wire nails, it's a shame that they are prohibitively expensive for structural use where they are, of course, not visible. One lb. of 2½" nails cost $2.49 and represents only 48 nails.

Catalogue available, $3.75.

Cumberland General Store
Rt. 3
Crossville, TN 38555
(615) 484-8481

Several types and sizes of cut nails come from The Renovator's Supply, from 1½" tacks to 8" spikes. Discounts apply to large orders.

Black pyramid-head screws don't offer the kind of technical advantage over today's screws enjoyed by cut nails over their modern counterparts, but they are the most appropriate fastener for use with wrought ironwork. They come in four sizes, ⅝" to 1¼", 25 to a package, and range in price from $1.40 to $2.10.

Catalogue available, $3.75.

The Renovator's Supply
71 Northfield Road
Millers Falls, MA 01349
(413) 659-3542

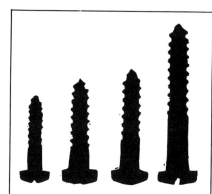

Dutch Door Quadrant

Dutch doors seem to have a whimsical quality. Perhaps it has something to do with their enabling you to have the door both open and shut at the same time. This reversible quadrant is made of solid brass and contains a nylon washer that maintains constant tension when the top door is closed. The price is $16.

Catalogue available, $2, refundable with purchase.

The Renovator's Supply
71 Northfield Road
Millers Falls, MA 01349
(413) 659-3542

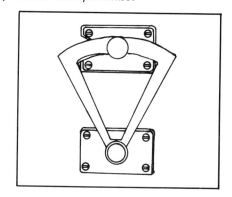

Doorstops

This reproduction of a Williamsburg doorstop has the distinction of being both very useful and very inexpensive. R. Hood & Co. is selling them for $2.50 apiece.

Brochure available.

R. Hood & Co.
College Road
Meredith, NH 03253
(603) 279-8607

The Subſcriber begs leave to acquaint the Publick that he is offering for sale at the moſt reaſonable prices, Goods & Neceſſaries of Iron, hand forged in the neateſt manner and finiſhed with Oil & Lampblack.

R. Hood

WILLIAMSBURG
STYLE
DOOR STOP

Letter Plates

Fine brass letter plates both plain and fancy can be had from Locks & Handles. Each is coated with a protective lacquer which for some time obviates the need for cleaning with anything but a damp cloth.

Brochure available.

Locks & Handles
8 Exhibition Road
London, SW7 2HF
(01) 584-6800

One source for letter plates on this side of the Atlantic is Period Furniture Hardware. Its heavy-gauge wrought-brass plate has an external flap covering the 7½" x 2" opening.

Catalogue available, $2.

Period Furniture Hardware
P.O. Box 314, Charles Street Station
123 Charles Street
Boston, MA 02114
(617) 227-0758

A rope-design letter plate in cast solid brass from Bona's Heritage Collection is very elegant, indeed, and sells for nearly $90.

Catalogue available, $3.

Bona Decorative Hardware & Mouldings
2227 Beechmont
Cincinnati, OH 45230
(513) 232-4300

Sash Hardware

Among the little things that can add to the period flavor of an old house are brass sash locks, bolts, and pins. The Renovator's Supply stocks a pressure-plate sash lock which fixes a window at any desired opening. A spring-loaded bolt comes with three strikes to hold the window in different positions. The bolt retracts when the knob is turned. A spring-loaded sash pin passes through the side of the sash and into a hole in the frame. Each costs $5.40, $9.25, and $3.60, respectively.

Catalogue available, $2, refundable with purchase.

The Renovator's Supply
71 Northfield Road
Millers Falls, MA 01349
(413) 659-3542

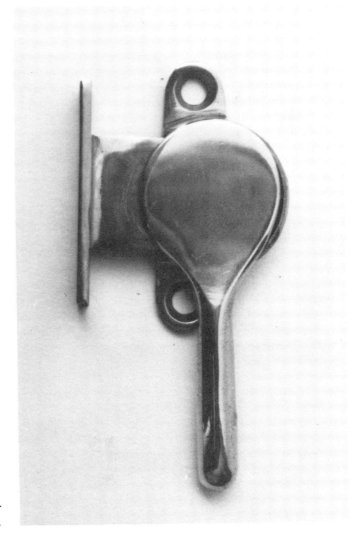

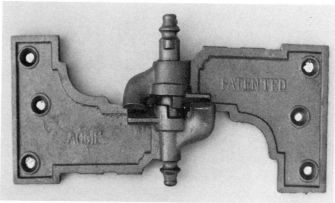

Lift-off shutters can be secured with the "Acme" type of shutter hinge. Each set is marked "right" and "left" and indicates as well which side goes on the house and which on the shutter. Prices range from $9.90 for a set that measures 3⅛" when open to $39 for a 9" spread. Two intermediate sizes are also stocked.

Catalogue available, $2, refundable with purchase.

The Renovator's Supply
71 Northfield Road
Millers Falls, MA 01349
(413) 659-3542

Shutter Hardware

Nothing can ruin a shutter faster than having it slammed against the house by gusting winds—not to mention the damage to the house itself. A properly weighted shutter dog keeps it in place and at the same time adds a decorative element to the house. D. James Barnett's simple iron shutter dogs are a reasonably-priced $9 to $10 a pair.

Catalogue available, $1.

D. James Barnett, Blacksmith
710 W. Main Street
Plano, IL 60545
(312) 552-3675

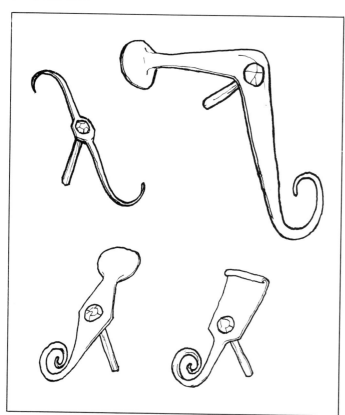

Bathroom Hardware and Fixtures

The sight, earlier this year, of a modern bathroom sink with the chrome legs removed and replaced with wooden turnings for "atmosphere" in a Victorian home—an atmosphere more than matched by the American eagle decals on the toilet seat—prompts us to repeat, verbatim, our stand on bathroom decor: "We remain adamantly opposed to dolling up the bathroom. If you already have a room which is fitted out with antique fixtures that work, keep them in place. They may require some cleaning up, perhaps even a new application of porcelain. Or if the bathroom in your new old house is in complete shambles, you will have to start anew and might as well consider something that fits the general decor. But if you are fortunate enough to have a perfectly fine modern bathroom, leave it as it is, adding only a bit here and there to take away the medicinal look. For some strange reason, the bathroom has become the kitschiest room in the house, new or old. Perhaps it is our modern tendency to spray away any evidence of natural human functions. In any case, please don't tart up the john with a wicker throne for a toilet or with covers for everything in sight."

Wooden Toilet Seats

Although wooden toilet seats—especially those with a natural finish—might conjure images of a musty boarding house and a line-up outside the bathroom door, it is today a common enough addition to the restored bathroom, and a welcome one at that. We're living, God help us, in the age of the foam-filled "soft" toilet seat. Spite isn't our usual forte, but we wish a severe bilious attack to the perpetrators of this latest distortion of the idea of "comfort."

The natural comfort afforded by an oak toilet seat makes it an easy choice over the chilly plastic variety we've become accustomed to. The richly-grained seats feature what the quaintly-named Head's Up terms a "triple-cross laminate construction to prevent cracking or splitting." Available in a standard and an elongated version.

Brochures and dealer list available, $1.

Head's Up, Inc.
14452 Franklin Avenue
Tustin, CA 92680
(714) 544-0500

Domestic Environmental Alternatives carries a variety of antique bathroom fixtures, including toilet seats, in its northern California store.

Brochure available.

Domestic Environmental Alternatives
495 Main Street
P.O. Box 1020
Murphys, CA 95247
(209) 728-3860

Toilets

Spurred by the success of their tiny independent competitors, more and more major manufacturers of largely "commercial" products are beginning to cash in on the restoration market with quality lines of old-fashioned merchandise. The Kohler Company has been a major producer of bathroom fixtures for home and industry for many years. It has recently introduced a line of "nostalgic" fixtures which includes a Victorian high-tank or pull-chain toilet. The "Vintage" model's tank has a lining to help prevent condensation; its brass chain, piping, and pipe supports are available in either polished chrome or polished 24-carat gold finishes.

Brochures available, 50¢.

Kohler Company
Kohler, WI 53044
(414) 457-4441

A particularly elegant version of the pull-chain toilet is offered by Sunrise Specialty. It is supplied with a solid-oak tank, a copper liner, and all-brass fittings. A matching oak seat is affixed to a china bowl. It is currently priced at $615.

Catalogue available.

Sunrise Specialty
2210 San Pablo Avenue
Berkeley, CA 94702
(415) 845-4751

The owners of Domestic Environmental Alternatives do more than sell physical goods. Their operation is based on the belief that traditional methods of sewage disposal are injuring the environment and that technology now exists that offers us some reasonable alternatives to continued pollution of land and water. DEA offers as part of the solution the waterless Swedish "Clivus Multrum" system for the home. Waste gradually slides down the layered soil and peat moss, is decomposed by "friendly" microbes, and ends up in a storage chamber after losing nearly 95% of its volume on the way. This could be the answer to one of the great nightmares of homeowning—repairing or replacing a defective septic system. Check your local ordinances carefully if you think this might be an alternative for you.

Brochure available.

Domestic Environmental Alternatives
495 Main Street
P.O. Box 1020
Murphys, CA 95247
(209) 728-3860

Amongst John Kruesel's many antiques are a few truly vintage toilets and bathroom fixtures. Drop him a line and see what he may now have in stock.

John Kruesel
R.R. 6
Rochester, MN 55901
(507) 288-5148

CROSS SECTION of the CLIVUS MULTRUM COMPOSTING TOILET

ROOF VENT PIPE
GARBAGE CHUTE
STOOL
FLOOR LEVEL
HINGED DOOR
VENTILATOR PIPES
BAFFLE
BAFFLE
SOIL LAYER
PEAT MOSS LAYER
CONCRETE FOUNDATION
BASEMENT FLOOR

Tubs and Sinks

As more and more people move into old houses, those willing to throw out their ancient tubs are becoming fewer and fewer. Still there *are* some dudes who don't appreciate the charm of such clawfoot antiques and pass them on to such suppliers as Domestic Environmental Alternatives. As with any source of antique objects, what is not on the floor today may be brought in—and sold—tomorrow. Call or write for information on the firm's current collection.

Brochure available.

Domestic Environmental Alternatives
495 Main Street
P.O. Box 1020
Murphys, CA 95247
(209) 728-3860

The unobtrusive "Caxton" vitreous china oval lavatory is designed for installation under marble or tile counter tops. It comes in 11 colors (plus white) and in two sizes, 17" x 14" and 19" x 15".

Brochures available, 50¢.

Kohler Company
Kohler, WI 53044
(414) 457-4441

At 19" wide by 17" deep this compact vanity might slip into a tiny downstairs bathroom. The vitreous china sink is offered in white, papyrus, or sand. Choose faucets to match other hardware in the room.

Brochures and dealer list available, $1.

Head's Up, Inc.
14452 Franklin Avenue
Tustin, CA 92680
(714) 544-0500

Hardware

Re-fitting the bathroom of an old house can present a problem in that historically-authentic, well-made bathroom fittings are often difficult to come by. So-called "period" bathroom fittings often attempt to go back to flamboyant historical eras long before the introduction of the bathroom to the private house, and frequently they turn out to be wild boudoir objects of ludicrous vulgarity. If you insist on gold-plated "Renaissance" faucets, O.K. But we've seen the turn-of-the-century sinks of the Vanderbilts and the Roosevelts, and even of the parvenu Ringling brothers; they all used the same plumbing hardware available to jes' plain folks.

A particularly fine range of Edwardian-era fixtures is imported from England by Watercolors, Inc. At once handsome and eminently practical, these authentic designs in solid brass and gunmetal with white porcelain insets are, alas, quite dear, and are available only through decorators, designers, architects, and contractors. The ½" basin mixer with adjustable pop-up drain sells to decorators, etc. for $400.

Brochure available to the trade.

Watercolors, Inc.
Garrison, NY 10524
(914) 424-3327

A restored kitchen would be doing well, indeed, to contain this solid-brass fixture with a soap dish and white china handles. It is also available as a wall mount and sells for $228.

Catalogue available.

Sunrise Specialty
2210 San Pablo Avenue
Berkeley, CA 94702
(415) 845-4751

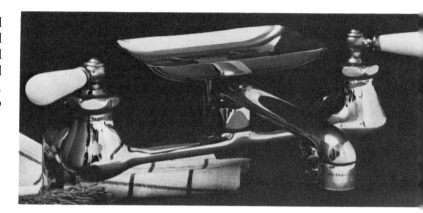

Not all brass fittings need be terribly expensive. Nor is cost a measure of authenticity. Among the many fascinating sundries sold by the Cumberland General Store are a soap dish with a copper sponge dish and a brass toilet-paper holder which sell for $34 and $5.60, respectively.

Catalogue available, $3.75.

Cumberland General Store
Rt. 3
Crossville, TN 38555
(615) 484-8481

Using the northern Midwest's many fine examples of Victorian architecture as inspiration, one Minneapolis firm carries a complete line of plumbing fixtures and appropriate accessories. Victorian Reproduction Enterprises caters to both the wholesale and retail trades and boasts of having the largest quantity of authentic Victorian reproductions in the world.

Catalogues available, $5, refundable with purchase.

Victorian Reproduction Enterprises
1601 Park Avenue South
Minneapolis, MN 55404
(612) 338-3636

Laundry Machines and Tubs

Should you not feel compelled to wash and dry your clothes in a modern machine as sophisticated and energy-expending as a lunar excursion module, there are several alternatives short of trekking down to the stream each morning to beat your clothes on a flat stone.

The James Washer certainly takes us back to the 19th century, but does not totally ignore the technology of the 20th. All moving parts slide on nylon surfaces to reduce wear on both the machine and the operator. Put in only enough water needed for the size of the load—it works just as well with one gallon as with the maximum of 15. The rewards for such austerity? Economy in the use of soap, water, electricity; increased muscle tone. Price? $130.

The Lovell Clothes Wringer can be affixed to the James Washer or to a round tub. Its steel frame has a rustproof aluminum finish. Roller pressure is adjusted by turning the screw on top of the frame. It is warranted 5 years for family use and sells for $82.29.

The 33½-gallon "Dub-L-Tub" can be used for washing clothes, kids, or dogs. The top inside dimensions are 23¾" x 42¾"; overall height is 11". It weights only 10 lbs. and sells for $43.23.

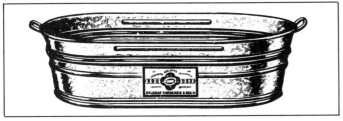

Catalogue available, $3.75.

Cumberland General Store
Rt. 3
Crossville, TN 38555
(615) 484-8481

Furniture Hardware

Have you seen what passes for furniture hardware these days? A trip to the local home and garden supermarket may not convince you that the world is coming to an end, but you may return home shaken out of your belief that Armageddon is light-years away. Escape from the sleaze of the moment by collecting the catalogues of the many reputable producers of fine-quality furniture hardware listed in the following pages. Proper pulls, escutcheons, latches, hinges, and other hardware fittings are available in both stamped and hand-forged pieces, and their styling ranges from the 17th century through the present.

Hinges and Latches

Very few antique iceboxes are now being used for keeping things cool. Many are not even intact. The Renovator's Supply carries replacement hinges and latches that might help reclaim one that's not too far gone. A cast-brass hinge, 2⅝" x 4", ⅜" offset, sells for $8.90. A brass latch, 1¼" x 2½", is $18.30.

Catalogue available, $2.

The Renovator's Supply
71 Northfield Road
Millers Falls, MA 01349
(413) 659-3542

Faneuil's offerings run a fascinating gamut from Colonial to modern. Among the former are latches suitable for simple pine cabinets and for finer mahogany furnishings.

Catalogue available, $2.

Faneuil Furniture Hardware
94-100 Peterborough Street
Boston, MA 02215
(617) 262-7516

Faithful reproductions of Colonial iron cabinet hardware (among other practical objects) are sold by The Weather Vane. The "H" and "HL" hinges pictured here come in 3" and 4" lengths and can be ordered either flush or with a ⅜" offset, the latter being suitable for, say, kitchen cabinets.

Catalogue #78 (black iron hardware), $1.

The Weather Vane
347 S. Elm Street
Greensboro, NC 27401
(919) 272-3797

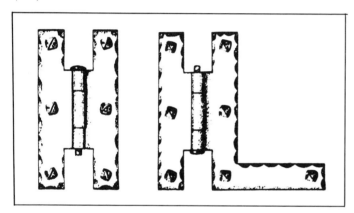

From Steve Kayne's forge and anvil are a Moravian heart-design strap hinge and a mortised hasp, both of which are made for a wooden chest.

Catalogues available, $2.50.

Steve Kayne
17 Harmon Place
Smithtown, NY 11787
(516) 724-3669

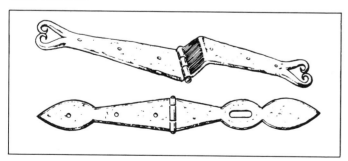

Drops and Pulls

The original William and Mary pulls were sand cast and hand

chased with fine chisels to achieve simple floral patterns in the back plate. Period Furniture Hardware carries at least three distinct designs for pulls and a like number of coordinated drops. They have full-size and miniature Chippendale pulls with a half-dozen bail handles to choose from as well.

Catalogue available, $2.

Period Furniture Hardware Co., Inc.
P.O. Box 314, Charles Street Station
123 Charles Street
Boston, MA 02114
(617) 227-0758

Another Boston outlet for a variety of drops and pulls is Faneuil Furniture Hardware. Like Period Furniture, Faneuil spans many stylistic categories, from 17th-century brasses to today's plexiglass.

Catalogue available, $2.

Faneuil Furniture Hardware
94-100 Peterborough Street
Boston, MA 02215
(617) 262-7516

Solid-brass Victorian bin pulls selling for under $3 (less if you buy 8 or more) can be ordered from The Renovator's Supply. Each is relatively simple in silhouette and reflects the decorative motifs of the period.

Catalogue available, $2.

The Renovator's Supply
71 Northfield Road
Millers Falls, MA 01349
(413) 659-3542

The premier manufacturers of 17th- and 18th-century hardware are Horton Brasses and Ball and Ball. Each has extremely high standards and each is capable of doing custom work of the most demanding nature. No lover of old houses should be without the catalogues of these fine companies.

Catalogue available, $1.25.

Horton Brasses
P.O. Box 95
Nooks Hill Road
Cromwell, CT 06416
(203) 635-4400

Catalogue available, $2.

Ball and Ball
463 W. Lincoln Highway

Exton, PA 19341
(215) 363-7330

Knobs

By the late 19th century porcelain had become a popular material from which to manufacture knobs for furniture as well as doors. Left undecorated, porcelain knobs could be handsome in their simplicity or, adorned, colorful additions to household furnishings.

Catalogue available, $2.

The Renovator's Supply
71 Northfield Road
Millers Falls, MA 01349
(413) 659-3542

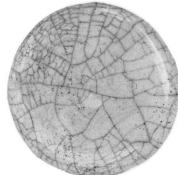

That knobs formed of brass, bronze, or sheet steel were not eclipsed by porcelain or china, is witnessed by the variety of stamped and "compressed" knobs offered by many suppliers. Victorian Reproduction Enterprises is a likely source for such period hardware.

2 catalogues available, $5 each.

Victorian Reproduction Enterprises
1601 Park Avenue South
Minneapolis, MN 55404
(612) 338-3636

As its name tells us, this outfit specializes, and, given the numbers of Americans interested in their Colonial heritage, does so with good reason. In the realm of knobs the company offers brass ones as small as ⅜"; walnut, maple, and mahogany as large as 2"; and clear opal knobs 1¾" in diameter.

Catalogue available, $2.50.

18th Century Hardware Co., Inc.
131 E. 3rd Street
Derry, PA 15627
(412) 694-8421

Escutcheons and Rosettes

An escutcheon forms the entry point for a key in a door, chest, or cabinet and may be either a simple shield or oval or ornately decorated. It is usually the only piece of hardware visible on that side of the door except for the knob or handle and the rosette behind the knob.

In restoring a period door or cabinet which has more recently suffered from alterations which have left oversize holes, a suitable escutcheon and/or rosette can help hide cosmetic sins at the same time they return the piece to its nearly original incarnation.

Faneuil and Period Furniture Hardware carry escutcheons and rosettes appropriate for 18th-century applications; H. Pfanstiel Hardware has several types of rosettes available; and Horton is a good source for Victorian escutcheons.

Catalogue available, $2.

Faneuil Furniture Hardware
94-100 Peterborough Street
Boston, MA 02215
(617) 262-7516

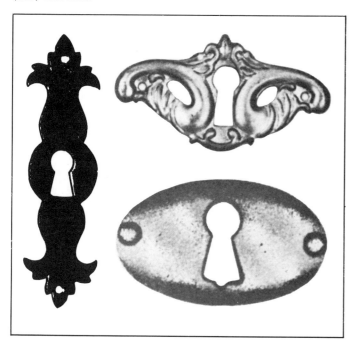

Catalogue available, $2.

Period Furniture Hardware Co., Inc.
P.O. Box 314, Charles Street Station
123 Charles Street
Boston, MA 02114
(617) 227-0758

Catalogue available, $2.

H. Pfanstiel Hardware Co., Inc.
Jeffersonville, NY 12748
(914) 482-4445

Catalogue available, $1.25.

Horton Brasses
P.O. Box 95
Nooks Hill Road
Cromwell, CT 06416
(203) 635-4400

Kitchen and Miscellaneous Hardware

The old house can greatly profit from attention to details. This does not mean we must slavishly attend to every particular in order to wipe out all traces of modernity. Such a task, aside from its great difficulty and cost, is quite impractical, especially in the kitchen. But by careful choice, many traditional objects can be put to proper use to enhance the period decor and enrich the experience of the user.

Kitchen Crane

Very few of us would want to bend over the hot hearth year-round the way Abe Lincoln's mother must have done over this one in Lerna, Illinois, but if you want to replace an old rusted-out crane with one that actually works, get in touch with Steve Kayne. He made the one shown here.

Catalogues available, $2.50.

Steve Kayne
17 Harmon Place
Smithtown, NY 11787
(516) 724-3669

Utensil Racks

A sturdy black iron utensil holder from The Renovator's Supply features a scroll and ram horn design, extends 6″ from the wall, is 12″ wide, comes with 6 S-hooks, and retails for $12.10.

Catalogue available, $2.

The Renovator's Supply
71 Northfield Road
Millers Falls, MA 01349
(413) 659-3542

Toasting Forks

Today, this toasting fork and combination fork and spatula are more likely to be used for marshmallows, hot dogs, and hamburgers than for rabbit legs and fritters. Each shows a high degree of craftsmanship.

Brochure available.

The Blacksmith Shop
R.R. 2, 26 Bridge Road
Orleans, MA 02653
(617) 255-7233

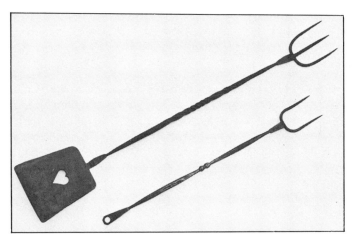

Spatulas and Ladles

Newton Millham has faithfully reproduced from an original New England design this ironware ladle and matching spatula. His extensive repertoire of kitchen utensils also includes racks, choppers, forks, trivets, skillets, and gridirons.

Catalogue available, $1.

Newton Millham—Star Forge
672 Drift Road
Westport, MA 02790
(617) 636-5437

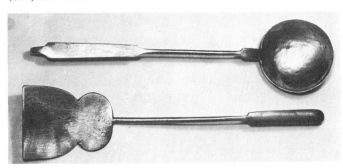

If you are at all daunted by the prospect of using ironware in the kitchen, then the products of this blacksmith-whitesmith might interest you. Whitesmithing involves the art of applying fine decoration to the simpler designs of the blacksmith's trade.

This usually consists of incising and filing or the applying of brass or copper inlay or overlay decoration. Thomas G. Loose is a practitioner of the art, of which these brass and iron ladles are examples.

No catalogue, but will reply to inquiries.

Thomas G. Loose, Blacksmith-Whitesmith
R.D. 2, Box 203A
Leesport, PA 19533
(215) 926-4849

Hearth Roasters

An accomplished Midwestern blacksmith hand-forges a hearth roaster by means of which most fireplaces can be the source of deliciously-cooked meats. The long-handled roaster is placed atop glowing coals and can also be used to toast bread or rolls.

Catalogue available, $1.

D. James Barnett, Blacksmith
710 W. Main Street
Plano, IL 60545
(312) 552-3675

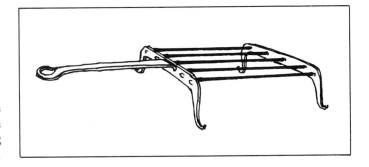

House Force Pumps

We occasionally see an old house that still has little more than the first or second generation of primitive indoor plumbing which, once you get used to it, isn't all that bad. House force pumps like this one can be had for about $85 through the Cumberland General Store.

Catalogue available, $3.75.

Cumberland General Store
Rt. 3
Crossville, TN 38555
(615) 484-8481

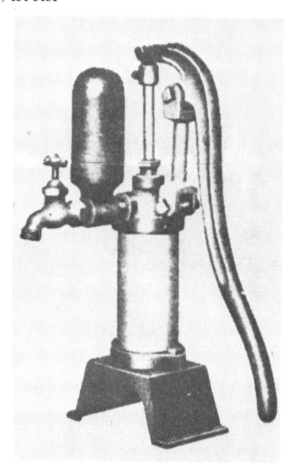

Hooks and Hangers

Whether a hook is stripped down to bare essentials—a "J" with a spiked end, for instance—or is a gaudy, shiny brass thing with curlicues and flourishes, it still serves the function of a hanger and is a handy thing to have in any room in the house.

Faneuil has a fairly ornate lion's-head hook which is 4" in height and projects 2" from the wall. It could serve just as well behind a door as in a hallway, but why hide it?

Catalogue available, $2.

Faneuil Furniture Hardware

94-100 Peterborough Street
Boston, MA 02215
(617) 262-7516

A wonderful three-pronged brass hat and coat hook that sells in the neighborhood of $20 can be ordered from Period Furniture. Even if you don't wear hats, this is a nice touch for the Victorian house.

Catalogue available, $2.

Period Furniture Hardware Co., Inc.
P.O. Box 314, Charles Street Station
123 Charles Street
Boston, MA 02114
(617) 227-0758

Four iron hooks of the very simplest kind can be ordered from Renovator's Supply for $1.40 each. Two are standard "john" types that differ only in length and projection, one is a short gooseneck, and one is an open-eyed spike designed to be driven into a beam or masonry.

Catalogue available, $2.

The Renovator's Supply
71 Northfield Road
Millers Falls, MA 01349
(413) 659-3542

Brackets and Other Hangers

Adequate shelf space is a must, regardless of the size of the house or the size of the family. If shelving is to be put up, or if plants are to be hung out of the way, why not conform their hardware to the style of the rest of the house? The Colonial home, for example, might best be served by an iron plant hanger and S-hook made by D. James Barnett. It projects 8" and costs $5.50.

Catalogue available, $1.

D. James Barnett, Blacksmith
710 W. Main Street
Plano, IL 60545
(312) 552-3675

Your budgie won't go off its feed if you hang its cage by a chain from Woolworth's, but you might like to treat yourself to a fancy Victorian polished-brass hanger which pivots in a wall bracket. A $20 indulgence, but why not?

Catalogue available, $2.50.

18th Century Hardware Co., Inc.
131 E. 3rd Street
Derry, PA 15627
(412) 694-8421

A cast-brass Victorian shelf bracket lends itself to positioning in just about any room. It measures 6¾″ x 5¼″ and is sold by the pair at $12.50

Catalogue available, $2.

The Renovator's Supply
71 Northfield Road
Millers Falls, MA 01349
(413) 659-3542

Tools

If you think back to high school days, you may recall the shop teachers admonishing you for, say, using a claw hammer on a cold chisel. Use the right tool for the job! you'd hear. You may have learned painfully that a ball-peen hammer won't shatter the cold chisel's brittle steel, but a claw hammer will. Or you may have witnessed the consequences of using a rip saw to go across the grain on a table top you'd put so much time into. Depending on the job, perhaps you can get away with an inadequate assortment of tools. After all, most odd jobs don't require much more than a basic hammer, saw, ruler, some common sense, and a steady hand. But when you're dealing with tasks of considerable complexity, or when you're faced with the possibility of destroying something that's one-of-a-kind, or of even injuring yourself, then you've got to sit down and make careful plans—and these plans include getting your hands on the right tools for the job.

Paint Removers

Old-house owners know that sooner or later their castle—be it cottage or mansion—will have to be repainted. But first, the old paint must be painstakingly removed. A welcome addition to the scraper's arsenal is the Grind-O-Flex, a wheel full of abrasive cloth flaps that will fit on an electric drill and can sand flat or contoured surfaces. It is available in fine, medium, and coarse grits and retails for $6.45.

Belt sanders are another popular tool for paint removal. Their greatest drawback, however, is that their belts quickly clog up with old paint and wood. An $8.05 abrasive belt cleaner held against the turning belt can prolong the life of the belt up to four times. This means fewer trips down the ladder and out to the hardware store.

2 catalogues available, $1.50.

Woodcraft Supply Corp.
313 Montvale Avenue
Woburn, MA 01801
(617) 935-5860

Scrapers

Some of the most efficient scrapers are the kind that require on-ly elbow grease for power. A set of 8 sharp contour blades and a handle can help you design new moldings or prepare to refinish old ones.

Catalogue available, $1.

Garrett Wade Co.
302 Fifth Avenue
New York, NY 10001
(212) 695-3360

Putty Remover

If you've ever tried to remove hardened putty from windows, you know what a chore it can be. Brookstone sells a knife specifically designed for the task. A pointed blade cuts through putty when tapped with a hammer from behind. If it saves you some aggravation, it's worth its $7.50 price.

Catalogue available.

Brookstone
127 Vose Farm Road
Peterborough, NH 03458
(603) 924-9511

Pry Bar

No greater friend hath a salvager of old buildings than a pry bar that doesn't destroy what is being dismantled. The tremendous leverage afforded by the long handle and the deep prying surface below the fulcrum combine to lift across a wide throw, thereby avoiding split timbers. The price is $22.50.

Product list available.

Wikkman House
Box 501
Chatsworth, CA 91311
(213) 780-1015

Finishing Trowels

Marshalltown is worth noting here not because its products are hard to find (they're carried by most good hardware stores and masonry supply houses), but because their range of tools reflects the degree of specialization in masonry and dry wall construction. Choosing the correct tool for your needs will pay dividends in the quality of the finished project. Use a flat finishing trowel for masonry and a curved one for dry wall, for example. For 75¢ Marshalltown will send you *Troweling Tips and Techniques*, a handy 24-page booklet.

Catalogue available.

Marshalltown Trowel Company
P.O. Box 738
104 S. 8th Avenue
Marshalltown, IA 50158
(515) 754-6116

Moto-Tool

If the kind of restoration work you have in mind requires painstaking hand operations, a Dremel tool might help. Not unlike a dentist's drill in principle, the hand-held "Moto-Tool" can grind, buff, cut, sand, and polish. Dozens of tools and

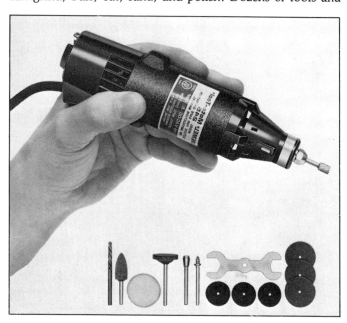

motors are available. The model 245, shown here, sells for $41.95.

Catalogue available.

Dremel, Division of Emerson Electric Co.
4915 21st Street
P.O. Box 518
Racine, WI 53406
(414) 554-1390

Honing Guide

Sharpen your chisel and plane blades at precisely the right angle. A simple honing guide takes the guesswork out of sharpening. It accepts blades as narrow at $\frac{1}{16}$" or as wide as $2\frac{5}{8}$". Frog Tool Co. will send one to you for $9.50. (And order the Frog catalogue, too; it's one of the best in the business.)

Catalogue available, $1.

Frog Tool Co.
700 W. Jackson Blvd.
Chicago, IL 60606
(312) 648-1270

Mitre Box

A professional carpenter's mitre box can be a very expensive investment, but, then, a carpenter makes dozens of critical cuts every working day, especially if he specializes in finishing work. For the occasional craftsman who must replace some molding or do similar mitre jobs, Garrett Wade has a $24.10 beech mitre box with adjustable saw guides. A compatible back saw is about the same price.

Catalogue available, $1.

Garrett Wade
302 Fifth Avenue
New York, NY 10001
(212) 695-3360

Band Clamp

One excellent solution for clamping irregular sections (columns, furniture frames) is the band clamp, an adjustable canvas belt capable of withstanding a 2,800 lb. load. A 10′ band sells for $41.75.

Catalogue available, $1.

The Woodworkers' Store
21801 Industrial Blvd.
Rogers, MN 55374
(612) 428-4101

Form-A-Gage

The Preservation Resource Group is the U.S. source for this

most useful restoration tool. If you have ever tried to duplicate a molding, you know that a profile gauge is essential. Without one, your only alternative is to take down a piece of molding and use that as a guide. The form-a-gage is especially sensitive to the often complex contour of the period molding as each rod in the instrument is suspended in a uniform magnetic field. This insures that each rod responds identically. Once you have the profile, the rods can be locked into place very securely. The cost is $24.50, plus $1.50 for postage and handling.

The Preservation Resource Group, Inc.
5619 Southampton Drive
Springfield, VA 22151
(703) 323-1407

Tool Bag, Safety Goggles, and Dust Mask

For ease in moving your tools from place to place, Garrett Wade carries a 20″ and a 24″ tool bag made of heavy white canvas covered on the bottom with an abrasion-resistant rein-forced vinyl laminate. The handles and straps are of harness leather, and the bag opening is reinforced with a steel frame for stiffness. The smaller bag is $43.50; the larger, $46.50.

Attention to safety should be a required part of every project. Make sure power equipment is properly grounded and guards are in place. Brace scaffolding against the racking and twisting effects of sudden wind gusts. Wear protective gear such as safety goggles and a dust mask when sanding or grinding. If you must work with toxic varnishes or other chemicals in poorly-ventilated areas, invest in an approved respirator.

Catalogue available, $1.

Garrett Wade
302 Fifth Avenue
New York, NY 10001
(212) 695-3360

Other Suppliers of Hardware

Consult List of Suppliers for addresses.

Architectural Hardware

Hinges

Ball and Ball
Cohasset Colonials
R. Hood & Co.
San Francisco Victoriana
Wallin Forge
Williamsburg Blacksmiths

Door Knobs

Acme Hardware
Elegant Entries, Inc.
P. E. Guerin, Inc.
William Hunrath Co.
Period Brass, Inc.
Ritter & Son
San Francisco Victoriana

Door Knockers

Baldwin
Horton
Period Furniture Hardware
Pfanstiel
Ritter & Son

Latches and Bolts

Ball and Ball
18th Century Hardware
R. Hood & Co.
Steve Kayne
Noel Wise Antiques

Locks

Baldwin
Ball and Ball
Newton Millham
Noel Wise
Period Furniture Hardware
San Francisco Victoriana
Victorian Reproduction Enterprises

Nails and Screws

Cohasset Colonials
Tremont Nail Co.
Woodcraft

Letter Plates

Baldwin
Noel Wise Antiques

Victorian Reproduction Enterprises

Sash Hardware

Ball and Ball
Cumberland General Store
Ritter & Son

Shutter Hardware

Newton Millham
Steve Kayne
Period Furniture Hardware
Wallin Forge
Wrightsville Hardware

Bathroom Hardware and Fixtures

Wooden Toilet Seats

Fife's Woodworking
Shepherd Oak Products

Toilets

Head's Up, Inc.
Victorian Reproduction Enterprises

Tubs and Sinks

Bona
P. E. Guerin
Head's Up, Inc.
The National House Inn
Sunrise Specialty

Hardware

Bona
Fife's Woodworking
P. E. Guerin
Materials Unlimited
The National House Inn
Pfanstiel Hardware

Furniture Hardware

Hinges and Latches

18th Century Hardware
Horton
Period Furniture Hardware
Noel Wise

Drops and Pulls

Albert Constantine & Son

18th Century Hardware
Steve Kayne
Pfanstiel Hardware
The Woodworkers' Store

Knobs

Acme Hardware Co.
Ball and Ball
Sturbridge Yankee Workshop
The Woodworkers' Store

Escutcheons and Rosettes

Ball and Ball
18th Century Hardware
Noel Wise
The Woodworkers' Store

Kitchen and Miscellaneous Hardware

Kitchen Cranes

Robert Bourdon
Cumberland General Store
Newton Millham

Utensil Racks

The Blacksmith Shop

Toasting Forks

Richard E. Sargent
Spatulas and Ladles
Hubbardton Forge & Wood

Hearth Roasters

The Blacksmith Shop
Newton Millham

Hooks and Brackets

The Blacksmith Shop
Robert Bourdon
The Craft House
P. E. Guerin
Hubbardton Forge & Wood

Tools

Cumberland General Store
Iron Horse Antiques
Wallin Forge

"Atlantic" parlor stove, illustration courtesy of the Bryant Steel Works,
Thorndike, Maine.

4 Heating & Cooking

Changes in the way we heat our homes are coming as fast as the rise in oil and gas prices. Efficiency rather than extravagance is the byword of all thinking people. In the old-house field the clock is being turned back; we are returning to practices and forms which have not been in use for two or three generations or more. Many older homes were built at a time when central heating was a luxury enjoyed only by the wealthy; except for very crude hot-air systems, houses dating back even further—before the mid-19th century—were never supplied with anything more than antique "space heaters."

Consider the history of the parlor fireplace in a typical 250-year-old New England farmhouse. In the 18th century the fireplace rarely contained a stove; the open fire threw a modicum of heat during the colder months. A fireback may have helped to reflect more of the warmth into the room, and one of Count Rumford's ingenious firebox designs may have discouraged heat loss up the chimney. By the early 19th century a Franklin stove or some other wood-burning contraption could have been placed on the hearth or in the fireplace opening with the stove pipe vented through the chimney flue. By mid-century the family in residence might have graduated to a coal-burning stove. A generation or two later the home could have been fitted with a boiler fueled by coal which pumped out steam to radiators strategically placed in at least the first-floor rooms. Fireplaces had no real utility by this time, and many were boarded up or plastered over.

The use of coal and steam as well as hot-air sys-tems continued to dominate the heating field until World War II. Many of us are old enough to remember filling the stoker, removing the clinkers and ashes, and bleeding the radiators. And this we do not want to go back to. In the postwar period most coal systems were converted to oil or gas. The house was cleaner, the heating system much easier to maintain. The furnace itself took up much less room. Heat was distributed more evenly within the rooms through the use of baseboards. Many families decided it was time to open up the old fireplaces—not for heating purposes, but because they wanted to enjoy the charm of an open fire on a cold evening night. If our New England farmhouse was a typical one, then sometime during the 1940s or '50s it is likely that one or more fireplaces were returned to their original form.

And what is happening now? We are taking the next historical step—placing wood or coal stoves back into the fireplace opening or on the hearth. No matter how much we may admire the look of an open fireplace, the classic cozy hearth enshrined for years in decorating magazines and historical villages, we are being forced to use fireplaces in the way they were intended to be used—as heating units.

Residents of older homes can often profit from the ways in which such structures were put together. It helps, of course, to have a fireplace or two. Rooms which can be shut off one from the other are also much easier to heat than those with a modern "open" floor plan with one space flowing into another. While ceilings are often higher in old homes than in modern ones, fans can be used to recirculate much of the heat. Walls—both exterior and interior partitions —are likely to have been built with a thickness which retains heat in winter and wards it off during the summer. Windows and doors may be problem areas, but, once again, if properly maintained with storms and weather stripping, they will leak less than the thin materials used today in sash, panels, and framing.

Caution in making "energy-saving" investments is necessary for everyone. The number of fly-by-night operators attempting to cash in on our understandable preoccupation with saving fuel seems to increase geometrically each year. Although this is a minor concern, there are aesthetic considerations which come into play when shopping for a stove. Many of the designs on the market are gussied-up contraptions (the spread eagle in tin being a favorite decorative motif) which no more belong in a tasteful room than does a butterchurn lamp. But there are simple, handsome models which we feel will do the job of heating well in style. More important, of course, is that stoves burn efficiently and be properly vented. Flues must be cleaned after each heating season.

Many of the same safety, efficiency, and design considerations apply to cooking stoves. Not being in the least accomplished in the culinary arts, we are often surprised to see how efficiently and easily a master of the wood or kerosene cooking stove can operate. Antique models are still available and, increasingly, the need for new "old" devices is being met. The popularity of such cooking stoves probably will remain limited, but, on the other hand, if the sands of Araby begin to shake violently, we're ready to learn how to cope with the oil crisis at an old-fashioned range if need be. The flue for the old kitchen stove is still in place.

Antique Mantels

Suppliers of restoration materials seem, for the most part, to be as well stocked with wood and marble mantels as they are with old doors. This should not be too surprising when you consider how many old houses fall under the wrecker's ball every year. It is fortunate that most such antiques can be removed intact, none the worse for the experience, and transported to one of the scores of important dealers throughout the country. This is an area in which the potential buyer should investigate several sources for the best quality and price and should not settle on a particular piece unless it is thought to be not only "perfect," but totally suitable for the new old house it is to occupy.

Antique mantels offered by Miami's Ye Olde Mantel Shoppe include both wood and marble varieties and for the most part date back to the 18th and 19th centuries.

Ye Olde Mantel Shoppe
3800 N.E. 2nd Avenue
Miami, FL 33137
(305) 576-0225

Some of the most striking mantels to survive from the last century are those made of cast iron. Designer Imports in Leawood, Kansas, imports some truly remarkable examples from England, ranging from ornate early Victorian to stylized Art Nouveau. The mantel shown here, termed "Serpentine," with

a "Mildmay dog basket" insert, is polished to resemble burnished pewter.

Brochure available.

Designer Imports
4701 College Blvd.
Suite 208
Leawood, KS 66211
(913) 381-6053

Reproduction Mantels

The full panorama of styles is reflected in the reproductions trade. The best quality pieces are indistinguishable from the originals because both materials and methods of manufacture have been duplicated. Some craftsman will design anew from sketches or will build around an existing piece. Still others produce mantelpieces on a near mass-production basis. The recommendations that follow incorporate the best of both worlds.

Bennington Bronze is a small manufacturer that is carving out a niche for itself in the highly specialized endeavor of designing and producing to order solid-brass and bronze mantels and andirons. The polished-bronze mantel shown here retails for over $4,000.

Information available on request.

Bennington Bronze
147 S. Main Street
White River Junction, VT 05001
(802) 295-9186

When fidelity to an original 18th- or 19th-century design is a first concern, the services of a historically-oriented craftsman are required. Norman Vandal is a Vermont-based cabinetmaker and housewright who studies period tools and construction technologies and uses both to recreate and restore all sorts of architectural components, including mantelpieces.

Brochure available, $1.50

Norman Vandal
P.O. Box 67
Roxbury, VT 05669
(802) 485-8380

At the opposite end of the spectrum from handcrafted custom pieces are the stock wood mantels produced by Readybuilt. This is not to suggest that Readybuilt's goods suffer unduly by comparison. Its mantels are constructed of the best-grade kiln-dried poplar; joints are mortised and tenoned, screwed and glued together. Stylistically, the selection of over two dozen models is weighted heavily in favor of late-18th and early-19th-century American types.

Catalogue No. 478, $1.

The Readybuilt Products Company
P.O. Box 4306
Baltimore, MD 21223
(301) 233-5833

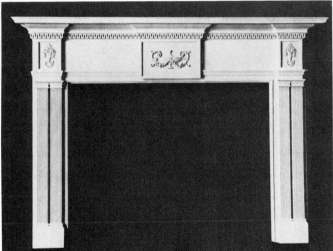

Shown here, with its double-reeded pilasters, double dentil molding, and urn motifs, is a Colonial mantelpiece appropriate for the more elegant period home. Its shelf is 6' 4" in length and has an opening width of 4' 2". All Readybuilt mantels are shipped with a white prime coat of paint, but upon request can be purchased unfinished for staining.

Fireplaces

Many old houses share an advantage over more recent dwell-

ings in that they often have not only a fireplace in the parlor or living room but one or two others on each floor. Usually these other fixtures were blocked off or walled over when central heating was installed. Now, as the clock seems to be turning back in favor of older sources of heat such as wood and coal, many home owners are repairing chimneys and fireplaces and returning them to service as either working fireplaces or stove installations. The activities of the H.S. Welles Fireplace Co. are aimed specifically at bringing old fireplaces up to modern building code specifications. The firm has been at work in the New York area for over 13 years.

H. S. Welles Fireplace Co.
209 E. 2nd Street
New York, NY 10009
(212) 777-5440

Some restoration projects require that a new period fireplace be built into a reconstructed building or that one be moved from its original location and re-assembled on a new site. Olde New England Masonry specializes in just this type of work and has more or less limited itself to the kinds of masonry practiced from about 1675 to 1800. If a particular fireplace part is needed on a job, chances are that this outfit will either have the replacement or can locate one.

Arthur Singer
Olde New England Masonry
27 Hewitt Road
Mystic, CT 06355
(203) 536-0295

Authentic regional English fireplace styles are reproduced from the originals by a California-based company. Builders or restorers of an American Tudor home, for example, might wish to recreate a period fireplace that is particularly suited to the blueprints of the house. The work is done with imported handmade bricks and is especially appropriate for locations which require a monumental flavor. The larger models might lend themselves to construction in compatible restaurants or inns.

Brochure available.

Dobson & Thomas Ltd.
838 Ninth Street
Suite #7
Santa Monica, CA 90403
(213) 394-5180

Chimney Pots

Chimney maintenance is not a pleasant affair—and any maintenance that goes beyond a simple annual cleaning is bound to be costly. Judging from the extremely high percentage of house fires caused by chimney problems, it is apparent that many of us would rather live dangerously than face the inconvenience and expense of routine inspections and care.

The chimneys of many older buildings were equipped with clay pots or tops which separated the surrounding masonry from the heat and sulphurous soot from fires below. They also kept out the elements and regulated drafts. These pots are still available today to replace old or missing ones or to install anew. The Superior Clay Corporation, a prominent manufacturer, touts chimney pots as "a beautiful way to protect your new home." Well, we think they are just as sensible for old homes, especially with today's proliferation of wood- and coalburning stoves.

Brochures available.

Superior Clay Corporation
P.O. Box 352
Uhrichsville, OH 44683
(614) 922-4122

Fireplace Accessories

Fireplace accoutrements far exceed in number what is actually necessary for the proper performance of a hearth. Admittedly, the distinction between necessity and luxury blurs when what is at first a mere convenience becomes something of inestimable value. Such might be the case, for example, with a kerosene firelighter that does away with short matches and singed fingers. Another way of viewing the array of needs and wants is to consider the value of an object as an enhancer of either performance (efficiency) or style (aesthetic appeal). The latter in a period house is closely related to appropriateness and authenticity. Installation of a fireback, for instance, can actually increase the efficiency of a fireplace; wrought-iron firedogs might be more stylistically sensible than fine brass andirons in a Colonial saltbox.

Andirons

"Functional art" is the way the designers at Bennington Bronze choose to describe their solid bronze andirons—and fine sculpture, needless to say, has often been expressed in the medium of bronze. Each stands over 18" high, weights 12 lbs., and is braced by a welded-steel log rest. The price per pair is $170. The andirons are also available in solid brass and in nickel-plated brass. Bennington's designers also undertake work based on historic documentation, photos, broken parts, or even samples of other household furnishings or hardware; they then custom cast the objects in whatever copper-based alloy is required.

Information available on request.

Bennington Bronze
147 S. Main Street

White River Junction, VT 05001
(802) 295-9186

In addition to the fine antique wood and marble mantels sold by Ye Olde Mantel Shoppe is a selection of andirons and tools reflecting a similar range of styles from Colonial through Victorian.

Ye Olde Mantel Shoppe
3800 N.E. 2nd Avenue
Miami, FL 33137
(305) 576-0225

The need for a more rustic colonial look is well served by D. James Barnett's substantial iron andiron topped with a brass finial. A pair sells for $100.

Catalogue available, $1.

D. James Barnett, Blacksmith
710 W. Main Street
Plano, IL 60545
(312) 552-3675

Tools

Among the accessories Designer Imports brings to this country from England is a simple but rather elegant set of brass fireplace tools—four in all—which hang about a brass caddy.

Brochures available.

Designer Imports
4701 College Blvd.
Suite 208
Leawood, KS 66211
(913) 381-6053

Bellows

Anyone who has used his or her lungs to fan an ember into a flame knows that about all you get is a face full of ashes and a dizzy spell. A solidly-built, dependable bellows takes the worry out of being close. George Soucy creates for $39.95 a pear-shaped, turtle-back bellows out of basswood, lamb leather, and brass tacks. The nozzle is turned from 1" diameter solid-brass bar stock, so it won't melt in the presence of hot coals.

Bellows by Soucy
1532 W. Shore Road
Warwick, RI 02889
(401) 737-3513

Firebacks and Grates

Original cast-iron firebacks, very few of which were made after the 18th century, were propped against the back of a fireplace to reflect heat out into a room. They also helped protect the masonry from the deteriorating effects of constant firing, a task which might explain why so few have survived intact to this day. We now depend on the talents of moldmakers to recreate the fireback designs of the past.

A. E. S. Firebacks cast this "Webb" fireback from a 1781 model. It stands 21" x 20" x ½", and weighs 46 lbs. Several other designs are also available.

Brochure available—send stamped self-addressed envelope.

A. E. S. Firebacks
27 Hewitt Road
Mystic, CT 06355
(203) 536-0295

Grates, or baskets as some types are more appropriately called, suspend logs and coals above the floor of a hearth and allow air to circulate around the fire. Some have legs, while others attach to, or rest on, the log rests of andirons. A portable basket is offered by Cumberland General Store. Its largest size—a front width of 24"—weighs 36 lbs. and sells for $56.40. It is made of cast iron, features a dumping bottom, and has a depth of 10".

Catalogue available, $3.75.

Cumberland General Store
Rt. 3
Crossville, TN 38555
(615) 484-8481

More elaborate (and costly) grates are produced by Kingsworthy Foundry Co. and reflect in their bold lines the solidity of English castles.

Catalogue available, $5.

Kingsworthy Foundry Co. Ltd.
Kingsworthy
Winchester, Hants. S023 7QG
England
Tel. Winchester 883776

Firescreens

A few minutes in front of a crackling log fire is enough to convince all but the most foolhardy of the need for a fine-mesh firescreen to contain those surprising little explosions that otherwise disperse sprays of golden embers across the rugs and floors. The marketplace is filled with scores of screens, many of them flimsier than stage props (although the worst is probably better than none at all). The best bet is to shop around and purchase the strongest suitable screen you can find and afford, avoiding along the way the little horrors that resemble the curtains of a puppet theater done up in a coat of mail.

An unusual alternative to a firescreen, but one that can be installed during the fireplace's idle summer months, is this ornate solid brass French folding screen. When open it measures 25" by 37" wide and is ideal for an equally ornate Victorian home. It can be folded like a fan and set aside when a fire is burning. The Renovator's Supply is currently selling this import for $89.95

Catalogue available, $2, refundable with purchase.

The Renovator's Supply
71 Northfield Road
Millers Falls, MA 01349
(413) 659-3542

Heating Stoves

The latest round of oil price hikes has us all tightening our belts another notch, and there is no reason to believe we won't be down a couple of more notches in the near future. Most of us seem to be more conscious now of energy conservation than we were just a few years ago. We're driving less, car-pooling more, and doing everything we can to plug up cracks around the house to cut down on our fuel-oil consumption. Add to this a willingness to invest a relatively small amount of money in insulation and storm windows (lacking in many older homes), and the fuel use really begins to plummet. A growing number of us are finding that wood- and coal-fired heat is another equally important way to dodge the escalating cost of oil.

Everyone wants to get on the woodstove bandwagon. New retailers are cropping up in vacant storefronts from coast to coast, and stores that sell other things take on stoves as a profitable sideline. Sporting-goods stores sell stoves; service stations sell stoves (talk about hedging one's bets!); and virtually every discount department store has its shoddy pot-metal clunkers from Taiwan. And some poor souls actually buy them.

We listed in previous Catalogues a number of manufacturers who at the time were the leaders in quality and dependability. Many of these names reappear on these pages because they retain their status against the busy and growing competition.

The folks at the Woodstock Soapstone Company have a good thing going, and for good reason: they manufacture and sell a simple, efficient, and very handsome wood stove that will heat 7,000 to 10,000 cu. ft. for 10 to 12 hours. The stove's simplicity and efficiency derive from the properties of the unusual material from which it is made. Soapstone, termed "perfect" for stoves by the Woodstock people, absorbs twice the heat of cast iron and radiates it evenly over a long period of time. There are no internal components to replace, no baffling system to adjust. The hand-fitted cast-iron frame is decorated with typically Victorian ornamentation. The stove stands 28" high x 26" wide x 20" deep and carries a price tag of $760. It should last a lifetime.

Brochures available, $1.

Woodstock Soapstone Co., Inc.
Box 223
Woodstock, VT 05091
(802) 672-5133

Rumor has it that coal-fired stoves are the wave of the near future, what with the difficulty of finding a dependable supply of wood in some parts of the country and the relative ease with which coal can be secured and stored. The All Nighter Stove Works is ready to meet the anticipated demand with its "Chubby Moe," which according to the manufacturer's literature is "the first 100% American-made cast-iron coal stove to be produced and on the market." (We assume they mean first *contemporary* stove to capitalize on the current demand.) "Chubby Moe" is capable of heating 1,500 to 2,000 cu. ft. Its capacity for nearly 60 lbs. of coal means that it can burn for as long as 36 to 40 hours on one load. Ashes can be removed conveniently through the drawer opening in front. The stove weighs 404 lbs. and is shipped fully assembled.

Literature available, $1.

All Nighter Stove Works Inc.
80 Commerce Street
Glastonbury, CT 06033
(203) 659-0344

The beauty of an original stove derives in part from the knowledge that everything about it is authentic, that it is not a self-conscious copy into which someone has wired a colored bulb to simulate throbbing embers. Authenticity is a key word at Grampa's Wood Stoves. Each one, like the "Art Jewel" parlor stove shown here, is fully restored to working order

with only original parts. Because Grampa's deals exclusively in original stoves, its stock changes constantly. And, incidentally, not all the stoves are wood-burners; many are fueled by coal.

Current listing available, $1.

Grampa's Wood Stoves
P. O. Box 492
Ware, MA 01082
(413) 967-6684

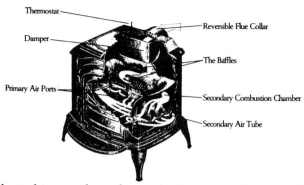

All the wood-burning stoves produced by Vermont Castings have the enviable feature that when their doors are swung open they can function like a fireplace without a fireplace's terrific inefficiency. The "Resolute," shown here in cutaway and as installed, is small enough to back neatly into smaller hearths, but can deliver up to 35,000 BTU's which is enough to heat about 7,000 cu. ft. The internal mechanisms channel preheated air evenly in the combustion zone. The secondary combustion chamber enables unburned gases to combine with preheated air to provide more efficient fuel consumption. A thermostat automatically controls the air intake to provide even heat output over long burning periods. .

Brochures available, $1.

Vermont Castings, Inc.
Randolph, VT 05060
(802) 728-3181

Antique Cookstoves

Cookstove technology reached its peak during the heyday of production, from 1890 to around 1920. Stoves for the average kitchen were designed to perform functions other than baking, boiling, and frying. They were called on to keep wash water hot for morning shaves, to heat the heavy clothes iron, to dry clothes, to warm adjoining rooms during winter, and to provide a cozy gathering place for family and friends. Today's slimmed-down electric boxes provide, alas, for only cooking functions.

The Good Time Stove Co. believes, and rightly, we think, that for anyone who is willing to split the wood and stoke the fire, nothing beats an honest-to-goodness antique cookstove. As its literature explains, "There is still virtually no choice on the

American market for a good quality cooking stove which offers all of the features that were standard on the old ones—warming ovens, water reservoirs, gas attachments, trivets, water jackets and various colored enamel finishes." The Glenwood "H," illustrated here, is typical of what you can find at Good Time.

Catalogue available, $1.

Good Time Stove Co.
Rt. 112
Goshen, MA 01032
(413) 268-3677

It is hard to imagine that there is any kind of stove made in the last two centuries that hasn't passed through Bea Bryant's shop in Thorndike, Maine. And at any given time about 200 reside in her large showroom, each one restored to "like new" condition. Many others are there only long enough to be repaired and are then returned to their owners. Some are very rare and some, like the Acme and Glenwood lines, are common old monsters. Aside from all the stoves that are for sale, the Bryant family has recently opened a stove museum to house some of the more noteworthy and historic coal and wood stoves.

Literature available.

Bryant Steel Works
R.F.D. 2, Box 109
Thorndike, ME 04986
(207) 568-3663

Stove Accessories

Heating and cooking with wood or coal require that we perform a variety of activities not necessary with modern electricity and gas: wood cutting and splitting, coal shoveling, fire lighting, and occasional ash removal. These important and inescapable duties demand a minimum of specialized accessories if they are to be done with a reasonable amount of efficiency. Suppliers' catalogues and warehouses contain plenty of the basics as well as numerous objects that aren't so much essential as they are convenient or just plain fun to own. The following selections represent a little of both.

Cleanliness may or may not be next to godliness, but it certainly bears directly on stove efficiency. Be sure to haul your ashes frequently, and do so with a long hoe and a closeable metal ash carrier like the ones pictured here. The 36"-long hoe is designed for drawing ashes from the deepest recesses of a stove. The "Ash Away" carrier has a 5-gallon capacity, so there is no need to run out to empty it with each cleaning. The lid keeps the contents from blowing around the house. The hoe sells for $13.10; the "Ash Away" for $22.50.

Catalogue available, $1.

The Blacksmith Shop
Box 15
Mt. Holly, VT 05758
(802) 259-2452

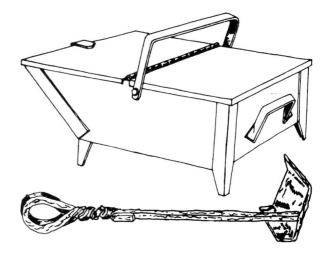

A coal hod is no less useful now than it was at the turn of the century—assuming you use it for carrying coal and not for planting philodendron, one of the curses inflicted on us by home and garden magazines. The Cumberland General Store sells a very simple one for $10.54. The corrugated body is wire-bound at the top and bottom and has a heavy flat bail and riveted ears.

Catalogue available, $3.75.

Cumberland General Store
Rt. 3
Crossville, TN 38555
(615) 484-8481

Don't skimp on stove pipe. This 22-gage pipe offered by Woodstock Soapstone Co. has features not found in most of that sold in "home center" hardware supermarkets. Because the seams are spot-welded, they cannot come apart; the heavier sheet metal provides extra protection against the deteriorating effects of heat and moisture. A 5" x 24" piece sells for $10; an elbow is priced at $12.

Fires demand attention whether you're dressed in overalls or in your Sunday best. And regardless of the state of your clothes there is the everpresent danger of singing your knuckles and of even more serious mishaps around hot stoves. Keep a pair of these heat-resistant leather gloves handy at all times. Woodstock sells them, and they're well worth a $10 investment.

The heat-retaining characteristics of soapstone, combined with its virtual impermeability, make it as much of a marvel in the kitchen as it is in the fine stoves featured earlier in the chapter. A soapstone griddle can be placed on a stove or over open flames and will perform like today's "non-stick" cookware. Since soapstone delivers slow, even heat it is ideal for cooking pancakes, for example. As an energy saver, it can be placed in an oven while other things are baking and can be then removed and used as a griddle with no source of heat but that which it has stored. It is sold in three sizes, 12" x 17", 8" x

15", and 10" x 12". The largest is priced at $39; the two smaller ones are each $32.

Brochures available, $1.

Woodstock Soapstone Co., Inc.
Box 223
Woodstock, VT 05091
(802) 672-5133

Other Suppliers of Heating & Cooking

Consult List of Suppliers for addresses.

Antique Mantels

Architectural Antiques
Victor Carl
Castle Burlingame
Felicity, Inc.
Gargoyles, Ltd.
William H. Jackson Co.
Materials Unlimited
Old Mansions Co.
Francis J. Purcell II
The Renovation Source, Inc.
R. T. Trump & Co.
Westlake Architectural Antiques
I. M. Wiese
Wrecking Bar (Dallas)

Reproduction Mantels

American Woodcarving
Architectural Paneling
Black Millwork
Decorators Supply
European Marble Works
Felber Studios
Focal Point
Fypon
Lone Star Plywood & Door Corp.
Old World Moulding

Fireplaces

Preway
The Readybuilt Products Co.
Thermograte, Inc.

Chimney Pots

Historic Boulevard Services

Andirons

Ball and Ball
The Country Loft
Cumberland General Store
The Essex Forge
The Harvin Co.
William H. Jackson Co.
Mexico House
Virginia Metalcrafters

Tools

Ball and Ball
The Blacksmith Shop
The Burning Log
The Country Loft
The Essex Forge
Steve Kayne
Stephen W. Parker
E.G. Washburne Co.

Bellows

Lemee's Fireplace Equipment
National Products Inc.
Period Furniture Hardware

Firebacks and Grates

Steptoe & Wife Antiques Ltd.
Helen Williams/Rare Tiles

Firescreens

The Blacksmith Shop
Hurley Patentee Lighting
William H. Jackson
Portland Williamette Co.
Ye Olde Mantel Shoppe

Heating Stoves

Atlanta Stove Works
Bow and Arrow Imports
Fisher Stoves
Guild of Shaker Crafts
Mohawk Industries
Pfanstiel Hardware
Portland Franklin Stove Foundry
Schrader Wood Stoves
Shenandoah Mfg. Co.
Washington Stove Works

Antique Cookstoves

Home and Harvest, Inc.
Kristia Associates
United House Wrecking

Stove Accessories

Cumberland General Store
House of Webster
Thompson and Anderson

Floorcloth design, English, 1851.

5 Floors & Floor Coverings

Everyone seems to admire beautiful wood floors. It wasn't always this way in North America. Architectural critics in the mid-Victorian period complained often about the uneven, scruffy appearance of pine flooring. Random-width boards, they said, were not at all fashionable or well made. Aesthetics aside, they were generally correct: little attention was paid to durable flooring materials. Softwoods such as pine had been used in the earlier years in place of better hardwoods. Not until the late 19th century did oak come into widespread use. It was then, too, that parquet flooring was introduced in mansions and villas.

Just how to restore or maintain a wood floor—of pine or oak, or even fancier hardwoods such as teak and mahogany—will always be a matter of argument. Many floors appear at first to require heavy sanding and a polyurethane coating. Dried-out soft pine flooring, however, will never hold a shine for long, and it does gouge easily. If sanding must be done, then it should be done gingerly, especially where pine is concerned. A rich finishing oil will renew the wood, and good old-fashioned wax is likely to do more good than a synthetic finish. At least these mixtures will not coat the fibers of the wood so that they have no resilience. Always resist if you can the temptation to make new what is old.

The owner of an old house often discovers that one floor has been laid over another, usually oak over pine. Before the ripping-up begins, however, think about whether or not it is worth it. Better yet, remove a few pieces in an inconspicuous area to see what condition the subfloor is in. It may be full of nail holes, the natural result of having served as the foundation for a second surface. The type of oak flooring most commonly found in late-19th and early 20th-century homes is of a much better grade than that used today. The strips are often wider, and the pieces themselves are thicker. Like many others, we prefer the random-width boards for their hand-crafted appearance, but oak can be just as fitting and attractive a material.

The use of synthetic flooring materials is a difficult problem to deal with. Modern vinyls, as pointed out later in this chapter, are really best suited to cover up the plywood underfloors of a new house. Few recently-built homes have floors; the vinyl or asphalt materials—in sheets or tiles—*are* the floors. The best of these—solid vinyls—have skyrocketed in cost, and there is now a trend back to the use of natural materials such as slate, brick, clay tiles, even concrete pavers in those areas where moisture can be a problem, such as the kitchen, bathroom, and front hall. If you need to replace flooring or to cover it up, you should carefully cost out the difference between a synthetic and a natural material.

Various kinds of floor coverings were used in the past to protect floors, to make them warmer and more comfortable, and more attractive. During the Colonial period most of these coverings were very simple—throw rugs, both braided and hooked, with rags used as the primary material. Oilcloth or canvas floorcloths also became popular in the mid-18th century and continued in use well into the 1800s. These handy coverings, fully explored in this chapter, have been rediscovered in recent years.

Area rugs, room-size rugs and carpets, and wall-to-wall carpeting multiplied in variety over the years. Oriental rugs were used only in the homes of the wealthy during the Colonial period and often served as table coverings rather than as objects to be stepped upon. Commercial rugs and carpeting only came into widespread use after the introduction of power looms in the 1840s and '50s. Then there seemed to be no end of possibilities for the housewife, providing her purse was ample enough. Axminsters, ingrains, and Brussels carpets flowed out of the mills of North America and England. Wall-to-wall materials seemed best at first to cover up what was than considered crude pine flooring; later in the Victorian period, the preference was for carpets or room-size rugs which left a display of highly-polished wood flooring on all four sides of a room. By the turn of the century, a retreat from carpeting was well underway.

Orientals began to be used in upper-middle-class homes; even Colonial-style oval and rectangular throw rugs had a vogue.

Floor coverings for today's historically-minded home owner can be of varying designs, forms, and materials. An exact period reproduction of a carpet may be necessary for a museum re-creation or historic house, but at home why not find a happy compromise? Anything shag-like is out, and most wall-to-wall materials are flimsy and appear to have been designed by color-blind artists. Well-designed Brussels reproductions of considerable durability are, however, available in both room and area sizes. These have been popular standbys for many years. Sears offered them in all its catalogues starting in the 1890s; unfortunately, mass-merchandisers now devote little attention to them, but rug merchants and department stores do.

Wood Flooring

There's nothing like real wood flooring—strips or planks that may squeak underfoot, that have a soft, warm patina that is the product of age. Boards need not be random-width to be charming; golden oak strips neatly laid across a Queen Anne parlor floor can be just as handsome. Most wood floors in North America are made of pine; that is, they were inexpensive. Architectural critics in the 1870s and '80s called them "unsightly" and recommended that they be at least partially covered up with rugs or carpeting. Today we love the display of wood and spend much time and money in "redoing" floors. Some are in such bad condition that they must be scraped, or, in the case of hardwoods, even sanded. Pine floors, however, should not be given such a harsh treatment, but should only be spot sanded. Polyurethane coatings should be avoided at all costs; they give a wood floor a glossy, uniform look. Hardwood floors can take a high shine of wax; pine is usually better left lightly polished.

Among the most prominent of the antique wood flooring suppliers are Kensington Historical Co., Craftsman Lumber, Maurer & Shepherd, and John A. Wigen Restorations. For addresses, consult the List of Suppliers.

Castle Burlingame

This New Jersey firm specializes in the sale of wide-board antique flooring and will also install and finish antique floors. Among the woods it stocks are pumpkin (white) pine, yellow and red pine, hemlock, oak, chestnut, and poplar. There are three useful booklets produced by the firm which can be ordered for $3.99 each, or $9.99 for the three: (1) "How and Where to Find, Buy, and Select Antique Wide-Board Flooring"; (2) "How to Install Antique Wide-Board Flooring"; and (3) "How to Sand and Finish Antique Wide-Board Flooring."

Castle Burlingame
R.D. 1, Box 352
Basking Ridge, NJ 07920
(201) 647-3885

Diamond K. Co., Inc.

Pine of the wide-plank variety is supplied by Diamond K. for use in flooring, wainscoting, and raised paneling. Much of the wood has been reclaimed from dismantled structures, but new wood—Canadian pine which has been air-dried for one year—can also be secured from this company.

Diamond K. Co., Inc.
130 Buckland Road
South Windsor, CT 06074
(203) 644-8486

Harris Manufacturing

Plank flooring ranging in width from 3" to 8" is produced in pine, red or white oak, and a teak called "Angelique." The thickness for all is ¾" and the material is available with a beveled or a square edge. The flooring is tongue and grooved and end-matched and is available either prefinished or unfinished. Illustrated is stained "Colonial Plank/Angelique Teak." Oak or pine pegs or "plugs" are available but, fortunately, not mandatory. "Colonial Plank" is also available in red and white

oak and in yellow pine. Harris distributors are found across the United States.

Catalogue available, 50¢.

Harris Manufacturing Co.
P.O. Box 300
Johnson City, TN 37601
(615) 928-3122

Kentucky Wood Floors

Random-width plank flooring (without plugs) can be ordered from Kentucky Wood Floors in plain white oak, plain red oak, ash or quartered oak, walnut or cherry, and Brazilian walnut. All this flooring is ¾" thick and tongue and groove. The firm is also a specialist in parquet flooring, examples of which may be found underfoot in The Metropolitan Museum of Art, the John F. Kennedy Center for the Performing Arts, and The White House. Strip borders can be ordered as well in plain white oak, quartered oak, or maple. These pieces are 2¼" wide, and ¾" thick. For fancy Victorian interiors, such contrasting woods may be very appropriate.

Brochure available, $1.

Kentucky Wood Floors, Inc.
7761 National Turnpike
Louisville, KY 40214
(502) 368-5836

Wood Mosaic

This firm produces handsome patterned wood flooring. Illustrated is the "Lincoln II" design which is preassembled to form 2' x 2' sections. All the flooring is today's standard ¾" for higher-priced materials. It is shipped unfinished and is available in white or red oak.

Brochure available, 25¢.

Wood Mosaic
P.O. Box 21159
Louisville, KY 40221
(502) 363-3531

Floor Refinishing

New York Flooring is one of the best of many companies that specialize in the refinishing of floors and has worked on a variety of jobs from The Metropolitan Museum of Art to a Columbus Avenue hardware store. It will, of course, undertake new installations as well and perform repairs, staining, etc.

Catalogue available, $3.

New York Flooring
340 E. 90th Street
New York, NY 10028
(212) 427-6262

If you are out in the New Jersey/Pennsylvania area, you might try to reach Colonial Wood, another refinisher and installer. The proprietor will let you know whether he thinks you *should* spend any money on your floors, and he has all the expertise to do a superb job if he agrees that it needs doing.

Colonial Wood
16 Water Street
Clinton, NJ 08809
(201) 735-9688

Ceramic Flooring

Next to real wood, real ceramic flooring is to be preferred by anyone willing and able to absorb the expense. If you have shopped around lately in the vinyl flooring market, however, you will know how expensive these oil-based products have become. Tiling and brick are beginning to look more and more attractive from a financial viewpoint alone. As far as real brick (and not fake imitations) is concerned, you are best off seeking out a supply of antique material. If the idea of unevenness bothers you (and it can be a problem), then consider the half-bricks or pavers which are available from many flooring and building suppliers. Ceramic tiles are fairly easy to locate,

although the selection available may be less attractive than you wish. Fortunately, baby blue, pink, and sunshine yellow are beginning to fade away into the pastel landscape as the 1950s themselves recede into memory, but enough vulgar designs remain on the market to satisfy any appetite for bad taste.

American Olean

You may very well find that the right tiles are made by American Olean. The American ceramic tile industry has not been able to protect some of its weaker members from the onslaught of vinyl and other synthetics, but some companies have not only survived, but are offering better and better products. Traditionally used in a front hall, kitchen, bathroom, or garden room, tiles, even those unglazed, have the advantage of being both very easy to clean and impermeable to burns. Contrary to popular belief, they are quite unbreakable. A good ceramic floor can last several generations or more; vinyl is good for perhaps a 20-year period. The white ceramic mosaic tile seen in the illustration is both very contemporary *and* traditional; there is no reason why something that is well-designed and made cannot be both. Other lines from American Olean that we find particularly appropriate for period rooms are "Primitive" (especially the "Hearth" and "Flint Blend" unglazed tiles); the very natural quarry tiles made in seven different shapes; and "Countertop Trim" tile for kitchens and bathrooms, a handsome substitute for cigarette-burned and kitchen knife-marred formica.

Product sheets available; "Real Ceramic Tile Kitchen Countertop Portfolio," $1.

American Olean Tile Co.
Lansdale, PA 19446
(215) 855-1111

Country Floors

This Manhattan emporium and distributor brings together the finest selection of imported tiles in North America. These products are imported from Italy, Spain, France, Portugal, Holland, Israel, and Mexico. Country Floor's catalogue ($5) illustrates well over 500 tile patterns in full color. The unglazed terra-cotta pavers from Mexico are extraordinarily handsome objects and are modestly priced; there are a number of shapes, and sizes vary. The brick pavers are available in 6" x 12" as well as 4" x 8½". Similar but less roughly cut and finished terra-cotta tiles are also available in the "Provence" line from France.

Country Floors, Inc.
300 E. 61st Street
New York, NY 10021
(212) 758-7414

Elon

This large firm also imports handmade tiles from Mexico for

both decorative and flooring uses. Of special interest to those with traditional tastes are the precast pavers in designs and solid colors, and marble tiles grained with pink or gray tones.

For information regarding your nearest distributor, contact:

Elon, Inc.
198 Saw Mill River Road
Elmsford, NY 10523
(914) 592-3323

H. & R. Johnson Tiles

Owners of Victorian homes are often at a loss as to where to turn for encaustic tiles. If you have visited the Arts and Industries building at the Smithsonian Institution, you may have noticed the extraordinary floor which was originally laid in 1876 (when the building was part of the Philadelphia Centennial Exposition) and recently remade by H. & R. Johnson. This company is one of Europe's leading specialists in the matching, laying, and restoration of encaustic tile floors. In addition to the Smithsonian building, it has authentically replaced some of the Pugin floors in the Palace of Westminster, London.

Any architect, builder, designer, or individual home owner who has an encaustic tile floor worthy of restoration or authentic replacement should send to the company for an initial questionnaire to enable a cost quotation to be prepared. Illustrated is the Smithsonian floor as remade by Johnson.

H. & R. Johnson Tiles Ltd.
Highgate Tile Works
Tunstall,
Stoke-on-Trent ST6 4JX
England
0782-85611

Stone Flooring

The use of marble, slate, and other natural stone materials has been limited largely in the past to homes of considerable cost and elegance. Marble, in particular, has always been a luxury item, even in those areas where it was produced in abundance —Vermont, Georgia, and Tennessee. Marble flooring was reserved for stylish entrance halls and such formal areas as drawing rooms. Both domestic and imported marble were available to the wealthy home owner. A number of the 19th- and early-20th-century town houses and villas found in Eastern seaport cities contain marble flooring from Italy and France.

Less expensive polished stone materials such as travertine and granite have been substituted for marble in many institutional and commercial buildings, but their use in houses has been slight. Slate flooring is much more likely to be encountered. During the 19th century it was quarried in large quantities in the New England and the Middle Atlantic states and shipped throughout the country. Slate production continues to this day at a much slower pace, but if competitive products such as oil-based vinyl tiles continue to rise dramatically in cost, this attractive stone may again find popular use. Properly sealed, it can be a most serviceable flooring material. Slate pavers are available from many stone dealers, and squares of the material are now being sold in a number of home centers.

In the past we have recommended various national or regional suppliers of natural stone products appropriate for flooring. If it appears that what you need is not available in your area, contact one of the following companies for advice. They are more than likely to direct you to possible sources.

Bergen Bluestone
404 Route 17
Paramus, NJ 07652
(201) 261-1903

Delaware Quarries, Inc.
River Road
Lumberville, PA 18933
(215) 297-5647

Marble Modes, Inc.
15-25 130th Street
College Point, NY 11356
(212) LE9-1334

Parma Tile Mosaic & Marble Co., Inc.
14-38 Astoria Blvd.
Long Island City, NY 11102
(212) 278-3060

The Structural Slate Co.
Pen Argyl, PA 18072
(215) 863-4141

Vermont Marble Co.
61 Main Street
Proctor, VT 05765
(802) 459-3311

Vermont Structural Slate Co.
P.O. Box 98
Fair Haven, VT 05743
(802) 265-4933

Vinyl and Asphalt Flooring

What can one say about these imitations? Very little. Linoleum did not replace wood flooring in the kitchen, but was laid over it as a covering in much the same manner as a canvas floorcloth of the Colonial era. Linoleum, however, is no longer produced. This is a pity. Sheet linoleum was not a gorgeous floor covering, but it was what it was—printed patterns on an oil-based material in designs that differed little from those used for wallpapers. There was very little attempt to imitate marble, terrazzo, wood, brick, etc.

Why do manufacturers of such modern vinyls feel that they have to produce stencil-like, stone-like, wood-like, brick-like patterns? Why? Because in modern homes these tiles or sheeting form the floor; there is nothing of real substance underneath. The dramatic upsurge in the use of vinyl flooring in recent years is, in many ways, similar to that which took place in wallpaper during the mid-19th century. With new technology at hand, thousands and thousands of patterns which imitated painted designs or luxurious fabrics could be printed at low cost. It was very handy to be able to cover up a crudely finished wall with a paper. The quality of printing, however, was often less than desirable. Wallpaper made in America became so vulgar, in fact, that by the end of the 19th century it was being used much less frequently by people of taste.

Kentile

We once again recommend several of the Kentile solid vinyl tile patterns—"Barre Slate" and those in the "Castilla" series which are of one color. Be forewarned, however, that prices are very high, and that you should cost out using natural materials such as slate or wood vs. the solid vinyl.

Literature available from most flooring dealers.

Kentile Floors
58 Second Avenue
Brooklyn, NY 11215
(212) 768-9500

Azrock Floor Products

These are not solid, but of vinyl composition, a combination of vinyl resin, asbestos fibers, coloring pigment, and inert filler. Consequently, they are less expensive than solid-vinyl tiles. Several patterns—"Thru-Onyx" and those of the "Cortina" series—may pass muster.

Azrock Floor Products
P.O. Box 531
San Antonio, TX 78292
(512) 341-5101

That's it folks, and we've looked at a good number of the vinyls and asphalts. All those lines dubbed "Concord," "1776," "Federal Parlor," etc., etc., are truly not right for an old house, their names notwithstanding.

Concrete Flooring

Believe it or not, concrete does not have to be ugly or covered over with vinyl. We've visited homes where concrete floors have been painted with a deep penetrating oil-based enamel and then highly polished. The effect is most handsome. There are also cement-based products which have become popular in recent years. It is hard to know what to term these—synthetic or natural? When used for wall facings—brick or stone—they are perfectly revolting. But some of the cement tiles used for flooring are worthy of consideration.

Z-Brick Flooring Products

This firm recently acquired the C-Tile Manufacturing Co. of Atlanta, Georgia, and is now producing and marketing various forms of flooring materials. The so-called "Rustic" pavers and the "brick" design are boringly regular shapes and about as authentic for an old house as vinyl siding. The squares —Marquis II Square—are, as illustrated here, quite handsome pieces. They are put down with Z-Brick Epoxy Floor Tile adhesive.

Literature available.

Z-Brick Company
Woodinville, WA 98072
(206) 485-7551

Floor Coverings

We frequently receive inquiries regarding the availability of documented period-design carpets. Rugs are not much of a problem since the art of woven, hooked, and braided rug making is very much alive. Rugs of a rather simple sort were the floor coverings used by most North Americans from the Colonial period through the 19th century. These might have been informally placed—in front of the hearth, at each side of the bed, beneath a dining table, in the front hall. Until the mid-19th century much of the flooring in the average house was not covered to any great extent. Although wall-to-wall carpeting was used as early as the end of the 18th century in the principal rooms of prosperous homes, it was not a practical or affordable commodity for most people. Carpeting in wide rolls became a reality for the general populace in the period following the Civil War. Widely adopted at the time were individual room-size carpets—Axminsters, Wiltons, Brussels, ingrains—produced here or in England. Oriental rugs or carpets became popular in the last several decades of the century as floor coverings.

It is nearly impossible to find many of the carpet designs which were used during the Victorian period either in room-size form or as wall-to-wall carpeting. Most Victorian carpets did not wear terribly well over the years, and, consequently, the market for antique carpets other than orientals is a slim one. The old-house decorator wishing to use appropriate designs has three alternatives to consider: (1) the custom-making of such material by one of several major mills; (2) the use of a reproduction commissioned from a mill by a museum or by a historical society; (3) the purchase of one of the newly-made adaptations offered by the many purveyors of commercial carpeting. The last alternative may not be as unsatisfactory as it appears. It is comforting to discover when shopping for carpets how little design has changed over the years. Carpet people— at least the buyers—are not the shag rug type.

Rugs

"Rug" is a term often used interchangeably in America with "carpet." A rug, however, is most properly a small-sized floor covering. The term derives from the coverings (ruggs) first used on the bed or as a type of lap cloth to cover the legs just as a shawl surrounds the upper part of the body. A rug is almost always cheaper than a carpet and, unlike the latter, is frequently hooked or braided rather than woven. We have offered a number of sources for hooked, braided, and woven rugs in previous years, and all these recommended firms remain quality suppliers.

Adams & Swett
380 Dorchester Avenue
Boston, MA 02127
(617) 268-8000

Country Braid House
Clark Road

Tilton, NH 03276
(603) 286-4511

Heritage Rugs
P.O. Box 404
Lahaska, PA 18931
(215) 794-7229

The Pilgrim's Progress, Inc.
225 Henry Street
New York, NY 10002
(212) 227-2772

Southern Highland Handicraft Guild
P.O. Box 9545
Asheville, NC 28815
(704) 298-7928

Christina Bergh

Colonial bed "ruggs" were treated with exceptional care and rarely were they allowed to slip onto the floor. It is questionable whether you would want to place Christina Bergh's hand-woven rugs in any other place except the wall. Many of her designs may be considered too contemporary for a period interior; others, like that illustrated, are reminiscent of the best woven folk materials. Each color used in tapestries, blankets,

shawls, and rugs is hand-dyed. If you visit the Santa Fe area, you would enjoy stopping at her shop and studio.

Christina Bergh
711 Camino Corrales
Santa Fe, NM 87501
(505) 983-3401

If you are "into" rug making yourself, then the following two suppliers of patterns and accessories are indispensable:

Catalogue available, $1.50.

Braid-Aid Company
466 Washington Street
Pembroke, MA 02359
(617) 826-6091

Booklet available, $1.50.

Heirloom Rugs
28 Harlem Street
Rumford, RI 02916
(401) 438-5672

Carpeting

Although the availability of documented reproduction carpeting is extremely limited, there is evidence that this situation is beginning to improve. as the following listings show.

Newbury Design

Historical reproductions of antique needlework rugs and Brussels and Wilton carpets are the specialty of this firm. These are the types of designs that may be appropriate for late-18th- and 19th-century American interiors. Illustrated are two such examples. The first was developed for The Metropolitan Museum of Art and is an adaptation of an antique needlepoint rug in Brussels carpeting; the second is an exact copy of an antique Brussels carpet commissioned by the restoration committee of the Old State Capitol, Iowa City, Iowa.

These reproductions are manufactured by a Wilton weaver in England under the supervision of Newbury. Some of the other designs which the firm has executed are a Victorian floral, English Regency or American Empire wreath and rosette pattern, and a "Turkey" pattern. The designs commissioned by various units of the National Park Service (Longfellow National Historic Site, Cambridge, Massachusetts; the Thomas A. Edison House, Orange, New Jersey; The Peterson House and The Frederick Douglass House, Washington, D.C.) are in the "public domain" and can be made available to other interested parties without payment of any sort of reproduction fee.

Brochures available.

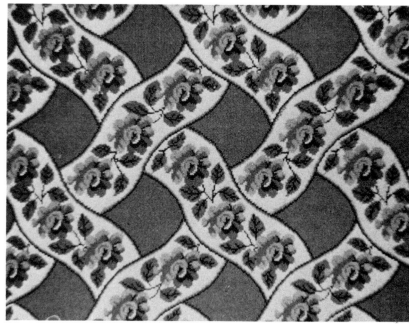

Newbury Design Inc.
P.O. Box 265
Wellesley, MA 02181
(617) 235-7293

Scalamandré

This firm's extraordinary collection of 19th-century reproduction carpets was described at length in previous *Catalogues*. They have been used in restorations from coast to coast. The Wiltons are made in England, and the ingrains at Scalamandré's own Long Island City mill. These designs—all documented meticulously—can be seen in such places as Independence Hall, the Smithsonian Institution, and the Metropolitan Museum.

Scalamandré products are available only through interior designers or the design department of select retail outlets. For information on such sources, contact Scalamandré.

Scalamandré Silks, Inc.
950 Third Avenue
New York, NY 10022
(212) 361-8500

Schumacher

Schumacher's new Victorian Collection is being launched this year in association with the Victorian Society in America. It is hoped that carpet patterns will be available in 1981. For further details on the first printed fabrics and wallpapers being issued by the company, see Chapters 7 and 8.

F. Schumacher & Co.
939 Third Avenue
New York, NY 10022
(212) 644-5900

Stark Carpet

Stark makes both a standard line and a documented series of carpets available for those needing historical materials. Examples from the stock Bouclé Collection are illustrated in *The Second Old House Catalogue*. These are 12'-wide Wiltons featuring sober geometric designs appropriate for both early and late 19th-century interiors. Just as interesting are the mid-19th-century carpets commissioned from Stark by various restoration groups. Illustrated is "Regency," a floral medallion within squares with a miniature border in gold, green, beige, red, and black. It has been used in one of the bedrooms of the Andrew

Johnson homestead in Tennessee. For further information, contact Mr. John Stark.

Stark Carpet Corp.
979 Third Avenue
New York, NY 10022
(212) PL2-9000

Floorcloths

These heavy canvas floor coverings are now considered the most authentic available for the traditional Colonial-period interior. Hand-painted and usually finished with several coats of varnish, they are very durable and easy to clean. There is no doubt that such oilcloths were in use in the New World as early as the 1720s; they seem to have become most popular in the late 18th century. At the time they were an inexpensive substitute for carpeting and were imported from England and produced domestically. The use of floorcloths continued well into the 19th century. Their use under dining room tables and parlor center tables and in halls and kitchens is well established.

Floorcloths, Inc.

In 1971 this became the first American firm to reintroduce floorcloths to the public. Since that time its craftsmen have executed traditional designs for many restorations and have created adaptations or contemporary designs for other patrons.

Literature available, $2.

Floorcloths, Inc.
P.O. Box 812
Severna Park, MD 21146
(301) 647-3328

Good Stenciling

The floorcloth designs of Nancy Good Cayford are much fewer in number than Floorcloths, Inc., but each is every bit as handsome. She has a traditional cube/geometric; another design termed "Sturbridge," taken from a cloth illustrated in Nina Fletcher Little's *Floor Coverings of New England Before 1800*; and "Crewel," an adaptation of a floor stencil that would be most fitting for a 19th-century interior. The standard colors are excellent; custom colors can be specified if desired. Rug sizes run from 2' x 3' to 12' x 14', with sizes over 6' wide seamed; runners are also offered.

Brochure available, $1.

Good Stenciling
Box 387
Dublin, NH 03444
(603) 563-8021

Craftswomen

The Craftswomen of Doylestown, Pennsylvania, first offered finished floorcloths but have since turned solely to the production of kits which give the buyer a chance to paint the design himself. Each kit contains heavyweight cotton canvas cut to size, a complete and detailed stencil pattern, Mylar sheets for cutting stencils, a marking pen for tracing the pattern onto the sheets, a bristle stencil brush, and all the instructions you need to execute the design and finish the floorcloth. Acrylics available from an art supply store are recommended as paint. Thirteen patterns are offered which require stenciling and six which call for only filling in of outlines. Sizes generally run from 3′ x 5′ to 6′ x 6′. A few of the patterns are adaptations of Amish quilt designs but, handsome as they are, they are not appropriate for use on floorcloths. A majority, however, are of the sort which would have been found underfoot in the 19th century. Illustrated, in the order of appearance, are "Laurel Wreath," "Victorian Border #1," and "Victorian Pattern with Checkerboard."

Catalogue available, $4.

Craftswomen
Box 715
Doylestown, PA 18901
(215) 822-0721

Floor Stenciling

From the early 18th until the mid-19th century, paint was probably the most commonly used "material" with which to cover and decorate floors. Wood floors were painted in solid colors, spattered, or adorned with stencil designs. The most accomplished stencil designs were usually executed by itinerant artists who, at the same time, could apply ornament around windows and doors, above the chair rail, and in the form of a ceiling cornice. The art of stenciling has become terribly popular once again, and space is devoted to such decoration in Chapter 8. Stephen Kelemen pays special attention to floors, and will undertake the restoration of stencil motifs, provide custom designs, and install a line of 6″ square wood tiles with painted geometric, floral, shell, and cloud motifs. These might be suitable for borders, overall or repeat patterns, or as a central medallion.

Stephen Kelemen
Design Associates
77 Main Road
Orient Point, NY 11957
(516) 323-3574

Other Suppliers of Flooring Materials
Consult List of Suppliers for addresses.

Wood Flooring
Architectural Antique Warehouse
Bangkok Industries
Blair Lumber
Dale Carlisle
The House Carpenters
Dana-Deck & Laminates
Early New England Restoration Co.
The 18th-Century Co.
The House Carpenters
Mountain Lumber Co.
Period Pine
Simpson Timber Co.
The Wrecking Bar (Dallas)

Ceramic Flooring
Parma Tile Mosaic & Marble Co.
Villeroy + Boch

Stone Flooring
The Bank
Carrara Marble Co. of America
Materials Unlimited
New York Marble Works

Vinyl and Asphalt Flooring
Armstrong Cork Co.

Floor Covering—Rugs
Carol Brown
Chapulin
Diane Jackson Cole
Henry Ford Museum and Greenfield VIllage
S. & C. Huber
Quicksand Crafts

Floor Covering—Carpets
Dildarian, Inc.
S.M. Hexter Co.
Charles W. Jacobsen
Kenmore Carpet Corp.
Rittenhouse Carpet

Floor Stenciling
Adele Bishop, Inc.
The Ceiling Lady
Gina Martin
Megan Parry
The Rambusch Co.
StencilArt
Stencilled Interiors

Reproduction six-light hanging fixture, English, c. 1820-35, courtesy of
Chapman Manufacturing Co., Avon, Massachusetts.

6 Lighting

Producers of lighting fixtures and accessories are among the most accomplished craftsmen in the restoration materials field. They have to adapt antique forms to technically-advanced uses without sacrificing the aesthetic qualities of the old. There are literally hundreds of craftsmen in this field who have successfully navigated such dangerous shoals, and the best of them will be found in this chapter.

There is very little literature available which will help you to decide how to use antique fixtures. All the experts are agreed, however, that objects never used for fixtures before, such as a candle mold, coffee mill, or a miniature ship's steering wheel, have no place in the home or anywhere else. The uniting of a modern electric accessory with a form never intended to receive it always results in an object of kitsch. Rather, turn to those traditional objects which held candles or burners of various sorts such as sticks, lanterns, sconces, glass bases, and iron, brass, and bronze holders. With the use of an adapter (available in most hardware stores or through lighting suppliers), one can almost instantly create an effective and appropriate modern fixture.

More complicated forms—chandeliers, gasoliers, indeed almost any hanging fixture—will require the expertise of a lighting specialist. Antiques are still available, but supplies of early forms are being depleted quite quickly. Victorian fixtures are also in great demand. Unless you are willing to spend a great deal of money and time in the search for true antiques which can be used in a practical manner, it may be better to choose a reproduction piece. These are made in every possible form by very knowledgeable, careful craftsmen.

How important is the matter of lighting in a period interior? This is a subjective matter for many involving a subtle appreciation of flattering levels of illumination. It goes without saying that homes in the past were not as brightly lit as they are today. When one moved from room to room, lights were not automatically switched on; rather, a portable source was carried along. This practice is well documented in pictures and paintings of people with chambersticks or small oil lamps in hand. In some series of historical sketches and photographs which illustrate various rooms in a house, the very same fixture may appear in two or three of the rooms.

Some of the most common domestic lighting devices are the hanging lamp or chandelier of the parlor, usually centered over a table to make reading possible; the bedside light; wall sconces or brackets; and portable lamps and lanterns. Fixtures made to hold candles were, of course, common in the Colonial period, and their use continued well into the 19th century. Today candles are used mainly for decorative effect, and there is no better way to provide soft illumination for short periods of time. Various kinds of oil-burning fixtures are also useful, but they, too, cannot supply as much illumination as we need on a daily basis. Kerosene lamps, for instance, are very useful standbys and can provide supplemental sources of light, especially at a time when electric bills are climbing each month.

Antique Lighting Fixtures

There was a time when every junkyard had its share of gasoliers and early electric light fixtures, when only "early American" devices had any value at all to collectors. But that time has long passed. The Victorian period is now far enough away in time to be duly appreciated, and even fixtures of the 1920s and the Depression years command astonishing prices today. Although the demand for authentic period lighting devices far exceeds the supply, good pieces are readily available in the marketplace if you happen to have both the pocket for the real thing and the insider's knowledge of where to find the best sources of supply. Descriptions of some of the most reputable dealers follow.

Roy Electric Co.

Roy Electric stocks a very large inventory of Victorian and turn-of-the-century gas and electric fixtures, sconces, lamps, shades, parts, lamp bases, and virtually anything pertaining to old lighting fixtures. It also can turn the old wreck you've been keeping in the attic into a functioning beauty, since it repairs, restores, refinishes, casts, plates, bends, polishes, lacquers, and rewires old fixtures as well. Shown is one of Roy Electric's original gas fixtures, so handsome in fact that the firm is planning a line of reproductions based on it and on other fixtures—all handcrafted and made from original molds.

Catalogue available.

Roy Electric Co., Inc.
1054 Coney Island Avenue
Brooklyn, NY 11230
(212) 339-6311

The Lily Collection

Lily offers a unique line of antique and custom lighting fixtures, including authentic antique lighting fixtures and shades predominantly of the period 1880 through the 1930s; original art bronze table lamps, wall sconces, and ceiling fixtures featuring antique patinas such as Tiffany green and Florentine gold; fine Dresden china shades and globes, designed and produced in its own studios; and custom pattern work and white metal castings for hardware and lighting fixtures. The firm works with commercial and residential clients and is always available for consultation on special projects.

Literature available, $5.

The Lily Collection
1313 N. Main Street
Ann Arbor, MI 48104
(313) 668-6324

City Lights

This spirited dealer in antique lighting (c. 1880-1930) sells ceiling fixtures and wall lights and sconces (gas, electric, or the two in combination), reading lamps, desk lamps, accent lamps (Art Nouveau and Art Deco), bridge lamps, and reading lamps. "At all times," the proprietors write, "we try to have unusual, interesting, or outrageous lighting" on hand. And they succeed admirably. City Lights restores its pieces to perfection, a lengthy process carefully spelled out in its interesting brochure.

Brochure available.

City Lights
226 Massachusetts Avenue
Cambridge, MA 02140
(617) 547-1490

The Lamp Shop

Although this shop is tiny, its small stock of Deco lamps and light fittings is always exceptional. As its prices are also very reasonable, no Deco connoisseur should miss it when visiting London. A selection of the stock on the day we visited it was as follows: original Deco "shell" light shades with chrome fittings to be clamped flush on the wall (£16 each); pewter lady on an illuminated crystal staircase (£65); pewter seal balancing a large illuminated crystal ball on its nose (£80); lady with illuminated pleated-glass skirt (£45); two pewter Pierettes sitting back-to-back on a large illuminated crystal ball (£70). You get the idea.

The Lamp Shop
24 Bedfordbury
Covent Garden
London WC2
England
(01) 836-3852

Brasslight

Steve Kaniewski so loves the old that he bought a commercial building in the historic Walker's Point neighborhood of Milwaukee to house both his business and himself. A dealer of fine antique lighting fixtures—Victorian gas, early electric, Art Deco, and other exquisite lighting fixtures from the past—Mr. Kaniewski prefers to accept inquires *by telephone.*

Brasslight of Historic Walker's Point
719 S. 5th Street
Milwaukee, WI 53204
(414) 383-0675

Sandy Springs Galleries

Boasting a showroom of about 7,000 square feet, Sandy Springs Galleries may at any one time have about 350 restored lighting fixtures and 150 sconces in stock, including antiques in brass, copper, wood, and wrought iron—most of them originally fueled by gas, candle, kerosene, or early electricity.

No catalogue, but telephone inquiries welcome.

Sandy Springs Galleries
233 Hilderbrand Drive, N.E.
Atlanta, GA 30328
(404) 252-3244

The following suppliers were recommended in the first two Old House Catalogues and remain primary sources of fine antique lighting fixtures:

London Venturers

This company specializes in authentic brass fixtures of the Victorian period and issues a catalogue of its holdings several times a year. Because of many requests to do so, it now carries a first-rate line of reproduction fixtures and shades.

Catalogue available, $1.

London Venturers Company
2 Dock Square
Rockport, MA 01966
(617) 546-7161

Yankee Craftsman

Bill Sweeney and his three sons take such pride in restoring period fixtures and in providing custom designs that their shop has taken on the very ambience of the late 19th century, a period they obviously love. Yankee Craftsman stocks a large inventory of antique fixtures; if you're looking for a specific type that the Sweeneys might have, they will send a photograph and information at no charge.

Yankee Craftsman

357 Commonwealth Road
Wayland, MA 01778
(617) 653-0031

Candleholders

If the golden age of the candleholder was the 150-year period between the middle of the 17th century and the end of the 18th, then, in a sense, that age is upon us again. In the past decade or so, although there were certainly progenitors during the Great Depression, a new breed of craftsman has sprung up—one that is not only respectful of the past, but one that is scholarly in its endeavors to re-master artistic techniques and procedures long thought to be lost. Although what follows is only a random sampling of the fine workmanship characteristic of today's craftsmen, it is sufficient consolation to even the most pessimistic old-house lover. Yes, the arts of the past will somehow manage to be passed on to our progeny. For starters, here are some examples of handcrafted candleholders by modern artisans that surely rival the glories of the past.

Hanging Candlestick

This candlestick, forged by The Blacksmith Shop, is a wonderful example of Yankee ingenuity. A hanging candlestick, it can be hung from mantels or from the backs of chairs to provide

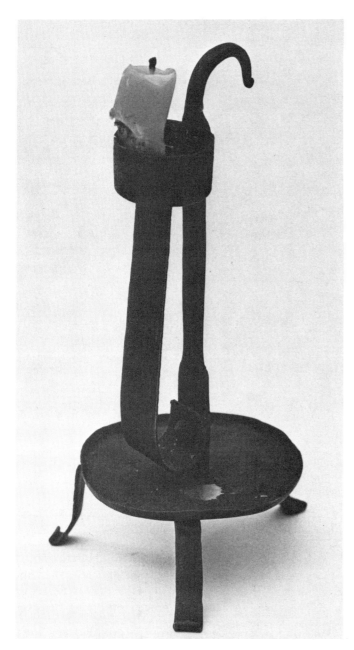

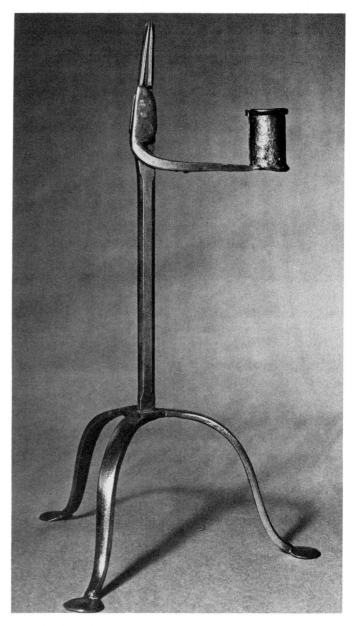

light in awkward places, and it can stand on its own as well.
Literature available.

The Blacksmith Shop
R.R. 2—26 Bridge Road
Orleans, MA 02653
(617) 255-7233

Candle and Rush Holder

Newton Millham handcrafts this fine reproduction of an early 18th-century three-legged candle and rush holder. The candle socket acts as a counterweight for the jaws of the rush holder. It is a bargain at $55.

Catalogue available, $1.

Newton Millham—Star Forge
672 Drift Road
Westport, MA 02790
(617) 636-5437

Hanging Candleholder

If your old house boasts exposed beams, especially in the kitchen, this device is hard to beat for portability (and for use in power outages). All you need is a well-placed hook, four

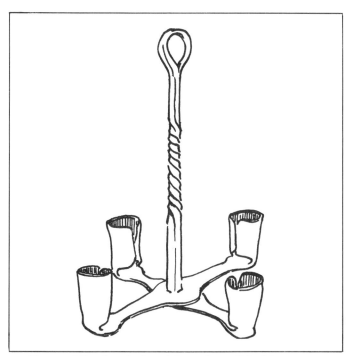

candles, and $30 for the hand-forged candleholder.

Catalogue available, $1.

D. James Barnett, Blacksmith
710 W. Main Street
Plano, IL 60545
(415) 552-3675

Candlestands

The Blacksmith Shop forges a graceful candlestand that is equipped with holders for both candles and rushes. The candle arm is completely adjustable. Another adjustable candlestand, but made for use on table tops, is forged by Newton Millham. Based on an 18th-century model, it features iron cups and sockets and a rooster finial. It is 31″ high and costs $135; a model to be used as a floor candlestand is also available.

Literature available.

The Blacksmith Shop
R.R. 2—26 Bridge Road
Orleans, MA 02653
(617) 255-7233

Catalogue available, $1.

Newton Millham—Star Forge
672 Drift Road
Westport, MA 02790
(617) 636-5437

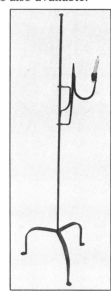

Chandeliers

A chandelier can be an object of ostentatious showmanship or a silent testament to good taste. The key to both is an unerring sense of correctness and of scale. Before selecting what's right for your living room or parlor, study both the architectural style of your house and the proportions of the room. A late-Victorian gasolier, obviously, looks preposterous in a Georgian room; and a fixture designed for a ballroom would be all but suffocating in a small sitting room. The suppliers that follow handcraft reproductions of museum pieces of virtually every style covering a 250-year period.

Wooden Colonial Chandeliers

L. D. Stevens handcrafts a line of graceful wooden Colonial

chandeliers. The model shown has ten lights and features candle plates of tin, candleholders finished in old iron (dark brown), and spindles that can be finished in walnut, pine, maple, mustard, old blue, red, and green. The fixture is 24" in diameter, 19" high, and sells for $186.

Literature available.

L. D. Stevens
Colonial Lighting Fixtures
2423 E. Norris Street
Philadelphia, PA 19125
(215) 435-5947

Selecting a representative lighting fixture from Hurley Patentee Manor is difficult since Stephen and Carolyn Waligurski produce nothing that is not an outstanding reproduction from the Colonial past. If their standads are high, no wonder: they are perhaps the only contemporary craftsmen to have restored their own headquarters and to have opened it to the public as a recognized national historic site. Shown here is the Waligur-

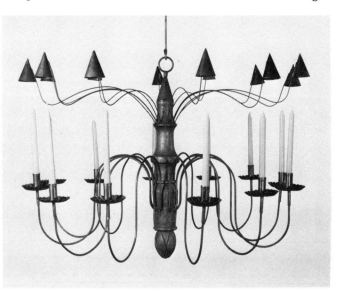

skis' "American Turkey" chandelier, a fine early multiple-lighted fixture with a tin extinguisher above each candle. Not illustrated are the 12 turkeys on rods inserted in the center post.

Catalogue available, $2.

Hurley Patentee Manor
R. D. 7, Box 98 A
Kingston, NY 12401
(914) 331-5414

Captain's Cabin Light

David Williams is one of the country's preeminent tinsmiths, and his handcrafted Colonial lanterns are well known to readers of *The Old House Catalogue*. For a change of pace, and to demonstrate Mr. Williams's versatility, we illustrate here this cabin light, just one of several chandeliers offered by The Village Lantern.

Brochure available, 50¢.

The Village Lantern
598 Union Street
N. Marshfield, MA 02059
(617) 834-8121

Wrought-Iron Chandeliers

The compatability of modern design with the sleek, curving lines of Colonial artifacts has long been recognized. Hubbardton Forge & Wood handcrafts a line of chandeliers that are *not* reproductions of 18th-century models. They are, rather, completely original and modern—and suggest an affinity with the very best Colonial design. We find them very nice indeed and recommend, in particular, the hand-wrought model with four arms joined together by a fireweld that opens into a distinctive and difficult-to-execute bauble ($56).

Catalogue available, $3, refundable with purchase.

Hubbardton Forge & Wood Corporation
Bomoseen, VT 05732
(802) 273-2047

Pewter Chandelier

Chandeliers in the Essex Forge collection are painstakingly re-created from authentic Colonial designs. The materials used in these fixtures—terne, iron, and tin—were all common to 18th-century tinsmiths. The firm's electrified chandeliers include real wax sleeves. The Devon model shown is 15¼" high, including the rings, and has a spread of 24". It sells for $162 if electrified, and for $135 if not.

Catalogue available, $1.

The Essex Forge
15 Old Dennison Road
Essex, CT 06426
(203) 767-1808

Charleston Chandelier

It almost demeans the chandeliers from King's to call them fixtures, since the company has specialized for three generations in reproducing the very best high-style designs of the past. The early Victorian chandelier shown here is accurate down to its smallest detail. It has brass rope turned arms with gas cut-offs and frosted etched shades, and is thickly hung with Waterford spear-point prisms and graduated festoons of crystal buttons.

A King's chandelier is not for the impecunious—this model costs $2,300—but the proprietors are correct when they say that their chandeliers are tomorrow's heirlooms.

Catalogue available, 50¢.

King's Chandelier Co.
Highway 14
Eden (Leaksville), NC 27288
(919) 623-6188

For those who admire the precision and accuracy of King's, but who could afford only to windowshop at its Leaksville showroom, we recommend Greene's Lighting Fixtures where a fixture is most certainly a fixture and not an heirloom. Greene's offers a wide range of chandeliers that will please the traditionalist who insists upon authenticity, but expects it at a reasonable price.

Catalogues available, $3.

Greene's Lighting Fixtures, Inc.
Chandelier Warehouse
40 Withers Street
Brooklyn, NY 11211
(212) 388-6800

Victorian Chandeliers

Techniques developed over 100 years ago are employed in the construction of each solid-brass chandelier produced by The

Classic Illumination, a specialist in reproduction Victorian lighting of high quality. All body pieces are spun by hand; each arm is bent and soldered by hand; then each piece is highly polished, assembled, and finished to the buyer's specifications.

Catalogue and list of dealers available, $3; brochure available, $1.

The Classic Illumination
431 Grove Street
Oakland, CA 94607
(415) 465-7787

The following sources stock Classic Illumination fixtures: Victorian Reproduction Enterprises; Olde Theatre Architectural Salvage Co.; Ocean View Lighting & Accessories; London Venturers Co.; The Conservatory; Woodbutchers; and A Touch of Brass. Consult the List of Suppliers for addresses.

Spanish Colonial Revival Chandeliers

Finding appointments suitable for the many southwestern houses built in the Spanish Colonial style is not easy; as a result of the now passé vogue for "Mediterranean" furniture, much junk abounds. Mexico House, however, is different; here quality is the rule and not the exception. Illustrated is the Valencia chandelier, perfect for the authentic Spanish Colonial Revival interior that used to be featured in Hollywood movies of the 1920s. Keep in mind that Mexico House also specializes in custom design work. If you live in a Spanish or Mediterranean house you will want to explore the firm's ability to duplicate virtually any design from photographs, drawings, or specifications—including such diverse products as gazebos, railings, grill work, and furniture.

Catalogue available, $1.

Mexico House
Box 970
Del Mar, CA 92014
(714) 481-6099

Hanging Lamp

When is a chandelier not a chandelier? When it's a simple unadorned hanging lamp, that's when. For narrow hallways and entryways, hanging lamps provide just the right amount of light and are far less ostentatious than chandeliers, and far more in scale. Hanging lamps are available in most period styles—from Colonial lanterns to simple late-Victorian gasoliers. The Washington Copper Works offers a hanging lamp, one of many styles, that is particularly elegant. Because it is basically a lantern, but without horizontal or spiral guards, it presents a reserved sophistication proper for many Colonial houses.

Catalogue available, $2.

The Washington Copper Works
Washington, CT 06793
(203) 868-7527

Table Lamps

There are few more difficult decorative chores than finding suitable table lamps for the period home. Most commercial products look ridiculously out of place or are such obvious fakes (butter churns with gingham shades; miniature force pumps with milk-glass globes) that the home owner resorts to occasionally dubious conversions of his own (5-gallon crocks and turn-of-the-century grocery tins equipped with harps and shades). What to do? We've recommended in the past the use of old kerosene lamp bases converted to electricity with adapters available at most hardware stores. We still think this a fine idea. But several of the suppliers listed in this book are coming up with ideas of their own. Some of them, we think, have missed the mark. "Paul Revere" lanterns with lamp shades growing out of the peaks look pretty silly to us, and we've rejected them even though they are produced by one of the most reputable firms we know. We offer here a couple of the better ideas, but acknowledge that the problem of locating suitable electric table lamps will be with us for at least a while longer.

Desk Lamp

Hurley Patentee Manor's 18th-century formal desk lamp is 28" high; its shade height is adjustable. The lamp is available electrified for $115 or as a candleholder for $10 less.

Catalogue available, $2.

Hurley Patentee Manor
R.D. 7, Box 98 A
Kingston, NY 12401
(914) 331-5414

Art Glass Lamp

We hate to say it, but much of the stuff masquerading as stained glass today is unadulterated junk. There are exceptions, however, and this art-glass lamp with Art Nouveau base is one of them. It is available in already assembled form or as a do-it-yourself kit. If your fingers are as nimble as ours, you'll prefer the finished lamp.

Catalogue available, $1.

Studio Design, Inc.
49 Shark River Road
Neptune, NJ 07753
(201) 922-1090

Floor Lamps

Electrified candlestands, in our opinion, are among the only "modern" lamps that do not look out of place in a Colonial house. They are also the most practical reading lamps ever devised. Place one behind an easy chair, and *voila*, instant comfort. These devices were immensely popular in the 1920s and have recently staged a well-deserved comeback. The best that we've yet seen are made by Michael Sutton at The Village Forge. The models shown here range in price from $40 to $60.

Catalogue available, $1, refundable with purchase.

Michael D. Sutton
The Village Forge
P.O. Box 1148
Smithfield, NC 27577
(919) 934-2581

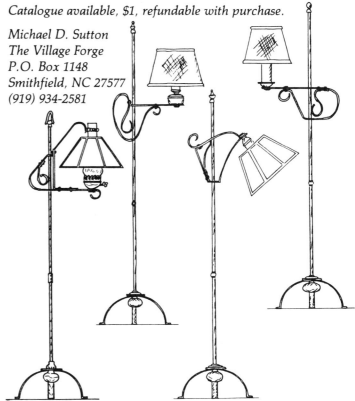

Oil and Kerosene-Burning Lamps

Kero-Electric Lighting

Pioneer Lamps & Stoves specializes in dual-fuel lamps and chandeliers, a development that will probably change the minds of old-house owners who have been reluctant in the past to depend to any degree on old-time kerosene lamps. Most of Pioneer's lamps can be ordered with an optional electric converter, and the lamp will operate on common household current. In the event of a power failure, all you have to do is unscrew the electric converter, replace it with the kerosene burner assembly, and the lamp is once more a source of reliable

emergency lighting. Shown here is only one of Pioneer's 115 models of wall, ceiling, table, and floor kero-electric fixtures.

Literature available; color slides of 42 models, $17, refundable after purchase.

Pioneer Lamps & Stoves
71 Yesler Way
Seattle, WA 98104
(206) 622-4205

Brass Chamber Lamp

Hurley Patentee Manor offers an early 19th-century whale oil lamp with oil container insert and wick enclosed in a brass font; the globe is included in the selling price of $40.

Catalogue available, $2.

Hurley Patentee Manor
R. D. 7, Box 98 A
Kingston, NY 12401
(914) 331-5414

Sconces

These simple wall fixtures provide a pleasant source of light in hallways, above fireplaces, or in the dining room above a sideboard. Most common are the flat tin candleholders that do not project very far from the surface of the wall. These are most often found with straight or crimped brackets which serve as reflectors of the light and deflect the heat from the wall itself. Sconces can also be rather elaborately designed. The type to be used depends on the basic decor of the room in which it is to be used. Most of the reproduction sconces are fitted as electric fixtures. They can be ordered, however, as plain candle-burning pieces.

17th-Century Sconces

Paul Grubb of Colonial Metalcrafters offers a reproduction 17th-century sconce that will be appreciated by those with discriminating tastes. Its elegant simplicity and fine workmanship enable it to be used in a formal Georgian living room or even in a country kitchen. The brass is antiqued, hand rubbed, and waxed to give the feeling of the original old-brass patina. It comes equipped with a candle follower that will enable the candle to burn twice as long and prevent it from dripping. It sells for $94. Colonial Metalcrafters offers several sconces of identical quality and subtlety.

Catalogue available, $3, refundable with purchase.

Colonial Metalcrafters
P.O. Box 1135
Tyler, TX 75710
(214) 561-1111

Lanterns

The lantern seems to have become a reluctant symbol of our Colonial past and is in danger, like the American eagle, of becoming the sole property of the red-white-and-blue kitsch purveyor. We've seen lanterns designed as planters, and miniature lanterns used as salt and pepper shakers. Luckily, the classic shape and functional simplicity of 18th-century lanterns have been preserved by a good number of serious modern artisans. A representative sample of their excellent handiwork follows.

Governor's Palace Light

This lantern, which would look smashing mounted on the wall of an 18th-century entryway, is one of many classic lighting devices handcrafted by Heritage Lanterns, a firm whose catalogue is a veritable lexicon of Colonial lighting.

Catalogue available, $2.

Heritage Lanterns
70A Main Street
Dept. OH80
Yarmouth, ME 04096
(207) 846-3911

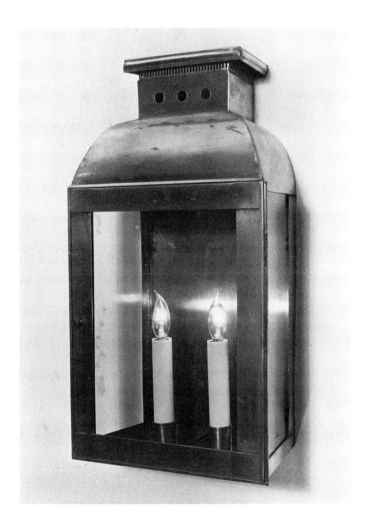

Hanging Lanterns

Maurice Murphy's handmade lanterns are anything but inexpensive, but such is the individuality of each of his pieces that one would be hard-pressed to realize that they are not authentic antiques. Shown is one example of Mr. Murphy's very fine work.

Information available.

Maurice J. Murphy
73 Burnside Street
Lowell, MA 01851
(617) 452-9339

Post Lanterns

Copper Antiquities produces a line of very handsome handcrafted lanterns and oil lamps. Each lamp is individually cut, fitted, and assembled, and care is taken in crafting the smallest detail. All parts are cut, formed, and hand soldered using the original tools and techniques known to Colonial copper-smiths.

Catalogue available, $1, refundable with purchase.

Copper Antiquities
79 Adams Road
West Yarmouth, MA 02673
(617) 775-7704

Lanterns and other lighting devices from The Washington Copper Works are preeminent in the field. The firm is not only renowned for its scholarly attention to the fine points of Colonial design, but for its attention to safety as well. It has applied for, and received, the Underwriters Laboratories' approval of its fixtures. We have previously recommended the work of Washington Copper in these pages and are pleased to do so again. Shown here is just one example of this company's craftsmanship.

Catalogue available, $2, refundable with purchase.

The Washington Copper Works
Washington, CT 06793
(203) 868-7527

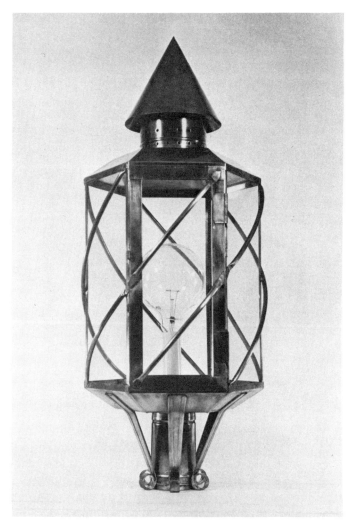

Entryway Lantern

How many period houses have been marred by an ill-considered entry light? Owners of Colonial homes will be pleased by Period Lighting's handsome carriage lantern, a design borrowed from an 18th-century Philadelphia street lamp. Its application over main entryways or expansive areas such as garages makes it an ideal light source compatible with 17th- and 18th-century structures. Period Lighting's catalogue features this fixture as well as some 75 other lanterns, chandeliers, and sconces, all of them first-rate reproductions of authentic period designs.

Catalogue available, $2.50.

Period Lighting Fixtures
Dept. 3
1 W. Main Street
Chester, CT 06412

Ornamental Lighting Posts

Have you ever wondered where the beautiful cast ornamental lighting posts in such cities as Washington, Philadelphia, Boston come from? From Spring City Electrical Mfg. Co., that's where. Under its present family ownership for over 50 years, Spring City's plant site for its foundry and fabrication facilities dates back to the Civil War era and represents an unbroken continuity of fine craftsmanship to the present day. The historic areas of cities and towns from coast to coast boast Spring City lighting posts, and it is more than possible that your own historic property might benefit from the firm's expertise. Shown here is the Franklin post, one of many models suitable for the period property.

Brochure available.

Spring City Electrical Mfg. Co.
Hall and Main Streets
Spring City, PA 19475
(215) 948-4000

Supplies

Anyone who has ever looked for a replacement part for a favorite lamp has probably been driven wild at the local home center supermarket searching through row after row of teeny plastic bags for something even vaguely similar to what is sought. Chances are that the victim of today's impersonal hardware emporium has given up and simply bought a new lamp. But rejoice. There is hope. The following firms should solve your spare parts problems with no trouble at all.

Colonial Lamp & Supply

In a word, Colonial is definitive. Its catalogue has to be seen to be believed; almost nothing is missing. The firm carries a full line of assembled lamps, burners, chimneys, shades, wiring devices, tools, brass candlesticks, chain, paint, Aladdin Lamp parts, lamp oil, prisms, harps, and (one almost weeps at the company's modesty) "many other lamp parts." "Thousands" is more like it.

Catalogue available.

Colonial Lamp & Supply, Inc.
P.O. Box 867
McMinnville, TN 37110
(615) 473-4759
(615) 473-6150

Coran-Sholes Industries

This long-established firm of manufacturers, distributors, and suppliers of lead, glass, and equipment for the stained-glass artisan publishes a catalogue rich in parts, kits, and objects necessary for anyone interested in stained glass and generous in lore and practical information. Its descriptions of the thousands of articles offered are models of clarity.

Catalogue available, $3, refundable with purchase.

Coran-Sholes Industries
P.O. Box 55
509 E. 2nd Street
South Boston, MA 02127
(617) 268-3780

Campbell Lamps

Campbell is an excellent source of parts for Victorian and early 20th-century lamps. Its selection of bases, shades, and brass arms is relatively small, but choice. Small *can* be beautiful.

Catalogue available, 60¢.

Campbell Lamps
1108 Pottstown Pike
West Chester, PA 19380
(215) 696-8070

Readers of these pages know that in the past we have highly recommended the products of Ball and Ball, Authentic Reproduction Lighting Company, San Francisco Victoriana, and Kenneth Lynch & Sons. We continue to do so with enthusiasm. Among its many hundreds of hardware products, Ball and Ball includes a fine line of expertly wrought lighting fixtures in the Colonial mode. Not explicit in its name is the fact that Authentic Reproduction Lighting specializes in handcrafted lighting of the Colonial period. The firm's catalogue ($2.30) should be in everyone's collection. San Francisco Victoriana, mentioned in many sections of this book, is preeminent in its field. Do not overlook its lighting catalogue ($5), invaluable for anyone interested in the Victorian period. As to Kenneth Lynch & Sons, what can one say that hasn't been said before? The prodigious output of this firm touches on virtually every subject pertaining to the restoration of the period house. Not to have the complete run of Lynch catalogues— "books" would be a more accurate term—is like attempting to be a physician without a copy of *Gray's Anatomy*. Write to Lynch for its current bibliography and price list. For the addresses of these firms, consult the List of Suppliers.

Other Suppliers of Lighting Fixtures

Consult List of Suppliers for addresses.

Antique Fixtures

Jerome M. Blum
Brasslight
The Cellar
Gargoyles, Ltd.
John Kruessel
Levy's Gasolier Antiques
Materials Unlimited
Nesle, Inc.
Old Lamplighter Shop
Joseph Richter, Inc.
Mrs. Eldred Scott
Robert W. Skinner, Inc.
Stansfield's Antique Lamp Shop
Westlake Architectural Antiques
Charles J. Winston
Richard W. Withington
The Wrecking Bar (Atlanta)

Candleholders

Authentic Reproduction Lighting
Baldwin Hardware
Ball and Ball
Lester H. Berry
Colonial Lamp & Supply
Colonial Williamsburg
Copper Antiquities
Henry Ford Museum and Greenfield Village
Guild of Shaker Crafts
Historic Charleston Reproductions
Hubbardton Forge
Hurley Patentee Manor
Steve Kayne
Mercer Museum Shop
Mexico House
Gates Moore
Stephen W. Parker, Blacksmith
Period Furniture Hardware Co.
The Saltbox
Sturbridge Yankee Workshop
The Village Forge
Wallin Forge
The Washington Copper Works
Wasley Lighting

Chandeliers

Alcon Lightcraft Co.
Authentic Designs, Inc.
Baldwin Hardware
Ball and Ball
Lester H. Berry
Chapman Mfg. Co.
Cohasset Colonials
Colonial Williamsburg
Frederick Cooper
Copper Antiquities
Dutch Products and Supply Co.
Empress Chandeliers
Farmington Craftsmen

Heritage Lanterns
House of Spain
Luigi Crystal
Kenneth Lynch & Sons
MarLe Co.
The Mercer Museum Shop
Metropolitan Lighting Fixture Co.
Gates Moore
Newstamp Lantern Co.
Packard Lamp Co.
Period Furniture Hardware
Period Lighting Fixtures
The Renovator's Supply
The Saltbox
Spanish Villa
William Spencer
William Stewart & Sons
Sturbridge Yankee Workshops
The Village Forge
Wallin Forge
Wasley Lighting
Wilson's Country House
World Imports

Table Lamps

Classic Illumination
Colonial Lamp & Supply
Colonial Tin Craft
Colonial Williamsburg
Frederick Cooper
Faire Harbour Boats
Henry Ford Museum and Greenfield Village
Greene's Lighting
Historic Charleston Reproductions
The Lily Collecton
Luigi Crystal
Magnolia Hall
Ephraim Marsh
Mercer Museum Shop
Sturbridge Yankee Workshop
Wasley Lighting
Washington Copper Works

Oil and Kerosene Lamps

Colonial Lamp & Supply
Copper Antiquities
Faire Harbour Boats
Heritage Lanterns
Sturbridge Yankee Workshop
Washington Copper Works
Wasley Lighting

Sconces

Authentic Designs
Authentic Reproduction Lighting
Ball and Ball
Brasslight
Classic Illumination
Colonial Tin Craft

Colonial Williamsburg
Copper Antiquities
Essex Forge
Greene's Lighting
Heritage Lanterns
Horton Brasses
Hubbardton Forge
Hurley Patentee Manor
The Lily Collection
Gates Moore
Newstamp Lighting
Period Furniture Hardware
Period Lighting Fixtures
The Renovator's Supply
The Saltbox
Shaker Workshops
Spanish Villa
William Spencer
William Stewart & Sons
Sturbridge Yankee Workshop
Village Lantern
Virginia Metalcrafters
Washington Copper Works
Wasley Lighting

Lanterns and Postlights

Colonial Metalcrafters
Colonial Tin Craft
Copper House
Essex Forge
Kingsworthy Foundry
The Lennox House
Kenneth Lynch & Sons
MarLe Co.
Mercer Museum Shop
Mexico House
Newstamp Lighting Co.
Period Lighting Fixtures
The Renovator's Supply
The Saltbox
San Francisco Victoriana
A. F. Schwerd Mfg. Co.
William Stewart & Sons
Sturbridge Yankee Workshop
Village Lantern
E. G. Washburne & Co.
Wasley Lighting

Supplies

B. & P. Lamp Supply
Classic Illumination
Duro-Light
Faire Harbour Ltd.
The Lily Collection
Kenneth Lynch & Sons
Pompei Studios
Rainbow Art Glass

Bedroom decorated by Liberty & Co. and photographed in 1897 by Bedford Lemere. Courtesy of The National Monuments Record, London.

7 | *Fabrics*

Fabrics are the decorator's delight. Ever since the mid-19th century they have been used to drape nearly everything in sight—windows, doors, furniture, walls, even fireplaces. Good period-design textiles provide a room with a pleasant, harmonious appearance; they may help to hide the irregular features of a surface, give a piece of furniture a more pleasing form, and protect the inside of a house from harsh exterior elements. The usefulness of such material is without question; how they are used is a completely different matter.

"Curtains" and "draperies" are terms that are used interchangeably today. Draperies, most properly, however, are fixed or stationary fabrics, and curtains are the hangings which can be drawn over a window or around an old-fashioned bed. The use of both types of textile furnishings was limited in the Colonial period. High-style Georgian Colonial homes often displayed examples of the draper's art at the windows, but the average dwelling place contained only a few pieces of homespun or cotton curtaining. There is ample documentary proof that this bare look continued to be the norm in many early 19th-century homes. As long as fabrics were handmade, their expense prohibited widespread use. The production of printed textiles in the 1840s resulted in a radical change. Suddenly many more people could afford to lavish various colorful effects in the parlor, bedroom, and dining room. Layer upon layer of fabric often hung over a window, a lambrequin and draperies being laid over curtains. Not until the late 19th century did the vogue for heavy draped effects begin to languish.

The use of upholstery fabrics parallels the history of window treatments. Very few pieces of furniture were padded in the Colonial period. One exception might have been the wing chair. Cushioned seats and padded backs were not unknown on chairs in the 1700s, but their use became common only in the 19th century. More elaborate forms developed throughout the 1800s with tufted and pleated effects being particularly favored. Overstuffing became the fashion and culminated in the so-called "Turkish" parlor sets which look as if they had been borrowed from a sultan's harem. Fringe was lavished on such pieces; antimacassars protected the fabric from hair oil and common dirt. By the 1880s and '90s there was the beginning of a turning away from plump furnishings and a return to the simpler styles known during the Colonial period. "Comfortables," as many well-endowed chairs were termed, continued, however, to find a ready market in the early 20th-century.

Finding antique fabrics for daily use is a difficult task and their use is very limited. They do exist, but such priceless documents are better stored away before they disintegrate further or should be framed suitably as the historical curiosities that they are. Good reproduction fabrics of all kinds are not difficult to find. In fact, as outlined in this chapter, the number-one problem is that of selection. There are so many patterns and types of materials vying for attention that it becomes difficult to know which way to turn. The suggestions as to suppliers will help in this respect.

A number of English firms are described for the first time. While buyers may find a trip to London impractical, this does not rule out the purchase of high-quality materials from English sources. Since fabrics are not generally heavy items, they can be shipped with some ease in response to mail orders. Readers who find that it is difficult to secure what they want from a North American manufacturer, distributor, or retailer will find the English firms very helpful.

Lightweight Print Fabrics

The selection of materials appropriate for bed and window hangings is complicated by one factor—the immense number of designs to choose from. Ever since cottons were first printed by machine in continuous rolls during the early 19th century, the buying public has been overwhelmed. Such printed textiles were often of dubious quality, and the situation today is not much better. The majority of printed cottons are cheap in most respects, the printing inexact and the colors less than aesthetically appealing. In part to rectify this problem, "documentary" prints—that is, designs based on fabrics known to have existed in the past—have been produced in the last 30 years. There are also "adaptations" of traditional designs which have been made available. Such higher quality textiles have become very popular in old-house circles.

This section of The Brand New Old House Catalogue *focuses on the producers and distributors of such better materials, most of the fabric being 100% cotton. Heavier fabrics are included in the upholstery/drapery section or in the section devoted to such plain materials as lace, dimity, rep, etc. A number of the suppliers of all sorts of fabrics are English manufacturers. As mentioned in the general introduction to this book, many British goods remain delightfully out-of-fashion and are, consequently, of considerable interest to old-house devotees.*

Laura Ashley

Bernard Ashley began printing textiles in a small workshop in Pimlico, London, in 1953, using the hand silk-screened method. His wife, Laura, designed small items. In 1974 the firm, with shops throughout Great Britain and the Continent, moved on to America. There are now six shops in the United States—in San Francisco, New York, Boston, Westport, Connecticut, Washington, D.C., Chicago—and a seventh due to open this November at Suburban Square, Ardmore, Pennsylvania. There are also four shops in Canada (Montreal, Toronto, Winnipeg, and Vancouver). In addition to printed cottons suitable for curtains or draperies, the company produces table linen, cushion covers, quilted fabric, and wallpaper.

Five factories in Wales and two in Holland are where the Ashley products are made. Best known are the "Country Furnishing" cottons, priced at $6.50 per yard; these are approximately 48" wide.

Ashley products can be purchased at fabric shops, through interior designers, and by direct mail in the continental U.S.A. by writing to the following address: Mail Order Department, Laura Ashley, Inc., 296 Rader Street, Port Newark, NJ 07114; or by visiting one of the Ashley shops. For further information, contact:

Laura Ashley
714 Madison Avenue
New York, NY 10021
(212) 371-0606

G. P. & J. Baker

This long-established English firm manufactures an enormous range of glazed chintz, printed cotton, cotton twill, and cotton and linen union. True to the original oriental inspiration of chintz in the 18th century (*chint* in Hindu originally meant spotted cotton cloth), many of Baker's designs show soft and elegant combinations of Chinese bird and plant motifs. They are naturally ideal for people possessing furnishings and objects of oriental origin or inspiration.

Not all designs are Far Eastern, of course, and one of the most attractive is the traditional "Provençal" (illustrated here), available in five colorways in cotton, wallpaper, and coordinated quilting material. In keeping with the traditional origins of many of Baker's fabric designs, "Provençal" was taken from a French 18th-century child's bodice.

One needn't make a trip to London to view or purchase many of these handsome textiles. If you are working with an interior designer, many of the designs are available through one of the following wholesale textile distributors: Brunschwig & Fils, Bailey & Griffin, Greeff, Lee/Jofa, F. Schumacher, Stroheim & Romann, Scalamandré, Clarence House, and Decorators Walk. For addresses consult the List of Suppliers.

G. P. & J. Baker Ltd.
West End Road
High Wycombe
Bucks HP11 2QD
England
0494-22301

Brunschwig & Fils

We are always pleased to show new fabrics from this well-established firm. Brunschwig has been associated in its documentary prints with such institutions as The Henry Francis du Pont Winterthur Museum, The Metropolitan Museum of Art, and the Cooper-Hewitt Museum of the Smithsonian Institution. The fabrics are printed in France, and, while the company's image suggests that only Colonial-style materials are available, there is, in fact, a wide selection of prints which are most appropriate for Victorian interiors. Illustrated in the order of appearance are some of both. All are 100% cotton.

"Petit Champs"—A documentary print which reproduces a French block-printed cotton of the 18th century now in the Winterthur collections. Colors are the original red and blue on cream, and one other colorway.

"Roses et Rubans"—A roller-printed challis was adapted for this Victorian-period reproduction. It is printed in its original colors—green ribbons on charcoal—and in two other combinations.

"Napoleon III"—Another 19th-century French challis inspired this reproduction in cotton. Pink and white peonies emblazon a green geometric background incorporating the fleur-de-lis. A second colorway has a background of slate blue.

Brunschwig fabrics are available only through interior designers or decorating departments of selected retail outlets. For information regarding these sources, contact:

Brunschwig & Fils, Inc.
979 Third Avenue
New York, NY 10022
(212) 838-7878

The Colefax & Fowler Chintz Shop

Colefax & Fowler is one of the reasons why we advise a trip to London if a major 18th-century interior restoration is planned. This elegant little shop is an offshoot of the famous Colefax & Fowler interior design partnership founded by John Fowler and Sybil Colfax in 1936. The firm has a scholarly knowledge of 18th-century English country house decoration and painting, and its specialist services include trompe-l'oeil, hand-painted furniture and floors, plus an exclusive range of painted wooden wall lanterns based on mid-18th-century originals. What has all this to do with American country houses of the 18th century? A great deal if you look into the matter carefully. Both before and after the Colonists formally became Americans, there was considerable dependence on the English for fashions in furnishings and architectural design.

The Colefax & Fowler chintzes are based on original designs of the 18th and early 19th centuries, and, although expensive, they instantly convey the air of muted tranquility typical of classic English and English Colonial house design. Several of the recommended designs are available through American wholesalers; the rest might be ordered directly from the English firm. Some of the patterns you will want to consider are "Old Rose," "Wellington" (distributed by Clarence House in the U.S.), "Caroline" (handled exclusively by Brunschwig & Fils in the U.S.), "Angouleme," "Berkeley," "Chatsworth," "Fuschia," and "Bailey Rose."

The Colefax & Fowler Chintz Shop
149 Ebury Street
London SW1W 9QN
England
(01) 730-2173/4

Colefax & Fowler (Interior Design)
39 Brook Street
London W1
England
(01) 439-2231

Cowtan and Tout

An American subsidiary of this famed London firm was established in 1925 at the behest of one of its American clients, J. Pierpont Morgan. Morgan preferred the firm's hand-blocked papers for the decoration of his several country properties.

Cowtan and Tout has since turned primarily to the manufacture of silk-screened prints, but it does maintain a limited stock of hand-blocked patterns. The fabrics consist largely of imported English chintzes, one example of which, "Karpurtala," is shown here.

Cowtan & Tout
979 Third Avenue
New York, NY 10022
(212) 753-4488

S. M. Hexter

Adaptations of traditional patterns are a specialty of this American firm. Hexter's fabrics and papers are widely available in North America. Illustrated, in order of appearance, are three well-printed cottons: "Khandesh," basically a 17th-century English floral design available in six colorways; "Banbury," an 18th-century arboreal English design printed in seven colorways; "Maxine," a graceful Art Nouveau design, a two-color design available in eight combinations.

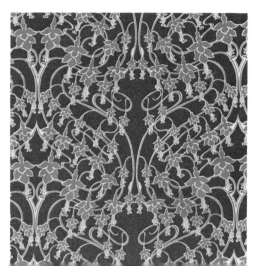

For information regarding Hexter fabrics, contact:

S. M. Hexter Co.
2800 Superior Avenue
Cleveland, OH 44114
(216) 696-0146

Liberty & Co.

Liberty & Co. is more than just a store—it is one of the great institutions contributing to the history of the decorative arts in England. Founded in 1875 by the Japanist, Arthur Lazenby Liberty, the shop was originally called East India House and played a significant role in the English Aesthetic Movement by its dissemination of oriental fabric designs. The fact that the Italian name for Art Nouveau is "stille Liberty" shows what an immense impression these fabrics made in Italy and elsewhere in Europe. They also became terribly popular in North America.

To this day, the store is famous for its huge range of printed fabrics, its jewelery department, and its delightful oriental rug department in which a profusion of rugs is hung bazaar-style over the rails of the central gallery. The building was remodeled in 1924-26 by E. T. and E. S. Hall to a solid Tudor design and it is always a pleasure for visitors to travel in the elevators which are lined with polished-oak linen-fold paneling, in keeping with the oak paneling throughout the rest of the shop. The store is scented throughout with potpourri, a quaint custom which never fails to delight customers.

If a trip to Liberty is out of the question, you might consider contacting the company's New York City store. They can supply you with information about sources of its fabrics in the United States and Canada.

On whichever side of the Atlantic you find yourself, try to get a look at the range of Liberty printed chintz. Composed of 100% cotton with a high satiny glaze, all these fabrics are floral in design and have the diffuse, faintly washed-out quality of the traditional English middle-class drawing room. All the designs are in two colorways. These are what is termed "furnishing fabrics." Of course Liberty also sells an enormous range of printed dress fabrics. Made from 100% cotton and printed with a profusion of floral designs, these fabrics are much less expensive than the "furnishing" type and are appropriate for lightweight curtains. When lined, they have all the body necessary for the window or for use as old-fashioned bed hangings.

Liberty & Co. Ltd.
Regent Street
London W1R 6AH
England
(01) 734-1234

Liberty of London
229 E. 60th Street
New York, NY 10022
(212) 888-1057

Mrs. Monro

This quaint shop, set in a quiet Knightsbridge street in London, keeps a small but very exclusive range of chintzes of great authenticity and charm. Founded some sixty years ago by the present Miss Monro's mother, the little company is now happily supplying chintzes to the grandchildren of early customers. Inquiries from foreign customers will be answered by mail, but a visit to the shop is strongly advised. Visitors intending to look at the chintzes need to be forewarned that the fabrics are not on public display. The lower floor of the shop is devoted to small items of antique furniture and to porcelain and prints; you must request an opportunity to examine the chintzes kept in an upstairs showroom.

These chintzes are primarily revivals of 19th- rather than 18th-century patterns, and, for those who like high-Victorian fabric designs, the star of the collection is "Bird Dog," a reprint of a Currier & Ives design of 1857. People who are mad about the unusual hand-painted look of these period chintzes will be especially interested in Mrs. Monro's exclusive hand-blocked line which sells at £17.50 per meter. Dear, but stunningly authentic.

Mrs. Monro Ltd.
11 Montpelier Street
London SW7
England
(01) 584-4011
*   589-0686*

Scalamandré Silks

Americans need not look beyond their own shores for fine examples of printed cottons. In the case of Scalamandré, home is the Long Island City, New York, mill which has produced some of the best documentary prints and adaptations for leading restoration projects. Both plain and glazed printed cottons

are numerous in the Scalamandré line. We have chosen to illustrate three which are representative of the quality and variety available: "Pillar," a glazed print based on an original document from the Essex Institute, Salem, Massachusetts, and most appropriate for an early 19th-century parlor; "Persian Symphony," a semi-glazed chintz, an adaptation of a 19th-century French pattern; and "Quail," a glazed-cotton design appropriate for elegant country interiors of almost any period.

Scalamandré fabrics are available only through interior designers and decorating departments of select retail stores. For information regarding these sources, contact:

Scalamandré Silks, Inc.
950 Third Avenue
New York, NY 10022
(212) 361-8500

F. Schumacher & Co.

We have previously featured some of the traditional fabrics

which Schumacher has produced in association with Colonial Williamsburg and other historical museums and restorations. The company remains an excellent source for well-produced curtain and drapery materials for the Colonial and early-19th-century period home. And now it is launching a new Victorian collection in association with The Victorian Society in America. Fabrics, available now, and papers (scheduled to be issued in 1981) are based on documents found from the period 1820-1918.

The interpretation of the long Victorian period in America is being handled with considerable care and expertise. Thirteen printed fabrics are included in the initial collection. Although Victoria's reign commenced in 1837 and lasted until 1901, the styles popular in America during her early years on the throne had their English origins in the 1820s. Similarly, the fashions popular in England during the 1890s continued in vogue in America in the following two decades. The patterns, with the dates of the original documents, are:

1820—"Kerchief Border," "Kerchief Stripe," and "Kerchief Petit," based on a printed cotton kerchief in the Schumacher museum.

1830—"The Queen's Aviary," which reproduces an English hand-blocked chintz from the Schumacher museum.

1840s—"Lottie's Lace," reproduced from a chintz in the Cooper-Hewitt Museum collection.

1850—"Corabelle" and "Melinda," adaptations of wallpaper borders in the Dornsife Collection of The Victorian Society; "Ferndale," a reproduction from a printed wool document at Cooper-Hewitt; and "Lucy's Love" and "Sarah's Delight," reproductions from dress fabrics at the Schumacher museum.

1860—"Grande Baroque," a reproduction from an original wool print in the Cooper-Hewitt collection.

c. 1890—"Lily" and "Lily Wisp," reproduced from the original document of the same name by Arthur Wilcock of England found at the Cooper-Hewitt Museum. "Lily Wisp" is adapted from the background of "Lily" to provide a companion print.

A line of woven fabrics and Victorian carpet patterns is planned for 1981 along with the wallpapers and related accessories such as borders, friezes, etc.

Schumacher fabrics and papers have been widely available for many years. A good number of the materials may be found in local paint, wallpaper, and fabric stores. If you need further information regarding standard Schumacher fabrics or the new Victorian collection, contact:

F. Schumacher & Co.
939 Third Avenue
New York, NY 10022
(212) 644-5900

Waverly Fabrics

Waverly was recommended in previous *Catalogues* for its

Sturbridge Village cotton prints. Although not as expertly printed as other designs from more expensive sources, they remain useful for curtains in less formal rooms. Waverly has many other adaptations of the early American variety at reasonable prices. All are to be found at fabric shops across the country.

Waverly Fabrics
58 W. 40th Street
New York, NY 10018
(212) 644-5890

Heavy Woven Fabrics

Quality textiles appropriate for period upholstery, draperies, valences, portieres, and furniture throws are more difficult to locate than printed cottons for curtaining. Cotton as a material is, of course, widely used in upholstery fabrics, but the devotee of the antique is often looking for something with more finish or at least a weave more complex than that found in a printed cotton. Linen, silk, wool, and such finishes or weaves as damask, velvet, and satin have the substance wanted for a draped form.

The natural materials are always the best to use, but it is impossible because of cost to ignore the combinations of natural and synthetic which are produced today. Despite the rising cost of petrochemical products which provide the basis for much synthetic material, natural fiber fabrics will still cost twice as much as a combination. Fabrics made up of only a synthetic should be avoided, however, since they rarely approximate either the texture or the colors of a period design. Dyes, for instance, will take to natural wool in a way that they won't to a substitute. Most of the heavy materials marketed today are of the 100% synthetic variety. Cottons may be a partial answer to this dilemma. Included in the following listings are producers of some very handsome materials of this type. All of these same firms also produce quality combinations as well as 100% natural fiber products. Handmade woven goods are also available, and for these, the reader is directed to the sections in this chapter entitled "Finished Goods" and "Plain Basics."

Brunschwig & Fils

Brunschwig's eminent position in the decorating fabric field was illustrated in the first section of this chapter. Its upholstery fabrics are similarly accomplished. Illustrated is one of them— "Cortez Woven Flamestitch." This woolen fabric is woven in Spain in a way that reproduces the look of a hand-embroidered *point de Hongrie.* Its five colorways are all traditional in hue.

Brunschwig can also arrange for textiles to be embossed to create a damask effect. Embossing is done by passing a fabric between two rollers, one of which has a raised pattern on its sur-

face, the other flat. All embossing is performed in France where the individual rollers are kept. Consequently, only fabrics made and stocked there can be used, but these include plain linen and moreen, mohair, wool, silk, cotton, and synthetic velvet. The effect of embossing depends on the individual textile and its thickness, pile, and contents. Brunschwig has samples of various patterns and effects and a book of designs arranged in stylistic periods.

Leave it to the French to be so clever and economical.

Brunschwig's fabrics and services are available only through interior designers. The firm will be glad to consult on particular problems. For further information, contact:

Brunschwig & Fils, Inc.
979 Third Avenue
New York, NY 10022
(212) 838-7878

Peter Jones

This well-established London emporium, housed in a handsome 1930s moderne building, contains a particularly well-stocked and clearly laid-out furnishing fabrics department. Besides keeping a representative range of fabrics by most of Britain's leading manufacturers, it is particularly good for several kinds of items.

Peter Jones manufactures its own line of plain linen "unions," very durable, coarsely-woven fabric composed of 54% flax and 46% cotton—thus the term "union" or combination of materials. This fabric is ideal for slipcovers subject to everyday wear and tear and for heavyweight curtains or draperies and upholstery. The plain unpatterned unions are particularly useful for people who have already selected a highly patterned wallpaper and are looking for a good simple upholstery fabric in a plain, subtle color. Coordinated papers and fabrics can be a bloody bore, as the English would put it.

Peter Jones also imports an interesting selection of Italian furnishing materials which are dignified in appearance and woven to traditional early and mid-19th-century designs combining silky stripes with tiny sprigs of flowers.

You won't find Peter Jones's special fabrics in the United States, and you are encouraged to write to the company.

Peter Jones
Sloane Square
London SW1
England
(01) 730-3434

Liberty & Co.

Much has already been said about this famed establishment. One of Liberty's best heavy fabrics lines is that devoted to union prints. Like the material from Peter Jones, it is made up of 54% flax and 46% cotton, and, once you have invested in it, it will last a lifetime. Although dry cleaning is recommended, it washes and irons perfectly well, providing you allow 5% for shrinkage on the first wash. Illustrated are two of the designs: "Briarwood," a busy bird and plant design; and "Lodden," a design adapted from William Morris.

Contact the New York store or London headquarters for further information.

Liberty & Co. Ltd.
Regent Street
London W1R 6AH
England
(01) 734-1234

Liberty of London
229 E. 60th Street
New York, NY 10022
(212) 888-1057

Scalamandré Silks

This leading American firm is *the* place where most everyone

would like to go for luxurious and expertly rendered woven fabrics. If you compare the cost of medium-priced synthetics which may last ten years on a chair or sofa with the higher-priced made for a lifetime, you may decide that paying more may cost you much less in the long run. And if you decide to do one thing at a time (not such a bad idea when you are attempting to restore an interior), the cost may be much more bearable. Shown are:

"Oak Hill" damask, an Italian-made 100% silk documented design reproduced for Essex Institute, Salem, Massachusetts. This damask was originally used at "Oak Hill" in Peabody, Massachusetts.

"Exotic Birds" lampas is made in Belgium for Scalamandré. A lampas is an intricately woven fabric with a double warp, and one or more picks are used; a special loom is required. The texture is extraordinary, and the design is worked in spun rayon against a cotton background.

"Stylized Sunflower" lampas is our favorite, especially as rendered in reds, navy, and tan on a sand color. It, too, is made in Belgium of cotton and spun rayon. It would be most appropriately used in a stylish late-Victorian setting.

"Bombay Bird" crewel is one of several such patterns imported by Scalamandré from India. Unlike many such handworked fabrics, it is of sturdy construction.

Scalamandré's fabrics are available only through interior designers or the decorating departments of select stores. For further information about sources, contact:

Scalamandré Silks, Inc.
950 Third Avenue
New York, NY 10022
(212) 361-8500

cent years, it was truly run-of-the-mill. There were various kinds of designs used in Victorian houses, and the quality and price did vary from item to item, but good lace was not difficult to obtain. Today it is coming back into use in restored homes and it provides a pleasant visual accent in less studied interiors. Lace is still made in America, but the reader may decide that the best sources are from overseas. Several English suppliers are included herein.

Carol Brown

This 90-year-old businesswoman continues to delight us with beautiful tweeds and woolens. She does not run a mail-order house, but personal attention is given to inquiries, and fabrics are available by the yard. Among these are durable non-synthetic fabrics for making bedspreads, curtains, and upholstery from Irish tweeds to khaki cloth to textured natural colored cottons. Carol Brown also offers ready-made blankets, bedspreads, rugs, and throws.

Carol Brown
Dept. OHC/80
Putney, VT 05346
(802) 387-5875

Peter Jones

This is one of the leading English suppliers of good lace. Since the material is so lightweight, you might want to consider ordering from overseas. All the patterns are made from 100% cotton or 95% cotton with 5% polyester content. Traditional motifs combining leaves, flowers, birds, and scallops are available in either pure white or champagne, a light cream color. Illustrated are two designs—"Balmoral" and "Chelsea".

Lace curtaining is very variable in price, although it must be said that Jones's prices are more reasonable than those found in the United States for the same level of quality. People who are furnishing on a shoestring and who cannot afford lace curtains should consider pure white cotton muslin, the traditional fabrics for English country cottage windows and used in North America for many, many modest homes. Muslin curtains require frequent hand washing and old-fashioned cold-water

Plain Basics

Some of the most useful furnishing fabrics are the simple ones —muslin, wool, linen, baize, serge, etc., which may be necessary for liners or can stand on their own as curtains or upholstery materials. A number of well-known commercial manufacturers stock such basics; they are also handmade by craftsmen according to well-established standards. A plain tweed, cotton, or linen fabric may be preferable to one with special finishing or printing. Not only may it be less costly than the fancy, it could be much more appropriate.

Lace is included in this category of plain basics because until re-

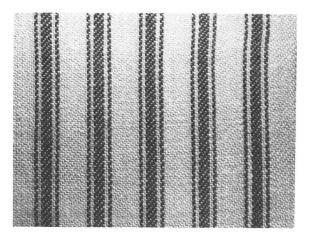

starching to keep them looking crisp and fresh, but they look charming when made with fairly deep hems for additional weight. You can probably find muslin in many close-to-home sources, but it is interesting to note that Peter Jones sells a pure white variety at the miraculous price of 47 pence (approximately $1) per meter (more than a yard). Muslin is also appropriate for summer bed hangings of the sort traditionally found in the warmer areas of North America.

Peter Jones
Sloane Square
London SW1
England
(01) 730-3434

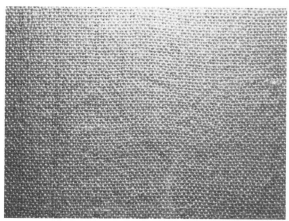

Sunflower Studio

In the last catalogue we reproduced Constance La Lena's "Sampler of Early American Fabrics"; unfortunately, black and white cannot do justice to the colors and textures which it features. Illustrated this time are, in order of appearance, pure linen, pure linen ticking, linsey-woolsey, pure linen check, and worsted wool damask. The last item is new for the home furnishings and restorations market. These materials are only a small part of the La Lena repertory. Of special interest to the old-house owner are such items as plain calico, corded cotton, dimity, and towcloth. Fabric swatches are available for 35¢, or 3 for $1, and must be requested with a stamped return envelope. Credit for them can be taken with an order.

Catalogue available, $2.

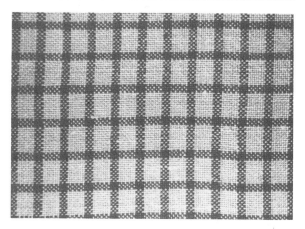

Constance Le Lena
Sunflower Studio
2851 Road B½
Grand Junction, CO 81501
(303) 242-3883

Scalamandré Silks

We have previously recommended such simple fabrics from Scalamandré as monk's cloth and homespun; there are many others of unusual quality such as 100%-cotton dimity in white with a slight raised and figured stripe. It can be used in bed hangings and for window curtains in a Colonial-period home. Illustrated is an American tweed, "Banners," of 78% wool and 22% nylon which is appropriate for sturdy chair cushions; the type of velvet cotton often used as covering is inadequate for more than occasional use. Scalamandré also offers an English vertical rep, "Dublin," of 100% wool.

Scalamandré fabrics are available only through interior designers or the decorating departments of major retail stores. For further information regarding sources, contact:

Scalamandré Silks, Inc.
950 Third Avenue
New York, NY 10022
(212) 361-8500

Finished Goods

Most of us have little time to work up our own finished fabric goods; and, if like this writer, one is noted for the "Frankenstein stitch," a horrible zig-zag appropriate for sewing up a monster's joints, there is no chance of turning out something that will approach its proper form. We still prefer, however, to buy fabric whenever possible. Money is not only saved this way, but we are absolutely sure of what fabric and pattern we will be getting when the work goes out to be done by others. There are, however, suppliers of finished goods who possess not only the skill to execute them with taste and ability, but have on hand a variety of quality materials to choose from.

We are also including in this section a source of information regarding canvas awnings. Four years ago we featured such ready-made supplies and underlined the fact that they are a practical energy-saving device. Now that it is impossible to run an air conditioner for very long without draining a public utility of its supply of kilowatts or one's wallet of dollars, awnings make even more sense.

American Canvas Institute

There are a surprising number of canvas awning suppliers left in North America; how they survived the 1950s and '60s flight to whole-house refrigeration is a mystery. The American Canvas Institute has literature which will convince you of the benefits of awnings if you still remain skeptical. As far as dealers are concerned, you can find them in every metropolitan area.

Literature available, 35¢ to cover postage and handling.

American Canvas Institute
10 Beech Street
Berea, OH 44017
(216) 243-0121

Nancy Borden

Period window curtains and bed hangings for Colonial-period homes, especially those in rural areas, can be supplied by Nancy Borden. The reproductions are based on actual museum examples, with adaptations made if necessary to fit your needs. Handwoven materials can be used if desired. Samples of these and of prints can be ordered at 50¢ each.

Nancy Borden
Period Textile Furnishings
187 Marcy Street at Strawbery Banke
Portsmouth, NH 03801
(603) 436-4284

Decorators Walk

Swiss-made tambour curtains have been popular in North America for many generations. These delicately embroidered fabrics are now mainly produced in polyester, but there are still some 100% cottons available. Decorators Walk sells two sets—both are embroidered batiste curtains (HC-77095 and HC-77094) featuring small floral patterns. They do require hand washing and are more expensive than most 100% polyesters, of which Decorators also has a large supply. Each curtain (sold only in pairs) is 44" wide by 3 yards long.

These products are sold through interior design firms and by select department stores. Contact the company for further information about sources.

Decorators Walk
125 Newtown Road
Plainview, NY 11803
(516) 249-3100

New Hampshire Blanket

It is surprising to discover how sleazy bed clothing has become in most local departments stores. One way to avoid the tasteful shopper's willies is to contact New Hampshire Blanket. The firm's 100% virgin wool blankets are made to be used and to be admired, and since the last time we featured them, two more designs have been added to the line. The newest is at the far right in the photograph. The size of each is 72" x 90"; the colors are natural, white, and indigo blue.

Flyer sent upon request.

New Hampshire Blanket
Main Street
Harrisville, NH 03450
(603) 827-3334

Jane Kent Rockwell

Period draperies, valences, bed hangings, and custom upholstery of a traditional sort provide the focus of the Rockwell interior design service. Draperies and other window hangings or fittings can be copied from old photographs. The service, however, is primarily a regional one and a visit to the shop is suggested. Nonetheless, inquiries from other areas are invited.

Jane Kent Rockwell
48-52 Lincoln Street
Exeter, NH 03833
(603) 778-0406

Trimmings and Other Decorative Accessories

We're perfectly happy doing without some of the frills and frumpy things which have crept into the decorating repertoire in recent years—yards of ball fringe, ruffled polyester valences, perky little tiebacks of velveteen. Somehow it all reminds us of Dorothy Parker's reaction to Winnie-the-Pooh: *it makes us want to "f'wow up." Yet, it must be admitted that trimmings have a place in high-style interiors of both Colonial and Victorian houses. Braid, gimp, tassels, fringe—these and other fabric articles properly finish off a curtain, drapery, or piece of upholstered furniture. Here are some suggestions for sources of trimmings and other fabric doodads.*

Constance Carol

Ready-made curtains in various Colonial styles from Carol have been featured in previous editions of this book, but never the trimmings. The firm is awfully big on so-called "Pilgrim" effects; the "Pilgrim Stripe Trim" is a grosgrain ribbon used for curtains, and an attractive one at that, even though, as the company is the first to admit, "They [the Pilgrims] may never have used it themselves. . . ." Other trimmings are more suitable for Georgian Colonial and early 19th-century fashions. These are primarily neatly woven floral designs and stripes of cotton. Carol is also a good source for a new line of accessories —tiebacks made from Waverly cotton fabrics.

Constance Carol has four mail order showrooms located on the East Coast: Plymouth, Massachusetts, Lexington, Massachusetts, Philadelphia, and Williamsburg, Virginia. Customers may place their orders by mail or by telephoning Carol's toll-free number: (800) 343-5921; in Massachusetts, (800) 242-5815. For the Collection of Fabrics and Trims, $4, and a 32-page, full-color catalogue, free, write to:

Constance Carol
P.O. Box 899
327 Court Street
Plymouth, MA 02360

Clare House

In the market for an extraordinary silk lampshade or other fancy silk fittings? They won't fit in with calicoes and pine, but may be just what you need with damask and mahogany. By appointment to H.M. the Queen as suppliers of lampshades and fittings, this English company specializes in making traditional fine silk lampshades to order. Unusual forms are gladly undertaken.

Clare House Ltd.
35 Elizabeth Street
London SW1
England
(01) 730-8480

Decorators Walk

Tapestry seat-backs and armrests and extremely beautiful tapestry borders in 3", 6", 8", and 12" widths are offered by this

American distributor. All are woven in Europe and express the very best of traditional design.

Decorators Walk products are sold only through interior design firms and by select department stores. For further information regarding sources, contact:

Decorators Walk
125 Newtown Road
Plainview, NY 11803
(516) 249-3100

Christiane Kahrmann

This imaginative English firm offers a range of exclusively designed borders, braids, tie-backs, and edgings for curtains, draperies, and upholstery which can make the difference between a mundane and a distinctive effect. These can be made up to your personal requirements.

Christiane Kahrmann
7 W. Eaton Place
London SW1X SLU
England
(01) 235-7484

Other Suppliers of Fabrics
Consult List of Suppliers for addresses

Lightweight Print Fabrics
Cohasset Colonials
Lee/Jofa
Old Stone Mill Corp.
Thomas Strahan
Stroheim & Romann

Heavy Woven Fabrics
G. P. & J. Baker
Clarence House
Gurian's
F. Schumacher
Stroheim & Romann
Watts & Co.
Waverly Fabrics

Plain Basics
S. C. Huber
Quaker Lace Co.
F. Schumacher

Waverly Fabrics

Finished Goods
Astrup Corp.
Carl Brown
Constance Carol
Country Curtains
Down Home Comforts
Grilk Interiors
The Hearthside
Norman's of Salisbury
Sunshine Lane

Trimmings and Other Decorative Accessories
Clarence House
Conso Products
Scalamandré Silks
F. Schumacher
Standard Trimmings

Wallpaper design in the "Persian" manner, English, 1850s.

8 | *Paints & Papers*

In both redecoration and restoration projects the use of paints and paper is basic. The easiest and most noticeable of all "home improvements" to make are those which can be produced with a new coat of paint or a fresh layer of paper. Fabric has been used as a wall covering in only the exceptional home since heavy embossed papers can so effectively simulate the look of textiles that such imitations are often mistaken for the real thing.

The development of the commercial wallpaper industry in the 19th century was directly related to the public's desire for various decorative effects. From the many manufacturers flowed flocked patterns which simulated an embossed fabric; printed paper designs of panels, moldings, friezes, cornices, wainscoting; patterns with flecks of gold or silver foil to suggest expensive hand-applied decoration; scenic papers or printed murals which imitated painted designs. All these papers are available again today—as documented designs or adaptations. The do-it-yourself home decorator may use them willy-nilly; the home restorer, however, seeks to match the proper paper with any remaining scraps of old paper that he can find, and, failing that, chooses a design which is stylistically fitting for the age of the house.

Eighteenth-century interiors were often without paper. There were hand-blocked designs of Colonial origin to be had, but only in a limited quantity and at a high price. Imported papers were popular with the well-to-do, a distinct minority among the settlers. The use of a paper was, then, not a realizable alternative for the majority of people. It is even question-able whether the choice of a paper rather than paint would have been exercised if the option had been available. Among the most popular of the early 19th-century papers were the so-called "plain papers," each consisting of a rather patternless wash of solid color with perhaps only a printed cornice design. It was difficult, however, to paint walls without a hard plaster finish, an uncommon improvement in most homes until the mid-1800s. The plain papers effectively covered up the irregularities and simulated the look of an oil paint.

When machinery was developed to handle the printing of papers efficiently, the sober-sided plain variety was doomed. So much more could be done, and was done from the 1840s on, to familiarize the public with the latest European and English fashions. What occurred in the decorative arts affected all furnishing design—a series of Victorian revivals of traditional motifs, symbols, patterns, and forms beginning with the Gothic and not ending until sixty years later with the Georgian Colonial and Tudor revivals. Papers, being among the most cosmetic of decorative touches, were particularly affected by the changing whims of fashion.

Today we see the same imitative process continuing. Designs embodying stencil patterns are particularly popular, and there are those which effect a flowery "country" chintz look. Now, however, there are also new papers based on old wallcovering patterns. In order to choose those which are appropriate, it is necessary to develop a good sense of what is, in fact, true period design and execution.

The home restorer is less likely to run into difficulty with period paint colors, although the painting of a Victorian house is often a matter of guesswork. One line of colors is now available (Devoe) and a second is on its way (Sherwin-Williams). We hope that there will be others, since the actual number of colors used in the 19th and early 20th centuries was much greater than that known in the Colonial period. The color schemes varied also from decade to decade in the 1800s for both interior and exterior work.

Paints

Ready-mixed paints were first introduced in America in the late 19th century. Before this time there were various commercial products available, but these required not only mixing but a sure sense of which ingredients would produce which shades on a consistent basis. Formulas were well known, but in practice each painting job was a "custom" one. Some standardization of colors in the years preceding the 1880s was achieved by two factors: a limited range of pigments that could be used, and a natural inclination to copy what was done by others.

The modern "Colonial" palette is much more diversified than that available to home owners from the 17th century to the early 19th. Some of the colors produced by commercial manufacturers today are true "documented" hues; the majority are adaptations of what was simply fictitious. Even less reliable research has been done on the colors used in the 19th century, although this situation is now being remedied, as the following listings indicate. In this respect, it is worth noting that most exteriors and interiors in the past were painted in that least imaginative of all colors—white. Despite the rages and remonstrances of contemporary critics, the custom persisted for years. White, relieved by a generous display of trim color, can be most pleasing, but in many cases—particularly in country homes—it presents only a vacant, monochromatic look.

Allentown Paint

In several years we'll give you the results of our test of Allentown's oil-based Pennsylvania-Dutch/Breinig exterior house paint. At this point, we are extremely pleased with the way in which our clapboards have taken to the application of "rich straw," and the shutters to "maroon." Allentown is America's oldest ready-mixed paint manufacturer and offers both lead-free oil-based and latex exterior products. We prefer the oil-based in almost any situation, especially one where moisture can be a problem; latex just won't "feed" and protect wood in the same effective manner as oil.

Allentown's selection of exterior colors is most appropriate for Colonial-period homes, but can be adapted for use on those of a later time. The interior colors are less interesting and authentic.

If you are unable to locate Allentown literature in your area, contact:

The Allentown Paint Mfg. Co., Inc.
East Allen & Graham Streets
Allentown, PA 18105
(215) 433-4273

Laura Ashley

Better known for fabrics and wallpapers, this country-style British firm also produces a line of interior paints which are especially designed to coordinate with its own furnishing materials. There is no reason in the world, however, why these delightfully conceived colors could not be used in a more general way. The "rose," "plum," and "burgundy" shades are particularly handsome and might be considered effective for 19th-century interiors. The Ashley colors are not recommended for most Colonial-style rooms.

The line is available in a vinyl-based emulsion paint as well as a satin-gloss. It is sold through the Ashley shops in the United States and Canada, and through Ashley's mail-order service. The shops are located in San Francisco; New York; Boston; Westport, Connecticut; Washington, D.C.; Chicago; Montreal; Toronto; Winnipeg; and Vancouver. A seventh is due to open at Suburban Square, Ardmore, Pennsylvania.

Mail Order Department
Laura Ashley, Inc.
296 Rader Street
Port Newark, NJ 07114

Cook & Dunn

The "Colormarvl" exterior house paint line—linseed oil-based—is designed for Colonial-style homes. There are 16 custom-mixed colors available, and they are adapted from those found in New England houses.

Cook & Dunn paint cards can be found in many home centers and paint stores; if you have difficulty finding them in your area, contact:

Cook & Dunn Paint Corp.
P.O. Box 117
Newark, NJ 07101
(201) 589-5580

Devoe's "Traditions"

The Devoe & Raynolds Co. was the first paint firm in recent times to develop a line of paint colors suitable for Victorian houses. In the "Traditions" line are 48 exact reproductions of colors offered in the 1885 Devoe book—*Exterior Decoration.* A reprint was issued in 1976 by The Athenaeum of Philadelphia in association with The Victorian Society in America. Unfortunately, this $35 book with color plates and paint chips is now out of print. The Devoe line, however, remains a most useful source for the Victorian home restorer. These are exterior paints only. They are produced in acrylic latex, a medium which may be less than satisfactory in some situations. Devoe has added 36 adaptations to the 48 reproductions, and altogether they form a bold, rich selection of colors ideal for late-Victorian houses in the Queen Anne or Eastlake, and Second Empire styles.

The Devoe brochure, with paint chips, also provides useful information on how to choose colors for various elements in a high-Victorian façade. If you are not able to locate this material, contact:

Devoe & Raynolds Co.
1 Riverfront Plaza
Louisville, KY 40402
(502) 897-9861

Dutch Boy

The exterior oil/alkyd and latex paints from one of America's leading manufacturers are not offered in "period" collections. With a little imagination, however, they can serve just as well as those specifically designed for the Colonial-style old house. They are limited in use for mid- and late-Victorian buildings.

Paint cards are available at many retail outlets; if you have difficulty in locating them or need further information, contact:

Tom Spencer
Dutch Boy Paints
Glen Ellyn Sales Office
Suite 307, Bldg. #6
799 Roosevelt Road
Glen Ellyn, IL 60137
(312) 858-7000

Fletcher's Paint Works

Residents of New Hampshire know all about Fletcher's; there are eight stores throughout the state owned by the company and featuring its authentic Colonial colors. It is about time that the rest of the country heard about this useful source. The paints are not available from other retail stores, but can be ordered by mail directly from the factory.

Fletcher's exterior oil-base and interior alkyd paints are more expensive than acrylic-latex emulsions, but this is true elsewhere. The saving, especially in exterior work, comes from their longer-lasting quality. The 15 available exterior colors and 20 interior shades are typical of those used in the mid-18th century through the early decades of the 19th. How authentic they may be for your house will depend on its age, style, and past manner of decoration.

Fletcher's Paint Works
Rt. 101
Milford, NH 03055
(603) 673-2300

Sherwin-Williams

We are eagerly awaiting the release of a new line of reproduction Victorian paints which will be suitable for more than late-19th century houses, but for the whole range of traditional architectural styles dating from the 1830s until 1900. Roger Moss of The Athenaeum of Philadelphia is preparing just such a collection for Sherwin-Williams, and it is due out in 1981. For further information, contact:

Sherwin-Williams Co.
101 Prospect Ave., NW
Cleveland, OH 44101
(216) 566-2000

Previously Recommended Paint Lines

Not individually written-up are five companies whose products have consistently won the approval of old-house people. These paints remain highly recommended: Cohasset Colonials by Hagerty (9 oil-base paints suitable for early American homes); Finnaren & Haley (32 "Historic Philadelphia" colors for interior and exterior work by stylist James E. Naughton in oil and water bases); Martin-Senour Paints for Colonial Williamsburg (the largest line of documented exterior and interior colors, but in latex only); The Old-Fashioned Milk Paint Co. (8 colors in dry powder form and made of milk products, mineral fillers, and pigments—for use on furniture); Turco Coatings Inc. (14 basic oil-base Colonial colors for exterior or interior use and 7 "intermixes" as well as 7 buttermilk paint reproduction colors for furniture, woodwork, and walls).

For the addresses of these companies, consult the List of Suppliers.

Stains and Varnishes

We have become so used to painted surfaces that the possibility that the exterior (or interior) walls of an old house might have been left in a natural state comes as a surprise. The weathered saltboxes and shingled homes of New England coastal areas are well known, but not as visible are the many houses in the hinterlands which have never seen a coat of paint. Pine clapboarding, cedar, cypress, redwood—all these and other woods can age gracefully if they are merely given a bit of loving care in the form of a bleaching oil or other finish. Stains can be applied in much the same manner as paint to give a surface a different color.

The woods used inside a house are usually given more attention. Paneling may require not only a stain or varnish, but wax as well. In any case, all of these treatments must be tendered with as much care as a professional paint job. The wrong finish can destroy an antique patina which has developed over many years; a polyurethane finish may effectively cover up the gouges and water stains of a generation, but can prevent the wood from breathing properly, thus encouraging brittleness and cracking.

The following products are presented as samples of the types of materials which can be used by the old-house owner. They are representative of the best which can be found today.

"Bar Flame" Fire-Retardant Coatings

Varnish can perform more than a decorative or protective function; as formulated in recent years, it can greatly reduce the flammability of wood products. This is a special concern of old-house owners. Anyone who has tried to remove paint from clapboards with a heating element knows how easily a fire can begin. Barnard Chemical Co. is noted for its special coatings for internal and external use. Whether you live in a frame house in an urban, small town, or rural area, it might be worth exploring the possibilities of further fire-proofing your building or buildings.

Barnard Chemical Co., Inc.
P.O. Box 1105
Covina, CA 91722
(213) 331-1223

P.O. Box 86
Stamford, CT 06901
(203) 356-1170

Cook & Dunn

This firm's line of stains for exterior use differs from many others in its very broad selection and in its alkyd fortified oil formulation. The last difference is very important, as the mixture keeps shingling, shakes, and boards from drying out. Cook & Dunn's list of stain names does not conjure up the usual Colonial images; indeed, such names as "Navajo Red," "Deep Canyon Blue," "Arroyo Beige" suggest a home on the range. But don't let this put you off if you are in an East Coast location. The colors are very similar to those found in most areas of North America. These are appropriate for both Colonial and Victorian-period dwellings.

Cook & Dunn stains are widely available in paint stores and home centers; if you need specific information as to sources, contact:

Cook & Dunn Paint Corp.
P.O. Box 117
Newark, NJ 07101
(201) 589-5580

Daly's Wood Finishing Products

These various commercial stains, sealers, and finishers are of very high quality. In Seattle, Washington, things can get rather damp, a situation that Daly's has learned to combat. Ben Matte tung oil stain and tung oil clear sealer are imported from Denmark and are used for interior decoration. The other products—SeaFin teak oil finish and Benite clear sealer are Daly's own products and have exterior uses as well. Benite is often used as an additive to oil-base paints and varnishes to improve adhesion and longevity.

If not available in your area, these products can be mail-ordered.

Daly's Wood Finishing Products
1121 N. 36th Street
Seattle, WA 98103
(206) 633-4204

Minwax

These products are known across the country. The red, white, blue and green (?) "Americolor" wood finishes are garish, but, if you can wink at this temporary burst of inappropriate patriotism, then you will discover some excellent and useful standbys. These best of these is probably the paste finishing wax; nothing has quite replaced this, although a floor polisher might make the job easier. Minwax has just introduced a new line of exterior wood finishes, semi-transparent stains, and preservatives. We haven't had a chance to try these out. The reader may wish to investigate.

Minwax Co., Inc.
Box 995
Clifton, NJ 07014
(201) 777-1924

Restoration Center

Also known as "Capability Brown," this firm is well equipped to help you with needs that may arise during the refinishing of furniture or of walls. It stocks effective paint removers, stains, and various other finishes. None of the products contain lye, a cheap ingredient often found at stripping shops and a potentially damaging one for such antique items as mantels, doors, and furniture. Mail orders invited.

Catalogue available.

Restoration Center
130 W. 28th Street
New York, NY 10001
(212) 242-5108

Watco-Dennis

Watco stains and finishes are often specified for use in major institutional and commercial building projects. The redwood finish is an excellent oil and resin mixture for that wood and for cedar; the Watco exterior wood finish is similarly recommended for other types of interior or exterior woods.

Watco-Dennis Corp.
Michigan Avenue and 22nd Street
Santa Monica, CA 90404
(213) 870-4781

Previously recommended suppliers of stains are Samuel Cabot, Inc. ("Old Virginia Tints," particularly appropriate for early period homes) and Turco Coatings, Inc. (paste wood stains and a clear paste varnish for interior use). For addresses, consult the List of Suppliers.

Stencil Artists and Other Decorative Painters

There was a time when one or another local painter could perform any number of interesting and special effects—graining, stenciling, fancy varnishing, marbling, among others. It was often the case that he was also a skilled paperhanger, and perhaps a plasterer as well. Home decoration was his profession, and the laying down of paint in even strokes was the least of his worries. Today there is little demand for special services and even fewer artisans capable of providing them. But the situation is not hopeless. During the great revival of interest in crafts during the past twenty years, some talented artists have stepped in to take the place of the old.

Adele Bishop

Probably the best known of contemporary stencil artists, Adele Bishop led the way in the revival of the craft. She has specialized in providing others with do-it-yourself kits. The designs themselves are quite authentic and are based on her experience. Illustrated is Bishop's first major home decorating project in 1959, a room in a 1797 Long Island sea captain's house. The decoration employs eleven different designs copied from a selection of 18th-century American wall designs.

Catalogue containing information on kits and supplies, $1.

Adele Bishop, Inc.
Dept. OHC/80
Dorset, VT 05251
(801) 867-5989

The Ceiling Lady

Despite her title, Judith Hendershot also likes to decorate floors and walls. She recreated Louis Sullivan ornamentation in the famed Auditorium Theater in Chicago and has executed very beautiful designs for businesses and home owners. A stenciled ceiling medallion, a wrap-around frieze, borders that define windows and doors—all these and more treatments are under her sure control.

Brochure available.

The Ceiling Lady
1408 Main Street
Evanston, IL 60202
(312) 475-6411

Alan Dodd

With the current revival of emphasis on printed wallpaper and textiles to give a room decorative interest, it is often forgotten that mural painting has a long and honorable place in the history of the domestic interior. Whether painted directly on the wall or on inset wooden panels, such paintings add an utterly unique historical touch to a room and can subtly underline the chosen color scheme and period flavor.

Alan Dodd is an English formal decorative painter specializing in the picturesque taste of the late 18th and early 19th centuries. Painted rooms and mural panels in trompe l'oeil, the Chinese, Gothic, rustic, Greek, or Egyptian Revival tastes are his particular strength. Sky ceilings, whether romantically atmospheric or classically austere, are another specialty. As well as painting and stenciling, this artist also consults on the design of such unusual landscape effects as garden pavilions and temples, shell grottoes, trellises, staircases, and bridges.

A talented and specialized artist, indeed. Illustrated is a corner of an entrance hall in a 19th-century house in the Kensington section of London. Dodd has many English patrons, but he would be delighted to discuss possible projects with North American clients.

Alan Dodd
295 Caledonian Road
London N1 1EG
England
(01) 607-8737

A. Greenhalgh & Sons

Alan Greenhalgh offers the kind of complete decorating services common in the past. Stenciling, painting, and wallpapering in a proper period manner are provided for owners of historic homes from Boston north to Manchester, New Hampshire, and west to Worcester. He is also willing to travel farther if the assignment warrants it.

A. Greenhalgh & Sons
Farwell Road
Tyngsborough, MA 01879
(617) 649-7887

Charles Hemming

Another English artist, Hemming is an excellent draftsman and colorist, but prefers to paint with a natural simplicity and vigor akin to the traditional school of naïve painting. Like most decorative painters, he is willing to work on a very large scale directly on the wall, but his natural preference is to paint such everyday rural subjects as lakes and cattle, using oil on small-to-medium wooden panels. This makes his art even more accessible to patrons overseas. He will want, however, to incorporate representations of the children or pets of the patron into the mural panels whenever possible. Illustrated is one of a series of four mural panels measuring 19″ x 28¾″ and painted

for a small Bloomsbury apartment. Hemming will also cut and execute stencils to order.

Charles Hemming
Flat above 176 Deptford High Street
Deptford
London SE8
England

Gina Martin/Milmar Studio

This craftsman offers two printed designs which can be purchased. Each is available with hand-painted swatches of color with the paint formula and complete instructions for stenciling walls. Other designs found in early New England houses are traced in outline full size and are sent with color notations. Prices vary from design to design.

Gina Martin is a good source for theorem patterns. She can lend a set of 69 authentic designs for your selection, each design consisting of the pattern and a color photograph. There is a $5 charge to cover postage and handling for the set; the prices of individual patterns range from $2.50 to $12.50 each, with the size ranging from 2″ x 4″ up to 15″ x 20″.

Gina Martin
359 Avery Street
South Windsor, CT 06074
(203) 644-1227

John L. Seekamp

The honorable tradition of wood graining is being continued in San Francisco by John Seekamp. He can restore work that has been damaged over the years, and grain, in his own words, "almost any surface that can be painted, including plaster and metal." Why was graining used in the past? Simply to make inexpensive and plain lumber look like much more expensive and beautiful woods.

Brochure available, $1.

John L. Seekamp
472 Pennsylvania Avenue
San Francisco, CA 94107
(415) 824-3493

Silver Bridge Reproductions

Stencil kits incorporating accurate reproductions of 18th- and early 19th-century designs are the specialty of this firm. Of particular interest to us is the Sturbridge Village fireboard kit, based on stencils found on a fireboard in the Village's collection. The price for this is $8; the kits include instructions and enough pre-cut stencils on oiled stencil board to effect the design.

Silver Bridge Reproductions
Box 49
New Braintree, MA 01531

The Toby House

Joanne Pirkle is a designer and decorator who also provides stencil patterns for use by others. The seven motifs illustrated here in Georgia's historic Bulloch Hall can be reproduced using clear vinyl stencils. These can be reused any number of times. The set, with instructions, is available for $35.

The Toby House
517 E. Paces Ferry Road, N.E.
Atlanta, GA 30305
(404) 233-2161

Wallpapers

The problem with papers for the past 150-or-so years has not been their availability, but their quality. In the mid-19th century paper was often used in place of paint for two reasons: badly finished walls would not take a coat of paint very easily; and papers were often cheaper to use than paints which had to be mixed from various ingredients. Once the printing presses were in place in the 1840s, the continuous rolls never seemed to stop flowing. Today the wallpaper books are usually heaped around the paint and paper shop or showroom, one heavier than the other, each calling for our attention with a smart collection name.

Paper was also brought to North America from England and France; the mills there were just as active. Hand-blocked papers, special luxury items in the 18th century, continued to be made here and abroad, as did hand-screened prints at a later date, but this production was minuscule in comparison to that produced on the assembly line. European papers were often better in design and printing than those made on this side of the Atlantic, and many wealthy Americans preferred them.

In selecting papers today the buyer should be aware that most have no historic documentation. Something called "Colonial" is vague to say the least. And the vision of what is "Victorian" is often limited to cabbage roses, an important motif, but by no means the dominant one. There are, however, Victorian papers which are based on true documents—remnants of antique papers. These are produced by a limited number of companies and are usually very high in price. Their printing must be very precise, and the number of colors or effects required may take more than one pass through a press.

Today's buyer of papers for an old house interior is fortunate, however, in many respects. The selection is so great that it is usually possible to find something which comes close to a period design and which is affordable. The companies and products described in the following write-ups do not begin to exhaust the possibilities, but they do suggest the alternatives among American and English suppliers that can be explored.

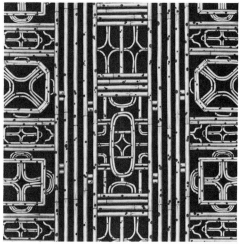

Charles Barone Inc.

The "Country Life Collection" is one of the seven books of designs which will interest the traditionalist; another is "Fresh Surroundings." Both include elegant small prints which may be comfortably used in country house interiors of almost any period. Barone will also custom print both fabrics and wallcoverings. If you wish to use the same design in both cloth and paper, this might be a good place to start your search.

Barone papers and fabrics are distributed throughout the United States and Canada.

Charles Barone Inc.
9505 W. Jefferson Blvd.
Culver City, CA 90230
(213) 559-7211

Brunschwig & Fils

As a source of fine French papers produced with the interests of North Americans in mind, Brunschwig has long been preeminent. The firm's fabrics have been surveyed in the previous chapter and are of the same high quality. Proper restoration materials can be found here, including those papers which are based on historical sources. Illustrated are three designs which are representative of Brunschwig's commitment to authenticity. These are, in order of appearance:

"St. Simeon," a Victorian paisley design which retains the flat ornamental quality of its document. It is printed in a six-color combination.

"Pavilion Fret," an adaptation of the faux-bamboo design found throughout the Royal Pavilion, Brighton, England.

"Teawood," a second adaptation from the Royal Pavilion, this based on the painted graining executed there in imitation of exotic woods. It is available in nine different colors—sand, raspberry, slate, citron, lime, shell, coral, sage, and grey.

Brunschwig & Fils papers are available only through interior design firms and decorating departments of select retail outlets. For further information regarding sources, contact:

Brunschwig & Fils, Inc.
979 Third Avenue
New York, NY 10022
(212) 838-7878

Greeff

This firm has long been noted for its quality American papers appropriate for Georgian Colonial and Federal interiors. Among the patterns of special interest are "Mattituck," "Kittery," "Stonybrook," "Thompsonville," "Londonderry," and "Northfield." As the names suggest, the origin of most of the designs is New England.

Greeff pattern books are to be found in many paint stores and home centers, and papers can be ordered through these suppliers. If you do run into difficulty, contact:

Greeff Fabrics
150 Midland Avenue
Port Chester, NY 10573
(914) 939-6200

Jones & Erwin

The designs of the late Hobe Erwin are classics in the field of American period decoration. Representative of the traditional papers available through the firm are "Hull Star," "American Fancy," "Federal Flower," and "Fruit Basket." Like those of Greeff, they are high-quality adaptations of papers popular among the prosperous citizens of the late Colonial and Federal periods when manufacturing was still a laborious handcrafted process.

Jones & Erwin papers can be ordered through paint and paper suppliers from coast to coast.

Jones & Erwin, Inc.
232 E. 59th Street
New York, NY 10022
(212) 759-3706

Osborne & Little

This firm can be best described as a fashionable English wallpaper manufacturer for people who like traditional designs with a degree of sophisticated modification. Osborne & Little's papers are not well-known in North America and deserve more attention.

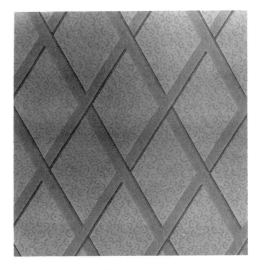

One of the company's most important collections is the "Folia Range" which consists of eighty wallpapers with twenty-eight coordinating fabrics. Illustrated are two representative designs from this line. These are surface printed to resemble the attractive, uneven, slightly textured effect usually achieved by block printing.

Osborne & Little Ltd.
304 Kings Road
London SW3 5UH
England
(01) 352-1456

Arthur Sanderson & Sons

Anyone visiting London should really make a stop at Sanderson, a giant emporium devoted to almost every kind of decorative fabric and paper known to have been produced in the past several hundred years. Some Sanderson materials make their way to North America, but not enough do. There are superb borders, heavy embossed papers (see following write up on San Francisco Victoriana), delicate designs based on chintzes, a "Hand Print Collection" and a "William Morris Collection," and many examples of flocked papers.

Arthur Sanderson & Sons, Ltd.
Berners Street
London W1A 2JE
England

San Francisco Victoriana

This enterprising firm of restoration specialists imports Sanderson's substitute for the long-gone Lincrusta-Walton; the heavily embossed papers are available in two lines— "Anaglypta" and "Supaglypta," the latter being "super weight." Prices per 33' roll are $30 for the lighter and $38 for the heavier. Between the two there are thirteen patterns available, and these can be painted any color you wish. Paper of this sort is suitable for wainscoting, ceilings, and walls in high-Victorian dwellings.

At last Victoriana has announced that it has on hand a supply of *antique* embossed wallpaper borders. These were manufactured in Germany between 1890 and 1915.

Sample packets available: antique embossed borders, $16; "Anaglypta," $8.50.

San Francisco Victoriana
2245 Palou Avenue
San Francisco, CA 94124
(415) MI8-0313

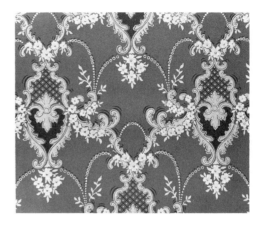

Scalamandré Silks

One of the advantages of turning to such a firm as Scalamandré for assistance is that you are able to take advantage of the company's many years of experience in reproducing antique papers for major museums and historical house associations. Once the prints are made up and struck, it is some time before they are put to rest. Most of the papers based on documents have to be custom ordered, but the cost will still be less than when the reproduction was first printed.

Scalamandré's 19th-century wallpaper collection has been featured in our first two catalogues. This time around, we are presenting documentary prints from recent Scalamandré restoration projects. Illustrated, in order of appearance, are two panel papers and a frieze paper from the Rosson House

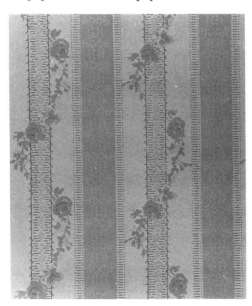

restoration; "Petersen House," a reproduction of the paper used in the Washington, D.C. bedroom where President Lincoln died; "Lawnfield," from President Garfield's house; and "Rose Swags" from the Central City (Colorado) Collection.

Scalamandré papers are available only through interior design firms or the decorating departments of select retail outlets. For further information regarding these sources, contact:

Scalamandré Silks, Inc.
920 Third Avenue
New York, NY 10022
(212) 361-8500

F. Schumacher

We have already spoken in the preceding chapter of the new "Victorian Collection" launched by Schumacher in association with The Victorian Society in America. Papers of the same fabric designs outlined previously are scheduled for release in 1981.

Schumacher has long been associated with Colonial Williamsburg, and we have featured many of these patterns in the past. These by no means exhaust the possibilities. The "Bucks County Collection," for instance, contains a number of very appropriate papers for 19th-century interiors.

Schumacher papers are available coast to coast in quality paint and paper stores, home centers, and department stores.

F. Schumacher & Co.
939 Third Avenue
New York, NY 10018
(212) 644-5900

Thomas Strahan

The papers and fabrics of Strahan are well known by admirers of late Colonial and Federal-style interior design. The "Charlesbank Collection" is representative of the very correct, formal designs which can be found.

Strahan papers are distributed across North America, but are most commonly stocked on the East Coast.

Thomas Strahan
10 New England Executive Park
Burlington, MA 01803
(617) 272-8980

Thibaut

This firm has been supplying wallcoverings since 1886 and has long sought to provide papers appropriate for various stylistic periods. Illustrated are two adaptations in the "American Colonial, Volume X" collection released this year: "Persian Gem" and "Josephine." Either might be as correct for the early Victorian period as for the Colonial. Thibaut is also a good place to check for real flocked papers.

Thibaut papers are distributed through various retail outlets and are available through interior designers. For further information on sources, contact:

Richard E. Thibaut, Inc.
P.O. Box 1541, General Post Office
New York, NY 10001
(212) 481-0880

The Twigs

Don't let the odd name put you off. This is a most professional firm. Museum curators often turn to the skilled artisans at Twigs to reproduce priceless papers. A reproduction of the Dufour "Monuments of Paris" (1814) can be found in the Richmond Parlor of the new American Wing of the Metropolitan Museum; Gore Place in Waltham, Massachusetts, has installed "Bird of Paradise," a reproduction of a 19th-century French paper. Illustrated here is "La Nancy" from the Nancy McClelland Collection and installed at the Boston Museum of Fine Art's Samuel McIntire room, "Oakhill."

If an organization (museum or historical group) is willing to have experts help it with the selection of correct papers for a period room and has the budget required for precisely documented and produced materials, Twigs is highly recommended. Its papers (and fabrics, too) are likely to last about as long as the originals they copy.

Twigs manufactures materials for sale only to interior designers, museums, and historical societies and associations.

The Twigs
76 Batterymarch Street
Boston, MA 02110
(617) 426-4069

Other Suppliers of Paints & Papers

Consult List of Suppliers for addresses.

Paints

Maine Line Products
Benjamin Moore & Co.
O'Brien Corp.
Ox-line/Lehman Bros. Corp.
Pittsburgh Paints
Pratt & Lambert

Stains and Varnishes

H. Behlen & Bros.
Cohasset Colonials
Deft, Inc.
Formby's
The Hope Co.
Illinois Bronze
United Gilsonite Laboratories

Stencil Artists and Other Decorative Painters

Stephen Keleman
Megan Parry
StencilArt
Stencil Specialty Co.
Stenciled Interiors

Wallpapers

Laura Ashley
G. P. & J. Baker Ltd.
Basset & Vollum
Louis W. Bowen
Clarence House
Colefax & Fowler Chintz Shop
A. L. Diament
S. M. Hexter
Katzenbach & Warren, Inc.
Old Stone Mill
Open Pacific Graphics
Reed Wallcoverings
Albert van Luit & Co.

A room furnished entirely with Historic Charleston Reproductions furniture by Baker.

9 Furniture

Well-made furniture will last for generations and appreciate in value. That which is handmade is the most valuable—whether it be a chair, table, sofa, bed, or chest. Despite all the changes in furniture design and manufacturing over the past 300 years, it is the individual craftsman's objects which are still the most admired and deserving of a place in the old house.

Considerations of cost and utility preclude the use of only antique furniture in most homes today. The situation in the past, however, was little different. At almost any given time, a parlor, to cite but one room, probably contained objects which had been gathered over two or three generations or more. Some were family heirlooms, others were probably simple hand-me-downs which were kept for utilitarian reasons, and a few were probably "new" pieces of throwaway value. The fashion for decorating a room *en suite*—that is, with matching pieces of furniture—did not become well established until the mid-19th century, and the vogue lasted only to the 1880s.

In the rush to fill period houses with antiques, it is often forgotten that use of the term "antique" has become hopelessly imprecise. It was once strictly limited by British customs officials to objects made before the Industrial Revolution. Now just about any object made before World War I is honored with this designation whether deserved or not.

There can be no hard-and-fast rules concerning the furnishing of an old house. Reproductions, if well-made (and every one of the pieces suggested in the following pages most certainly is), can be most useful and handsome additions to a room with period detailing. If you have a choice between a well-made antique and a well-made reproduction, by all means choose the older of the two, especially if the cost of the former is only slightly more. But, at the same time, be aware that the reproduction craftsman may have anticipated your needs for comfort. Use of back-breaking, antique ladder-back chairs at the dining room table, for example, is a preposterous exercise in antiquarianism for both family and guests who may never again come to dinner. Why not, instead, provide modern upholstered seating so that the meal can be enjoyed in comfort.

There are, of course, thousands of ill-made reproductions on the market; Colonial kitsch has been with us for so many years that it threatens to become a tradition. Now we are witnessing the growth of a similar phenomenon in the commercial arena of Victorian reproduction. It is only the true craftsman of the past and the present that you should patronize.

Reproduction Furniture

The search for reproduction furniture suitable for period rooms can either be an excruciating or an exhilarating experience. Those who can afford to furnish a house exclusively with antiques have an enviable problem—where to find the right piece at the best price. But those who have only a few precious pieces of the "real thing" and have to fill in with reproductions have a very real problem indeed—where to find furniture that approximates the lines and texture of period pieces without looking blatantly false.

There is no shortage of reproduction furniture on the market today. Every department store and furniture outlet has its "Paul Revere Room" or "Gaslight Parlor" awash with period "flavor." Here, unless one has an excellent sense of humor or an over-refined appreciation of the bizarre, the search for reproduction furniture can be excruciating, a strange journey through a world in which everything simulates something other than itself. A milking stool becomes an end table. The proportions of a blacksmith's toolbox are altered to become a magazine rack. The legs of a Victorian cigarmaker's workbench are shortened to become a "Colonial" coffee table. The top of a 17th-century gate-leg table is made to revolve as a "lazy-susan dinette." And when these pieces, and inventions even worse, fill the pages of mail-order companies, as they so frequently do, they are usually photographed against a decorative object along the lines of a wrought-iron bootjack pinup lamp.

On the pages that follow there is cause for exhilaration. More and more craftsmen are turning to the past for inspiration and are producing handmade furniture that can easily become the antiques of the future. In their work is the inherent reason for seeking out the very best reproductions. "Truly fine antiques are rare and becoming more so," one furniture maker writes. "For this reason, the collector must supplement them with reproductions; and he looks for those in particular which are truly documented, and are made and finished so that they will look at home with the old. The owner of any documented reproduction can feel the same satisfaction that the connoisseur of fine antiques feels when he has added another gem to his cherished collection." The suppliers that follow produce first-rate reproductions. Most craft their furniture by hand, and most will custom make pieces to order. A few large companies produce factory-made furniture that is sturdy, honest, and light-years away from the typical department store offerings. The best reproductions made today, and pictured herein, are imitations of 17th- and 18th-century furniture. For reasons unknown, most reproduction Victorian furniture is thus far uniquely dreadful.

Townsend Anderson

Townsend Anderson, whose many restoration services are enumerated in the first chapter of this book, is not only a master house joiner who can re-create museum-quality paneled

room ends and build 18th-century staircases, but a fine cabinetmaker as well. Pictured here is a hanging corner cupboard, a recent addition to a house he has restored in Middlebury, Vermont.

Brochure available, $1.

*Townsend H. Anderson
R.D. 1, Box 44D
Moretown, VT 05660
(802) 244-5095*

Ashley Furniture Workshops

Ashley Furniture Workshops is an English firm that manufactures classic 18th- and 19th-century chairs and sofas, upholstered in leather. The company specializes in handmade deep-buttoned Victorian chesterfield sofas and wing chairs. It also reupholsters original Victorian frames to order. Only the finest materials are used—first-quality grain-split hides; high-carbon double cone springs; new hair for stuffing. Hand-stained antique leathers reflect the traditional quality and finish from a total range of over 100 leather shades. All pieces are custom made to each client's individual order. Readers dismayed by the dreary reproductions of Victorian furniture usually found in the States will be pleased to learn that Ashley has a special mail-order service for American clients with door-to-door shipping to any destination in the U.S.A.

Catalogue available with price list in dollars, $2.

Ashley Furniture Workshops
3a Dawson Place
London W2
England
(01) 229-6013

Biggs

The Biggs Company has been specialists in 18th-century interiors and the exclusive purveyors of a line of handcrafted furniture since 1890. Biggs's expertise has been recognized by Independence National Historical Park, The Thomas Jefferson Memorial Foundation, and Old Sturbridge Village, all of which have authorized the company to reproduce fine pieces in their collections. Although Biggs reproductions are available in several stores, the company is perhaps unique among large firms in having a very friendly and very helpful mail-order department. This should be sufficient reason to order the company's large catalogue.

Catalogue available, $5.

The Biggs Company
Mail Order Department
105 E. Grace Street
Richmond, VA 23219

Barretts Bottoms

The story of David Barrett's chair business is simplicity itself: "I began making chairs because I needed a place to sit down. While furnishing our home, my wife and I tried to find good antique chairs and found that there weren't any to be had . . . and those we found were generally beyond repair or most uncomfortable. So I decided to make some chairs." And *what* chairs! Many are indebted to the original designs of Shaker furniture, although they are built on a larger scale for the comfort of us moderns. And still others are original ideas incorporating traditional design and contemporary styling. Because of the classic simplicity of each of the pieces, all of them will fit easily into any home, whether modern or antique. Illustrated (left to right) are David Barrett's Pennsylvania Country chair, Ohio Valley chair, and Shaker chair. Until you order the Barretts Bottoms catalogue, you'll have to take our word for it that Mr. Barrett's handcrafted tables, day beds, and benches are equally charming.

Catalogue available, $2.

Barretts Bottoms
P.O. Box 1245
Morgantown, WV 26505
(304) 292-2936

Robert Barrow

"The continuous arm Windsor chair," Robert Barrow writes, "appears to have been developed in the United States toward the end of the 18th century. Furniture of that period was made in small shops without benefit of power machinery. A craftsman, therefore, relied on his skilled hands and eyes to create a product that was well constructed, functional, and pleasing to the eye." This, of course, is exactly what Mr. Barrow does in crafting his exceptional Windsors, chairs that are made with the very tools that a Windsor chairmaker of the 19th century would have used. Robert Barrow's chairs are stamped and

numbered and are available in a variety of milk paint finishes (Windsors were usually painted) or in a stained and varnished finish. The colors, need we add, are all documented shades.

Brochure available.

Robert Barrow, Furnituremaker
412 Thames Street
Bristol, RI 02809
(401) 253-4434

Cane Farm

One trouble with reproduction furniture in general is that, if it is handcrafted by a master, it costs (and rightly so) almost as much as the antique it simulates; pay too low a price for it, and it is more than likely to be a piece mass produced by the kitsch purveyors and suitable as a repository for plastic philodendron. Cane Farm serves the very useful purpose of providing acceptable handcrafted reproductions for people who demand the best quality for the lowest possible price. Unlike the wares of so many producers of "Americana," there's little at Cane Farm to embarrass the fastidious. On the contrary, the careful buyer will be able to come up with a good number of very pleasant pieces. This hutch table, an early expression of American ingenuity, is a good example.

Catalogue available.

Cane Farm
Rosemont, NJ 08556
(609) 397-0606

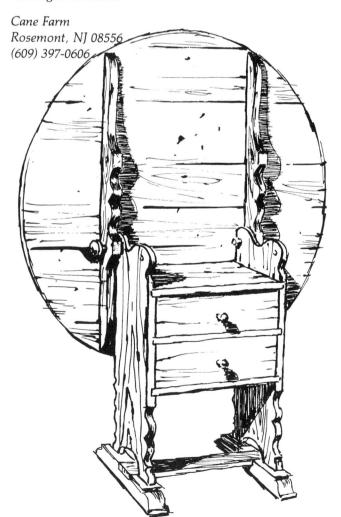

Brian Considine

With the knowledge that much original furniture of the 18th and 19th centuries is either unobtainable or prohibitively expensive, Brian Considine offers a custom-design service that helps to fulfill the needs of discriminating people for furniture built with the detail and integrity of fine antiques. Working directly with his clients, he will design any piece of furniture required, including any style of dining table, tall-case clock, bed, chair, or chest. Brian Considine is particularly adept at reproducing Shaker pieces, and it is no exaggeration to say that his handcrafted furniture reflects in every way the principles of purity, simplicity, and functionalism that guided the hands of Shaker artisans 150 years ago.

Literature available.

Brian Considine, Cabinet Maker
Post Mills, VT 05058
(802) 333-9598

Cornucopia, Inc.

This small firm, recovering from a disastrous fire that nearly wiped it out, is, like the mythological phoenix, emerging from the flames that consumed it. We list it here because its handmade reproductions of country furniture of the 17th and 18th centuries seem uncommonly honest and unpretentious. Its catalogue includes trestle tables, Windsor chairs, rockers, cupboards, and settees.

Catalogue available.

Cornucopia, Inc.
39 Main Street
Waltham, MA 02154
(617) 891-9472

Norman Crowfoot

With so many artisans and craftsmen working (traditionally) in the older sections of the East, residents of the Southwest can turn to the considerable talents of Norman Crowfoot who custom-crafts fine furniture from his workshop in Tucson, Arizona. Like other cabinetmakers trained in the techniques of the past, Mr. Crowfoot will work from photographs or measured drawings to reproduce virtually any type of antique furniture.

Inquiries invited.

Crowfoot's Inc.
Ponderosa Plaza
3831 N. Oracle Road
Tucson, AZ 85705
(602) 888-4493 887-4596

The Country Bed Shop

Handmade furniture from the Country Bed Shop is of distinc-

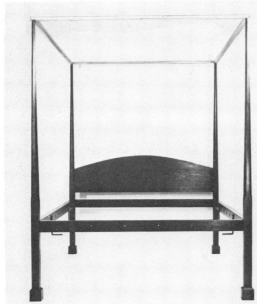

Gerald Curry

A cabinetmaker of the first rank, Gerald Curry reproduces quality 18th-century furniture entirely by hand, and entirely alone. He is the only worker in his shop and profits from the solitude reflected in the sensitivity and harmony characterizing his work. After thorough research and investigation, Mr. Curry has learned the various methods of design and construction that were employed by the distinct cabinetmaking regions of Colonial America. With this historical knowledge and intimate understanding of the woods used in his trade, he is able to re-create furniture of the same character as the furniture produced by the 18th-century masters—a truth illustrated by the exquisite pieces shown here. Mr. Curry prefers to make custom pieces and will work directly from photographs, books, or drawings. He is also more than capable of working in periods outside his favorite 18th century, provided that his standards of design and craftsmanship can be maintained.

Brochure available, $2.

Gerald Curry, Cabinetmaker
Box 1141
Auburn, ME 04210
(207) 784-6509

tive American origin and is documented from museum collections and other authoritative sources. The shop specializes in handcrafted 17th- and 18th-century country furniture reproductions, and, under the direction of Charles E. Thibeau, adheres strictly to traditional methods of fabrication. Hand-cut and fitted dovetails and mortise and tenon joints are employed; hand planes are used in moldings and on the underside or backs of panels; hinges are wrought at the forge. The result is furniture that stands in relation to department store "reproductions" as a diamond stands to a zircon. Although justly known for its beds, two of which are shown here, the shop crafts some of the finest early Colonial reproductions that we've yet seen. The Country Bed Shop will gladly make any style of country furniture from your sketch or photograph.

Catalogue available, $2.
The Country Bed Shop
Box 222
Groton, MA 01450
(617) 448-6336

Frederick Duckloe & Bros.

Duckloe has been making Windsor chairs since 1859 and is one of the few long-established furniture companies that does not pretend to be using the same methods of construction that it used at the outset of production. For Duckloe's first line of Windsors in 1859 was a complete failure—and the company was forced to rediscover in the 19th century the techniques that were used a century earlier in the 18th in order to bend and mold flawless straight-grained ash lumber into the accurate contours demanded of Windsor furniture. Having rediscovered these 18th-century techniques more than a century ago, it is no wonder that Duckloe has been selected by Independence National Historical Park to reproduce Windsor furniture from its collections, including the Bishop White settees pictured here.

Catalogue available, $2.

Frederick Duckloe & Bros., Inc.
Portland, PA 18351
(717) 897-6173

Craig Farrow

Using old tools and traditional carpentry, Craig Farrow produces handmade reproductions of fine 17th- and 18th-century American antique furniture. Mr. Farrow guarantees the authenticity of design and the durability of his work and will copy any original piece from either a photograph or a drawing.

Inquiries invited.

Craig H. Farrow, Cabinetmaker
149 Cornwall Avenue
Waterbury, CT 06704
(203) 757-6214

Historic Charleston Reproductions

A very fine selection of 18th-century reproductions is made by Baker Furniture for Historic Charleston, and the royalties from their sale are used to further the cause of preservation and restoration in Historic Charleston. Each piece follows as closely as possible the fine woods, the detail, and the decoration of the original. A few pieces, too costly to reproduce exactly, have been adapted and are listed in the catalogue as adaptations.

Catalogue available, $3.50.

Historic Charleston Reproductions
51 Meeting Street
Charleston, SC 29401
(803) 723-1623

Glen Hofecker

Glen Hofecker custom-crafts all types of period furniture, with a preference, however, for Newport-style Chippendale. All

pieces are individually made by Mr. Hofecker and two apprentices from woods that are carefully selected from the best hardwoods available today, primarily walnut, cherry, Honduras mahogany, and maple. All are hand-finished throughout and employ only the finest brasses to assure accuracy to the smallest detail. If you have a particular piece of furniture that you would like Mr. Hofecker to re-create, send him a picture or a description of it, and indicate the wood that you would prefer the piece to be made of. Once you approve the estimate of the cost involved, Mr. Hofecker will have a drawing of the piece made for your final approval before the job actually begins. Shown here are two examples of his work—a Newport-style lowboy and a gaming table accurately copied from a table at Stratford Hall, Virginia, where Robert E. Lee was born.

Inquiries invited.

Glen Hofecker
Rt. 1, Box 224A
Sugar Grove, NC 28679

Kittinger

Although this 114-year-old firm is a giant in its field, one need hardly make it a victim of today's "small is beautiful" mentality. If its reproductions were not of the highest quality, it could hardly have earned its distinction as the official reproducer of furniture from both Colonial Williamsburg and Historic Newport. This fact alone is sufficient reason to order Kittinger's very large catalogue of 18th-century furniture reproductions.

Catalogue available, $7.

Kittinger Company
1885 Elmwood Avenue
Buffalo, NY 14207
(716) 876-1000

Ephraim Marsh

Ephraim Marsh, to its credit, does not claim to produce handmade reproductions. Instead, it has sold for the past quarter of a century what it calls "distinctive furniture"—and in this designation it is correct. Not every lover of old houses is wealthy. On the contrary, as the preservation movement loses its aristocratic hauteur, more and more old houses are being restored by young couples with very middle-class pocketbooks. What are they supposed to use for furniture when a handcrafted table can run anywhere from $750 to more than twice that amount? Ephraim Marsh presents a reasonable alternative. In perusing its very large catalogue, the buyer with good taste and a moderate purse can find *honest* furniture free of the embarrassing embellishments and fake finishes characteristic of many mass-produced "reproductions." We have recommended Marsh furniture in the past and continue to do so. It is solid, straightforward, and economical.

Catalogue available, $1.

Ephraim Marsh Co.
Dept. 760
Box 266
Concord, NC 28025
(704) 782-0814

Mazza Frame and Furniture Co.

Here is an idea so basic, so practical, that one would like to credit its inception to the growing historic preservation movement. But, no, the Mazza Co. has been around for more than 60 years, providing the very same service that seems so novel today. Everyone knows that the art of the cabinetmaker results in the architectural frame of fine furniture, a furniture frame

that is then made functional by the art of the upholsterer. Since 1919 the Mazza Co. has specialized in the reproduction of distinctive frames of noted historic and artistic appeal. If you're in the market for a handcrafted reproduction of an 18th- or 19th-century original and can employ the services of a good upholsterer, why not consider acquiring the frame from Mazza. It may save you money in the long run, and you'll have invested in a piece infinitely superior to what you'd find in the best department stores. The photographs shown barely hint at the variety offered.

Brochures and photographs available.

Mazza Frame and Furniture Co., Inc.
35-10 Tenth Street
Long Island City, NY 11106
(212) 721-9287

Thos. Moser

The preface to Thos. Moser's handsome catalogue contains a brief statement about his firm's philosophy, one that should strike a chord in anyone who is struggling against economic realities to restore a house in the 1980s: "The continued existence of a small shop producing handmade furniture of absolute integrity defies all current laws of economics. Surrounded by mass production; unsympathetic government, the competition of highly capitalized multinational corporations measuring production in feet-per-minute, who fabricate furniture untouched by human hands; surrounded by all this, Thos. Moser Cabinet Makers continues to build furniture of uncompromising design and utility, one piece at a time by one craftsman. Our business is a 19th-century enterprise and shouldn't exist in today's world of planned obsolescence."

But it does exist and we are grateful. A Thos. Moser piece is, strictly speaking, not an exact replica of the past. Although derived from traditional designs, Moser furniture approaches uniqueness in form and construction and is "modern" in the best sense of the word. The knee table and continuous armchair pictured here illustrate this unique "modernity" which is perfectly at home in a Colonial interior. The chair is, of course, based on the traditional Windsor, but on close in-

spection it is unlike any Windsor of the past—and many times as comfortable. Thos. Moser encourages custom work to customers' specifications and will provide an estimate of cost upon the submission of a photograph or a measured drawing.

Catalogue available, $2.

Thos. Moser Cabinet Makers
Grange Hill Road
New Gloucester, ME 04260
(207) 926-4446

Simon Newby

Simon Newby, an English-born cabinetmaker and joiner, offers a rare specialty. Although he can (and does) execute popular 18th-century forms to perfection, he reproduces exquisite

pieces of 17th-century furniture that suggest in every detail the workmanship of the Pilgrim century. All of Mr. Newby's furniture is constructed, fitted, and finished with a minimum of machine tools. To reproduce the texture and finish of early woodwork, evidence of handwork is clearly visible, and, no less important, rigorous attention to detail and proportion is shown. Illustrated here are two of Mr. Newby's 17th-century tables, both made of English oak.

Brochure available.

Simon Newby
Cabinet Maker
P.O. Box C414
Westport, MA 02790
(617) 636-5010

Craig Nutt

Custom work is the specialty of Craig Nutt. Working from photographs or drawings, or from existing pieces if exact replicas are required, Mr. Nutt produces well-designed, pleasingly

proportioned furniture of high structural integrity. All pieces are carefully made, employing traditional joinery—pinned mortise and tenons, hand-cut dovetails, and other techniques of the past. That Mr. Nutt is an artist with wood is illustrated by the samples of his work shown here. His pieces have a simplicity and elegance found only in the work of master craftsmen. Craig Nutt is particularly interested in reproducing furniture of Southern origin, and the drop-leaf harvest table pictured here with a handsome corner cupboard has the feel of work produced in the Georgia Piedmont and in Alabama during the early 19th century.

Brochure available.

Craig Nutt Fine Wood Works
2014 Fifth Street
Northport, AL 35476
(205) 752-6535

Ole Timey Furniture Co.

Don't be put off by the down-home name of this tiny firm, a name more reflective of the 1960s when it was founded than of the high quality of its workmanship. Ole Timey specializes in the reproduction of 19th-century pine furniture and follows the construction principles of the well-built antique rather than

modern machine techniques. Shown here is a dry sink, which, while representative, is not completely typical of the firm's work since Ole Timey custom makes many of its pieces to the specifications of its clients. The company produces beds, cabinets, tables, mirrors, screens, and chests, but stocks a line of another maker's chairs, believing that the best chairs are made by chair specialists only. We like Old Timey's honesty.

Literature available.

Ole Timey Furniture Co.
Box 1165-A
Smithfield, NC 27577
(919) 995-6555

J. F. Orr & Sons

This firm produces a line of cupboards and dry sinks reproduced from originals in the possession of collectors, museums, and early inns. Each piece is faithfully constructed of wide hand-planed New England white pine and cut nails. Panel doors are mortised, tenoned, and pegged, while all appropriate shelves have plate grooves. In addition to cupboards and dry sinks, Orr makes trestle and drop-leaf tables.

Brochure available, 50¢.

J. F. Orr & Sons
Village Green
Route 27
Sudbury, MA 01776
(617) 443-3650

The Renovators Co.

If you live in a late-Victorian house and have decided to decor-

ate it in turn-of-the-century oak furniture, you're luckier than many old-house residents; good pieces are plentiful, and, although prices for them are escalating, many are still affordable. But what do you do about accents that finish a room, such as a period medicine chest or a hanging cabinet, pieces that were usually destroyed after outliving their utility? The Renovators Co. produces a line of cabinets in golden oak and will consider custom-building cabinets to a customer's own specifications. Shown here is one of Renovator's medicine cabinets; since it is individually crafted, it does not have the cheap look that is the bane of mass-produced Victorian reproductions.

Brochure available.

The Renovators Co.
Box 284
Patterson, NY 12563
(914) 279-3624

The Rocker Shop

In the past we've featured The Rocker Shop's famous Brumby rocker, which, over the years, has become a classic symbol of comfort and elegance. It has even become a valuable collector's item. As almost everyone knows, the Brumby has style, grace, and quality construction and workmanship. But what you might not know is that The Rocker Shop produces a solid-oak lap desk designed to fit across the arms of the Brumby and which renders the rocker convenient for writing. (Felt is attached to the underside to prevent scarring the rocker arms.)

Shown here is a child's rocker, handcrafted in solid oak with the same care that the company gives its adult rockers. The seat is handwoven of the finest canes, the arms are hand-wedged to the posts, the runners are offset and bolted to the chair, and the entire back section, including the back posts, is steam-bent.

Brochure and catalogue available.

The Rocker Shop of Marietta, Georgia
1421 White Circle, N.W.
P.O. Box 12
Marietta, GA 30061
(404) 427-2618

Thomastown Chair Works

A somewhat snobbish myth in certain antiques circles would have us believe that very little furniture of any worth was produced south of Baltimore. That the myth is unfounded hardly requires any proof from these quarters. That the deep South is still a fine source of furniture craftsmanship is attested to by the handmade products of the Thomastown Chair Works in Thomastown, Mississippi. The Thomastown ladderback is a very handsome piece, and its jumbo rocker, pictured here, surely epitomizes the "plantation rocker" of the Old South, a rocker that reflects the comfort and quality of Southern living. The quality of the rocker is obvious from its size (45″ high and 29″ wide), its weight (40 lbs), and from its construction—Southern oak for its strength, joints that are shrunk-fit for

trouble-free rocking (no glue used)—and from its handwoven seat and back of imported cane.

Literature available.

Thomastown Chair Works
Box 93
Thomastown, MS 39171
(601) 289-6560

Thonet

Thonet has been making furniture on two continents for almost two centuries. During this time, Thonet grew from a

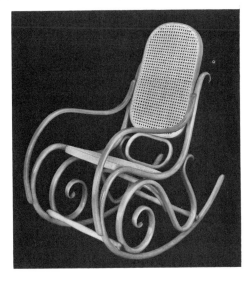

small craftsman shop to an international company that brought furniture production into the modern industrial world —and with no loss either to design or to quality. Many of the chairs first produced by Thonet have become furniture classics, and, as many people have discovered, the timeless modernity of Thonet pieces make them perfectly adaptable to the period house. The famous bentwood rocker, first produced in 1860, and illustrated here, is completely at home in any Victorian or modern interior. Also shown is the Vienna Cafe chair (1876).

Write to Thonet for list of retail suppliers and for brochures.

Thonet
491 E. Princess Street
P.O. Box 1587
York, PA 17405
(717) 845-6666

Trouvailles

If you're living in a house previously occupied by a well-traveled 19th-century industrialist of means, the chances are that your rooms were once filled with European and oriental pieces collected from 'round the world. Twenty years ago, furniture connoisseur David Israel, a collector of French country furniture, commissioned a French manufacturer to reproduce twenty pieces of furniture for sale in the United States—and Trouvailles was born. Today, if one is considering the acquisition of fine reproductions of precious furniture—all of it hand-

made—there is really no place that quite equals Trouvailles. At prices that range upwards to $8,000, Trouvailles pieces are anything but cheap. But, as Mr. Israel explains, 80 percent of the cost of each piece is in the hand labor. The exquisite *lac de Chine* piece shown verifies Mr. Israel's words; it represents 170 hours of custom work.

Brochure available, $2.

Trouvailles Inc.
P.O. Box 50
64 Grove Street
Watertown, MA 02172
(617) 926-2520

Up County Enterprise

The craftsmen of Up County Enterprise draw their inspiration and techniques from the furniture-building traditions of England and Colonial Philadelphia. They build furniture with the conviction that each piece built is a work of art—that is, that each piece is built from start to finish as a single work-in-progress, and that every process is completed by hand. Up County specializes in custom work. The piece undertaken may be a reproduction of an antique, an adaptation of a classic design to meet a particular need, or an original design. In each case, Up County craftsmen draw up careful specifications in consultation with the client, and, when appropriate, they work from photographs and measured drawings.

Literature available, $2, refundable with an order.

Up County Enterprise Corp.
226 Old Jaffrey Road
Peterborough, NH 03458
(603) 924-6826

Stephen von Hohen

Each of the 17th- and 18th-century country furnishings made by Stephen von Hohen is reproduced from an original antique in a private or museum collection. All the wood is hand-planed and the moldings are made with wooden hand planes in the Colonial manner. The firm offers country pieces of almost every sort: beds, cupboards, tables, chests, clocks, dry sinks, desks, looking glasses, and benches. Shown is a reproduction of the simple pine pewter cupboard at the Wayside Inn, Sudbury, Massachusetts.

Brochure available.

Stephen von Hohen
P.O. Box 485
W. Broad Street
Trumbauersville, PA 18970
(215) 538-1400

Robert Whitley

The Whitley rocker is a justly famous piece of American furniture. It is an original statement and not a copy. It derives from a tradition of chairmaking mastered in America, but it is also extremely contemporary in feeling and execution. The seat, arms, and back are shaped with great care to fit the human body. The rocker is both functional and aesthetically pleasing—an ideal combination in any period. We have recommended the Whitley rocker in the past, and gladly recommend it again.

Catalogue available, $4.

The Robert Whitley Studio
Laurel Road
Solebury, PA 18963
(215) 297-8452

Chairs—Continued.

73755 Dining Chair. If you want an easy sitting chair, and at the same time a beauty, this is one; made of hardwood and finished antique, highly polished and very strong; weight, about 14 pounds.

Wood seat, each..........$ 1.40
Per dozen................ 16.00
Cane seat, each......... 1.60
Per dozen................ 18.00

73756 Ladies' or Men's Large Arm Rocker, to match chair No. 73755; hardwood, has bolted arm, is highly polished and very strong; is very comfortable.

Wood seat, each. .$2.70
Cane seat, each.... 3.00

73757 A Fine Saddle Wood Seat Chair, can be used for dining or sitting room, more comfortable than cane seat; is made to fit; hardwood, finished antique; weight, about 13 pounds.

Each.....................$ 1.30
Per dozen.... .... 14.50

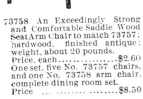

73758 An Exceedingly Strong and Comfortable Saddle Wood Seat Arm Chair to match 73757; hardwood, finished antique; weight, about 20 pounds.

Price, each................$2.60
One set, five No. 73757 chairs, and one No. 73758 arm chair, complete dining room set.

Price $8.50

73760 The Very Best Dining Room Set, made in the country for the money, very stylish; made of solid oak, nicely finished and very durable; finished antique.

Dining chair, weight, 13 pounds. Each....... .... 1.50
Per dozen.............. 17.00
Arm chair, weight, 18 pounds
Each.................... $2.40
One set, 5 chairs and 1 arm chair to match $9.25

73761 A Fine Quarter Sawed Oak Dining Room Set; highly polished and well made, cane seats, plain top and very rich and artistic.

	Each.	Per doz.
Dining chair; weight, 13 pounds....	$1.80	$21.00

Arm chair; weight, 18 pounds....... 3.00
One set 5 chairs and 1 arm chair to match, only.....................$11.00

Chairs—Continued.

73762 How is this for a fine Dining Room Set? Made of quarter sawed oak, highly polished and richly hand carved; boxed and bolted cane seat, well made and strong.

	Each.	Per doz.
Dining chair, weight, 13 pounds.....	$ 2.40	27.00
Arm chair, weight, 20 pounds........	4.25	

One set, 5 chairs and 1 arm chair to match, only.... ....15.00
Above set, with leather seats for...... 22.00

73763   73764

73763 If you want the best dining room set that can be had better get this. Perfect gems, carved selected oak or solid mahogany, all hand polished and water rubbed, leather back, with full spring leather seat. No better or finer goods made than this.

Diner, each, in oak......................$ 7.00
Diner, each, in mahogany........ .... 8.50
Arm chair, each, in mahogany 12.00
Arm chair, each, in oak 10.00

73770 A Large and Comfortable Wood Rest Dining and Sitting-room Chair, very showy and strong; a bargain; made of hardwood and finished antique. Weight, 12 pounds.

Each, only.............. $0.95
Per dozen................ 11.00

73775 Large Arm Rocker, to match 73770; very showy and strong, well made and nicely finished. Weight, 18 pounds.

Price, only................$2.20

73798 A Very Showy Cane Seat Sitting Room or Chamber Chair, hardwood, strong and comfortable; finished antique. Weight, 12 pounds.

	Each.	Per doz.
	$1.09	$12.00
Same in wood seat..........	.90	10.00

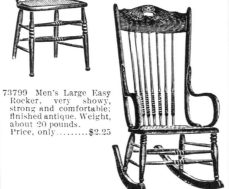

73799 Men's Large Easy Rocker, very showy, strong and comfortable; finished antique. Weight, about 20 pounds.

Price, only........$2.25

Chairs—Continued.

73801 A Large Arm Rocker to match 73753 chair. Made of solid oak, finely finished, very best make. Has a fine cane seat. Strong and comfortable. Weight, about 20 pounds. A bargain. Price only $2.98

73802   73802½

This is extra good value and will guarantee satisfaction,

73802 Fine Dining Room Set, made of solid oak, cane seat, backs are richly carved, very showy and pretty. Weight, about 12 pounds.

Dining chair, each, $1.60 Per dozen..... ....$18.00
Arm chair, each...... .... 3.00
Weight, about 25 pounds.
One set, 5 chairs and 1 arm chair to match.....10.25

73802½ Dining Room Set same as 73802 except made of elm, finished antique; 5 chairs and one arm chair for.................. .... 9.00

73803 Ladies' Rocker to match 73802, with brace arm, made of oak and finished antique; never sold for less than $3 00. Weight, 15 pounds.

Our price....................................... 2.00

73810

73820

73810 Rocking or Nurse Rocker, cane seat and back, maple stained imitation walnut, light and antique finish; weight, 13 pounds, Each......$1.40

73811 Rocker, same as 73810 except it has brace arms; weight, 14 pounds, Each 1.70

73820 Large Cane Seat and Back Rocker, bolted arms, well made, finished in imitation walnut, antique and light finish; weight, 20 pounds.... 2.00

73821 Rocker, same as 73820, except is made in solid oak and carved top; weight, 20 pounds. 2.40

73850 Large Wood Rocker, swell seat, scroll back, strong and comfortable, neatly decorated, finished in light or dark colors This is a much more comfortable chair than it looks; we can recommend it; weight, 19 pounds.

Each........ ......$2.00

Other Suppliers of Furniture
Consult List of Suppliers for addresses.

Beds
Bedlam Brass Beds
The Bedpost
Brass Bed Co. of America
Davis Cabinet
Guild of Shaker Crafts
Magnolia Hall
Ephraim Marsh
Thos. Moser
Lehlan Murray
Ole Timey Furniture
Reid Classics
Student Craft Industries
Townshend Furniture

Chairs
American Woodcarving
Cane Farm
Historic Charleston Reproductions
Brian Considine
Country Bed Shop
Crown of Fairhope
Frederick Duckloe
Davis Cabinet
Guild of Shaker Crafts
Hitchcock Chair
House of Spain
Ernest Lo Nano
Magnolia Hall
Ephraim Marsh
Louis Maslow & Son
Nichols & Stone
Southern Highland Handicraft Guild
Student Craft Industries
Sturbridge Yankee Workshop
Robert Whitley

Chests and Boxes
Brian Considine
Guild of Shaker Crafts
Ephraim Marsh
D. R. Millbranth
Thos. Moser
Craig Nutt
Ole Timey Furniture
Student Craft Industries
Townshend Furniture

Cupboards and Cabinets
Bittersweet
Ephraim Marsh
Thos. Moser
Craig Nutt

Restoration Unlimited
Student Craft Industries
Sturbridge Yankee Workshop

Custom Work
Bittersweet
D. R. Millbranth
Noelwood

Kits and Plans
Albert Constantine & Sons
Cohasset Colonials
Crown of Fairhope
Minnesota Woodworkers
Peerless Rattan & Reed
Woodcraft Supply

Mirrors
Brian Considine
Holmes Co.
Magnolia Hall
Student Craft Industries
Ephraim Marsh
Rococo Designs
Vintage Oak Fixtures

Settees and Benches
Bittersweet
Historic Charleston Reproductions
Country Bed Shop
Lennox Shop
Magnolia Hall
Ephraim Marsh
D. R. Millbranth
Thos. Moser
Ole Timey Furniture
Santa Cruz Foundry
Townshend Furniture
Vintage Oak Furniture

Tables
American Woodcarving
Bittersweet
Historic Charleston Reproductions
Country Bed Shop
Ephraim Marsh
Mexico House
Thos. Moser
Lehlan Murray
Craig Nutt
Townshend Furniture
Robert Whitley
Vintage Oak Furniture

Baskets by Coker Creek Crafts, Coker Creek, Tennessee.

Ann Hawthorne

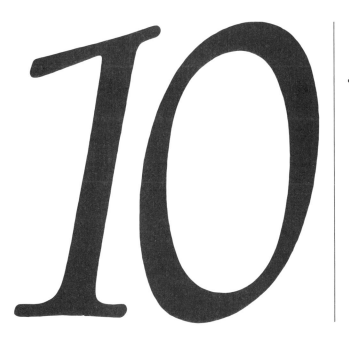

10 Accessories

Small though they may be in importance, handsome decorative accessories can add visual interest and sometimes even a useful touch to an old house. Such objects as clocks, weather vanes, pottery, and colorful china are not necessities, but they are just the sort of extras that help to make a house a home and give its decoration some personality.

All of the objects recommended in the following pages are made by modern artisans. They are not antiques, although the methods and patterns followed are thoroughly based on tradition. Forms, too, resemble those from the past to a striking degree. The materials used are natural, not synthetic. The personal commitment to imaginative, well-wrought work is clearly evident in the objects themselves. There are far easier ways to make a good living than laboring at the forge, kiln, or workbench.

Antique accessories of the same quality and form may be priced several times more than reproductions or adaptations of old designs, and the profit therefrom keeps the dealer in business. We have no argument with those who make their livelihood by saving and selling such treasures, but there is a special kind of satisfaction that comes from helping to support present-day artistry. It is easy to decry most of the products of our materialistic society; the average gift shop is stuffed to the brim with absolutely worthless trash that cannot even be recycled. That is why it is such a pleasure to collect the work of living craftsmen whether they are employed by large companies or in workshops, or whether they labor in the luxury of solitude.

Garden Ornaments

Readers of these pages are well acquainted with the prodigious output of Kenneth Lynch & Sons in almost every decorative area pertaining to the restoration of an old house. Mr. Lynch calls his catalogue of garden ornaments "an encyclopedia"—and he's not exaggerating. Almost 800 pages long, hardbound, and weighing more than 6 pounds, it is a veritable cornucopia of statuary, urns, fountains, pedestals, lawn furniture, and almost anything else for the garden that one could think of. This fanciful frame for a topiary giraffe is 9′ tall and is only one of an entire menagerie of topiary beasts—and only one item among the thousands in the catalogue.

Catalogue available, $27.50; condensed version, $7.50.

Kenneth Lynch & Sons
Box 488
78 Danbury Road
Wilton, CT 06897

Equally known to readers of *The Old House Catalogue* is the Robinson Iron Corporation, whose urns and vases, fountains, statuary, posts and standards, and garden furniture have attained national renown. Shown here are representative Robinson pieces, but they barely hint at the variety of the company's offerings, all of it accurate to the smallest detail in its reproduction of the past.

Some of Robinson's most interesting work is in the field of historic preservation and custom casting. The company is capable of restoring partially destroyed originals to their former grandeur by recasting missing components. Those familiar with The Courtyard in Montgomery, Alabama—a recreation of the French Quarter in New Orleans—or with the restoration of the Monroe Park fountain in Richmond, Virginia, have already witnessed Robinson's expertise in restoring the artifacts of outdoor spaces.

Brochure available, $3.

Robinson Iron Corporation
Robinson Road
Alexander City, AL 35010
(205) 329-8484

Those seeking to re-create the gardens of an English country house on their old-house grounds would do well to consult the catalogue of Chilstone Garden Ornaments, the equal of Lynch or of Robinson in the United Kingdom.

Catalogue available.

Chilstone Garden Ornaments
Sprivers Estate
Horsmonden, Kent TN12 8DR
England

Weather Vanes

The weather vanes carried by Ship'n Out, a firm specializing in reproductions of nautical antiques, are fashioned of solid copper. Shown is the classic trotter model. It sells for $195.

Catalogue available, 50¢.

Ship'n Out
Harmony Road
Pawling, NY 12564
(914) 878-4901

Cape Cod Cupola's catalogue has page after page of weather vanes, including an extensive selection of full-bodied pieces. These celebrated copper vanes are handmade on rare molds, over 100 years old. The motifs are hand-hammered of pure copper, beaten down into the old molds. The cow model shown, just one of a menagerie of century-old animal vanes, sells for $300.

Catalogue available, $1.

Cape Cod Cupola Co., Inc.
78 State Road
North Dartmouth, MA 02747
(617) 994-2119

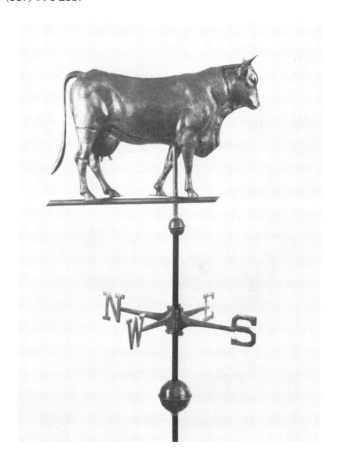

Handmade Baskets

Ken and Kathleen Dalton's baskets reflect the crafts traditions of southeastern Tennessee, and their materials and methods of weaving follow the old customs for making white oak split baskets—from searching out the right tree to shaving each split to the size needed in each basket. Shown here are rectangular

Ann Hawthorne

rib baskets in three sizes. The Daltons' skill and the variety of their artistry in wood weaving are evident in the photograph selected as the frontispiece to this chapter.

Brochure available; send stamped envelope.

Coker Creek Crafts
P.O. Box 95
Coker Creek, TN 37314
(615) 261-2157

Similar baskets of high quality are made in Rindge, New Hampshire, where the Taylor family, three generations of them, have been weaving ash baskets for years. The Taylors use ash because it is a tough elastic hardwood that wears well through the years, and they finish their baskets with oak hoops and handles.

Brochure available.

West Rindge Baskets, Inc.
Box 24
Rindge, NH 03461
(603) 899-2231

Clocks

What mantle is complete without a clock? But the prices of antique timepieces, with the exception of the most common late-Victorian clocks, is well beyond most of us. A lighthouse clock, for example, would be perfectly correct in an early 19th-century parlor, but, if you could wrest one away from a collector, the accomplishment would set you back many thousands of dollars. The stores and catalogues are full of reproduction clocks, most of them dreadful imitations featuring battery-driven pendulums that eliminate one of the loveliest of old-house sounds, the mechanical ticking of a clock. Happily, a new generation of fine craftsmen is moving in to fill the void, just as young cabinetmakers have given new life to the reproduction of classic furniture.

R. Jesse Morley, a cabinetmaker, designs and builds one-of-a-kind antique (and modern) clocks in wall, shelf, and floor

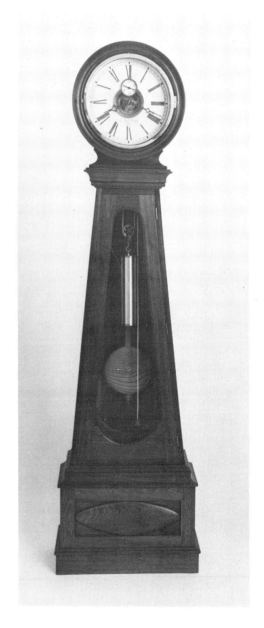

styles. His small firm can work from sketches or photographs or can supply designs conforming to particular requirements and preferences. Mr. Morley works in all types of wood, producing each clock individually by hand. By adhering to the highest standards of cabinetwork, Morley produces a functional antique of the future whose excellence, reflected in these photographs, is immediately recognized.

Literature available.

R. Jesse Morley, Cabinetmaker
88 Oak Street
Westwood, MA 02090
(617) 762-8184

spoons—a baby spoon, teaspoon, and demi-tasse spoon—reproduced from 19th-century originals and worked in the traditional manner; and hand-raised Sterling-silver porringers that can be ordered with bowls in three different sizes—2¼", 4", or 6".

Fine Metalwork
Deanne F. Nelson
Box 43
Bishop Hill, IL 61419
(309) 875-3400

Silver

The price of antique silver, as everyone knows, has made it well beyond the reach of many. Fortunately, there are craftsmen at work today making objects that will almost certainly become collector's pieces. One of these, Deanne F. Nelson, is a goldsmith and silversmith working at the historic Swedish colony of Bishop Hill, Illinois. Shown are three Sterling-silver

Pottery, Porcelain, and Glass

With the proliferation of craftswork in the 1960s and '70s, more people came to call themselves "potters" than one could shake a stick at. This is not to deny that the recent past has produced many potters of distinction and accomplishment, but anyone who has ever banged his head on a pot hung from macramé "imported" from Berkeley, California, knows how the word "craftsmanship" has been abused and demeaned of late. We list here a few authentic artists in clay—potters whose work can readily complement the period home.

David R. Farrell and Mary L. Livingstone at Westmoore Pottery make traditional earthenware and stoneware pieces modeled on English and early American originals. Their handmade wares include candlesticks, bowls, jars, pans, molds, pitchers, crocks, mugs, and virtually anything that would have been found in a Colonial kitchen. Shown are salt-glazed churns.

Broadside and price list, 50¢.

Westmoore Pottery
Rt. 2, Box 159-A
Seagrove, NC 27341
(919) 464-3700

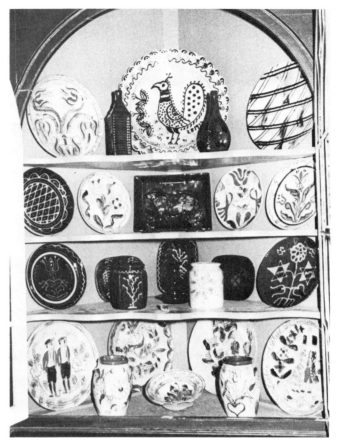

The free-flowing look of Cedar Swamp stoneware is achieved through the controlled application of cobalt-blue slip by hand brushwork and the employment of the traditional slip-cup method. The pieces—crocks, pitchers, churns, jars, etc.—have been inspired by those of the old Norton Pottery in Bennington, Vermont.

Brochure available.

Cedar Swamp Stoneware Co.
1645 Main Street
West Barnstable, MA 02668
(617) 362-9906

Lester and Barbara Breininger are specialists in the art of sgraffito and slipware and use traditional methods and century-old plate molds to produce their exceptionally accurate Pennsylvania-German pieces. Their work is displayed in museum collections and has been the subject of several magazine articles. These examples of their wares visually explain why.

Literature available.

Lester and Barbara Breininger
476 S. Church Street
Robesonia, PA 19551
(215) 693-5344

A lavish Chinese export porcelain service, the Sacred Butterfly pattern in pumpkin and gold on white, came to Charleston by fast clipper ship in 1800. It is now displayed in Charleston's Nathaniel Russell House and has been handsomely adapted for Historic Charleston Reproductions by Mottahedeh. The service includes a five-piece place setting and serving and accessory pieces.

Catalogue available, $3.50.
Historic Charleston Reproductions
51 Meeting Street
Charleston, SC 29401
(803) 723-1623

18th-century knife box.

Brochure available, 50¢.

The Candle Cellar and Emporium
1914 N. Main Street
Fall River, MA 02720
(617) 679-6057

The Liberty Village Foundation, a community of artisans retailing their wares in Flemington, New Jersey, sells very fine reproductions of Art Nouveau glass made in Liberty Village's Vandermark Glasshouse. A line of custom-made tiles in the same style is also offered. The wonderfully iridescent colors of Art Nouveau glass can in no way be approximated in a black-and-white book, so we suggest that you write for a set of photographs to examine.

Photographs available with a $5 donation to this non-profit organization.

Liberty Village Foundation
2 Church Street
Flemington, New Jersey 08822
(201) 782-8550

Acid-Etched Mirrors

The technique of etching glass with acid developed in the 18th century. Known as "French embossing," it gradually became a popular art, reaching a robust climax of sophistication in the late 19th century in Paris and London where its application to flat glass windows, mirrors, and glass gas lamp shades has never been excelled. With the entire Victorian period rejected by "moderns" of the 20th century, the practice declined, and by 1930 "French embossing" was a lost art. The current revival of interest in things Victorian has now revived the craft, and among its most knowledgeable practitioners is Rococo Designs, a small craft workshop specializing in acid-etched glass and mirrors, one of which, "Chinese Lattice," is shown here. All of the firms mirrors are framed in hardwood. Rococo

Woodenware

The Candle Cellar handcrafts several handsome wooden accessories, including candleboxes, wall shelves, tool boxes, match holders, and saltboxes—all modeled after artifacts of the Colonial past. Illustrated is a reproduction in pine of an

Designs can also make etched windows for any interior or exterior use and can copy old or partially broken windows for restoration.

Catalogue available, $1.50.

Rococo Designs
417 Pennsylvania Avenue
Santa Cruz, CA 95062
(408) 426-2741

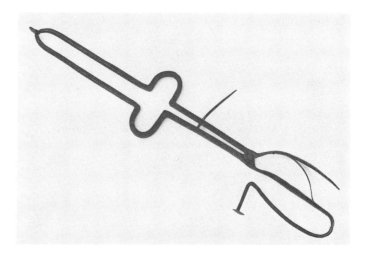

Miscellanea

Among the many handcrafted objects made by The Blacksmith Shop are two that are exceptional in charm and utility. The first, a truly ingenious device, is a bottle tilter (properly, a port tilter). The bottle is laid in the cradle, which is slowly tilted by turning the end handle. Whether Colonial winebibbers used such a Rube Goldbergish contraption, we can't say. But it will surely please today's oenologists. The second piece is a set of pipe tongs. One end is finished off with a tobacco stopper for tamping tobacco, and it also has a pricker for unstopping the pipe bowl. Both pieces, of course, are made of hand-wrought iron.

Literature available.

The Blacksmith Shop
R.R. 2—22 Bridge Road
Orleans, MA 02653
(617) 255-7233

Here is an item that even the most perfervid aficionado of Victoriana may have found difficult to locate until now. The late Victorians rarely kept anything uncovered, and simple lamps were no different from bare piano legs that were forced to wear skirts. The Custom House offers this Victorian lamp shade in both lace and handcrafted crochet.

Catalogue available.

Custom House
P.O. Box 38
South Shore Drive
Owl's Head, ME 04854
(207) 236-4444

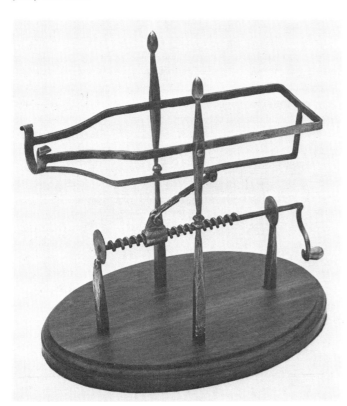

Other Suppliers of Accessories
Consult List of Suppliers for addresses.

Garden Ornaments

Renovator's Supply
Santa Cruz Foundry
Tennessee Fabricating

Weather Vanes

Renovator's Supply
Wilson's Country House

Clocks

Colonial of Zeeland

Metalware

Bernard Plating Works
Colonial Casting
Hampshire Pewter Co.
Jay Thomas Stauffer

Pottery

Sun Tree

Woodenware

Orleans Carpenters

Mirrors

I. Schwartz

Miscellanea

Green Boughs (Colonial firescreens)
David Lawrence (antique birdcages)
Morgans (Art Deco radios)

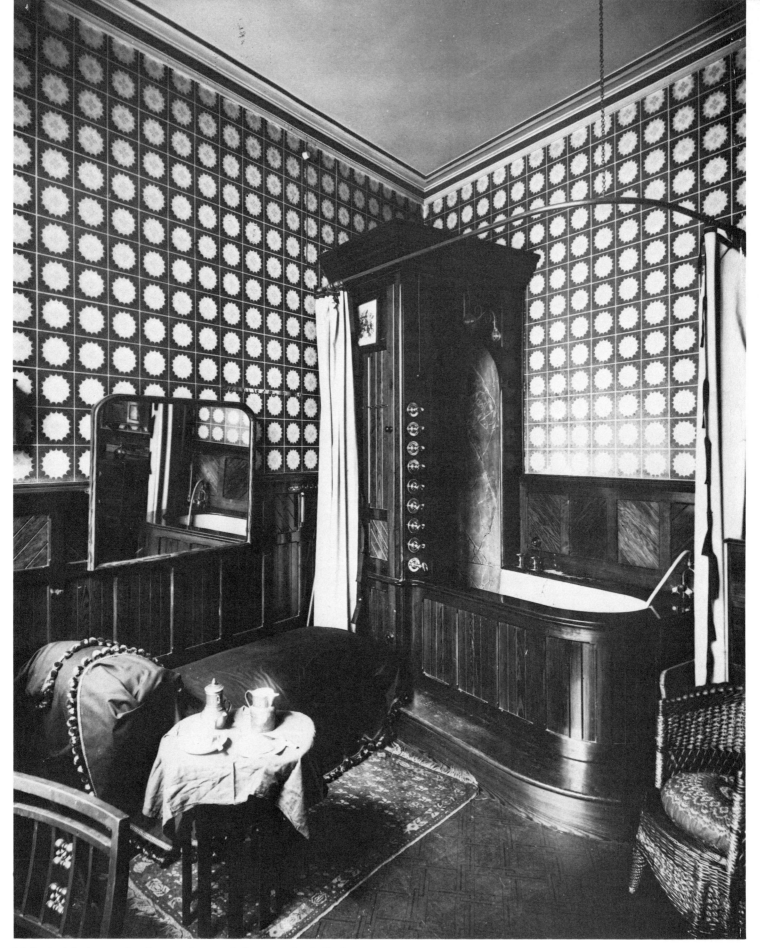

Mechanized bathroom, London, as photographed in 1893 by Bedford Lemere. The bath is of marbled earthenware and is cased in mahogany with brass taps and controls, including two to make "waves." Courtesy of The National Monuments Record, London.

List of Suppliers

AA-Abbingdon Ceiling Co., Inc.
2149 Utica Avenue
Brooklyn, NY 11234

Acme Hardware Co., Inc.
150 S. La Brea Avenue
Los Angeles, CA 90036

Acquisition & Restoration Corp.
1226 Broadway
Indianapolis, IN 46202

Adams and Swett
380 Dorchester Avenue
Boston, MA 02127

A. E. S. Firebacks
27 Hewitt Road
Mystic, CT 06355

Alcon Lightcraft Co.
1424 W. Alabama Street
Houston, TX 77006

The Allentown Paint Mfg. Co., Inc.
East Allen & Graham Streets
Allentown, PA 18105

All-Nighter Stove Works, Inc.
80 Commerce Street
Glastonbury, CT 06033

Allwood Door
345 Bayshore Road
San Francisco, CA 94124

American Woodcarving
282 San Jose Avenue
San Jose, CA 95125

American Building Restoration
9720 S. 60th Street
Franklin, WI 53132

American Canvas Institute
10 Beech Street
Berea, OH 44017

American Olean Tile Company
1000 Cannon Avenue
Lansdale, PA 19446

Amherst Woodworking and Supply
P.O. Box 464
North Amherst, MA 01059

American Stair Systems, Inc.
4323-A Pinemont Street
Houston, TX 77018

Amsterdam Corp.
950 Third Avenue
New York, NY 10022

Townsend H. Anderson
House Joiner
R.D. 1, Box 44D
Moretown, VT 05660

Arch Associates/Stephen Guerrant
874 Green Bay Road
Winnetka, IL 60093

Architectural Antiques/L'Architecture
  Ancienne
410 St. Pierre Street
Montreal, Quebec H2Y 2M2
Canada

Architectural Antique Warehouse
17 Bentley Avenue
Ottawa, Ontario K1P 6H6
Canada

Architectural Emphasis, Inc.
1750 Montgomery Street
San Francisco, CA 94111

Architectural Heritage of Cheltenham
The Manor
Swindon Village
Cheltenham, Gloucestershire
England

Architectural Ornaments
P.O. Box 115
Little Neck, NY 11363

Architectural Paneling, Inc.
979 Third Avenue
New York, NY 10022

Architectural Salvage of Santa Barbara
726 Anacapa Street
Santa Barbara, CA 93101

Architectural Specialties, Inc.
850 S. Van Ness Avenue
San Francisco, CA 94109

William Armstrong and Associates
Craftsmen in Stained Glass
20 Dalton Street
Newburyport, MA 01950

Art Directions
6120 Delmar Street
St. Louis, MO 63112

Artifacts, Inc.
702 Mt. Vernon Avenue
Alexandria, VA 22301

Artistry in Veneers, Inc.
633 Montauk Avenue
Brooklyn, NY 11208

Ashley Furniture Workshops
3A Dawson Place
London W2
England

Laura Ashley, Inc.
714 Madison Avenue
New York, NY 10021

The Astrup Company
2937 W. 25th Street
Cleveland, OH 44113

Atlanta Stove Works, Inc.
P.O. Box 5254
Atlanta, GA 30307

Atlas/Sancar Wallcoverings
206-214 Ditmas Avenue
Brooklyn, NY 11218

Atwood & Tremblay Associates, Inc.
40 Timber Swamp Road
Hampton, NH 03842

Authentic Designs
330 East 75th Street
New York, NY 10021

Authentic Reproduction Lighting Co.
P.O. Box 218
Avon, CT 06001

Azrock Floor Products
P.O. Box 531
San Antonio, TX 78292

Babcock Barn Homes
P.O. Box 484
Williamstown, MA 01267

Backlund Moravian Tile Works
Box 154
Key Largo, FL 33037

Bailey and Griffin
1406 E. Mermaid Lane
Philadelphia, PA 19118

G.P. & J. Baker, Ltd.
West End Road
High Wycombe
Bucks HP11 2QD
England

A. W. Baker Restorations, Inc.
670 Drift Road
Westport, MA 02790

Baldwin Hardware
841 Wyomissing Boulevard
Reading, PA 19603

Ball and Ball
463 W. Lincoln Highway
Exton, PA 19341

B & P Lamp Supply, Inc.
Box P-300
McMinnville, TN 37110

Bangkok Industries, Inc.
1900 S. 20th Street
Philadelphia, PA 19145

The Bank, Architectural Antiques
1824 Felicity Street
New Orleans, LA 70113

Joan Baren
Sag Harbor, NY 11963

Barclay Fabrics Co., Inc.
7120 Airport Highway, Box 650
Pennsauken, NJ 08101

Barnard Chemical Co.
P.O. Box 1105
Covina, CA 91722

Barnard Chemical Co.
P.O. Box 86
Stamford, CT 06901

D. James Barnett, Blacksmith
710 West Main Street
Plano, IL 60545

Barney Brainum-Shanker Steel
  Company, Inc.
70-32 83rd Street
Glendale, Queens, NY 11385

The Barn People
P.O. Box 4
South Woodstock, VT 05071

Charles Barone, Inc.
9505 W. Jefferson Boulevard
Culver City, CA 90230

Barretts Bottoms
P.O. Box 1245
Morgantown, WV 26505

Robert Barrow
412 Thames Street
Bristol, RI 02809

Bassett & Vollum, Inc.
217 N. Main Street
Galena, IL 61036

Barbara Vantrease Beall Studio
23727 Hawthorne Boulevard
Torrance, CA 90505

Ellen Beasley
P.O. Box 1145
Galveston, TX 77553

Bedlam Brass Beds
19-21 Fair Lawn Avenue
Fair Lawn, NJ 07410

H. Behlen & Bros.
Rt. 30 N.
Amsterdam, NY 12010

Robert W. Belcher
1753 Pleasant Grove Dr., NE
Dalton, GA 30720

Charles Bellinger/Architectural
  Components
P.O. Box 246
Leverett, MA 01054

Bellows by Soucy
1532 West Shore Road
Warwick, RI 02889

S. A. Bendheim Company, Inc.
122 Hudson Street
New York, NY 10013

Bendix Mouldings, Inc.
235 Pegasus Avenue
Northvale, NJ 07647

Bennington Bronze
147 S. Main Street
White River Junction, VT 05001

Bergen Bluestone
404 Rt. 17
Paramus, NJ 07652

Christina Bergh
711 Camino Corrales Road
Santa Fe, NM 87501

Bernard Plating Works
660 Riverside Drive
Florence, MA 01060

Bernardini Iron Works, Inc.
418 Bryant Avenue
Bronx, NY 10474

Berridge Manufacturing Co.
170 Maury Street
Houston, TX 77026

Lester H. Berry
1108 Pine Street
Philadelphia, PA 19107

Bestwood Industries, Ltd.
P.O. Box 2042
Vancouver, B.C., Canada

Beveled Glass Industries
900 North La Cienega Boulevard
Los Angeles, CA 90069

Beveled Glass Industries
979 Third Avenue
New York, NY 10022

The Biggs Company
Mail Order Department
105 E. Grace Street
Richmond VA 23219

Birch Hill Builders
P.O. Box 416
York, MA 03909

Adele Bishop, Inc.
Dept. OHC/80
Dorset, VT 05251

Bittersweet Furniture
P.O. Box 5
Riverton, VT 05668

Black Millwork Co., Inc.
Lake Avenue
Midland Park, NJ 07432

The Blacksmith Shop (Lighting)
R.R. 2, 26 Bridge Road
Orleans, MA 02653

The Blacksmith Shop
P.O. Box 15
Mount Holly, VT 05758

Blaine Window Hardware, Inc.
1919 Blaine Drive
Hagerstown, MD 21740

Blair Lumber Co., Inc.
Rt. 1
Powhatan, VA 23139

Blenko Glass Co., Inc.
P.O. Box 67
Milton, WV 25541

Jerome W. Blum
Ross Hill Road
Lisbon, Conn. 06351

Norton Blumenthal
979 Third Avenue
New York, NY 10022

Bona Decorative Hardware
2227 Beechmont Avenue
Cincinnati, OH 45230

Nancy Borden
187 Marcy Street at Strawbery Banke
Portsmouth, NH 03801

Robert Bourdon
Wolcott, VT 05680

Louis W. Bowen, Inc.
979 Third Avenue
New York, NY 10022

Bow and Arrow Stove Co.
11 Hurley Street
Cambridge, MA 02139

Larry Boyce
1307 Baker Street
San Francisco, CA 94115

Braid-Aid Co.
466 Washington Street
Pembroke, MA 02359

Brass Bed Company of America
2801 East 11th Street
Los Angeles, CA 90023

Brasslight of Historic Walker's Point
719 S. 5th Street
Milwaukee, WI 53204

Sandra Brauer/Stained Glass
364-B Atlantic Avenue
Brooklyn, NY 11217

Lester P. and Barbara Breininger
476 S. Church Street
Robesonia, PA 19551

The Broad-Axe Beam Co.
R.D. 2, Box 181-E
Brattleboro, VT 05301

Brookstone
127 Vose Farm Road
Peterborough, NH 03458

Paul M. Broomfield
30 Main Street
Carolina, RI 02812

Carol Brown
Dept. OHC
Putney, VT 05346

T. Robins Brown
12 First Avenue
Nyack, NY 10960

Bruce Hardwood Floors
4255 LBJ Freeway
Dallas, TX 75234

The Burning log (Eastern Office)
P.O. Box 438
Lebanon, NH 03766

The Burning Log (Western Office)
P.O. Box 8519
Aspen, CO 81611

Brunschwig & Fils, Inc.
979 Third Avenue
New York, NY 10022

Bryant Steel Works
R.F.D. 2, Box 109
Thorndike, ME 04986

Wm. Ward Bucher
1638 R Street, N.W.
Washington, DC 20009

Cabot Stains
1 Union Street
Boston, MA 02108

Douglas Campbell Co.
31 Bridge Street
Newport, RI 02840

Campbell Lamps
1108 Pottstown Pike
Dept. 21
West Chester, PA 19380

The Candle Cellar & Emporium
1914 N. Main Street
Fall River, MA 02720

The Cane Farm
Rosemont, NJ 08556

Capability Brown Limited
130 W. 28th Street
New York, NY 10001

Cape Cod Cupola Co., Inc.
78 State Road
North Dartmouth, MA 02747

Victor Carl Antiques
841 Broadway
New York, NY 10003

Dale Carlisle
Rt. 123
Stoddard, NH 03464

Constance Carol, Inc.
P.O. Box 899
Plymouth, MA 02360

Henry Cassen, Inc.
125 Newtown Road
Plainview, NY 11803

Castle Burlingame
R.D. 1, Box 352
Basking Ridge, NJ 07920

Cedar Swamp Stoneware Co.
1645 Main Street
West Barnstable, MA 02668

The Ceiling Lady
1408 Main Street
Evanston, IL 60202

Ceilings, Walls & More, Inc.
Box 494, 124 Walnut Street
Jefferson, TX 75657

Celestial Roofing
1710 Thousand Oaks Boulevard
Berkeley, CA 94702

Century Glass Inc. of Dallas
1417 N. Washington Street
Dallas, TX 75204

Chapman Manufacturing Co.
481 W. Main Street
Avon, MA 02322

Chapulin
Rt. 1, Box 187
Santa Fe, NM 87501

Cherry Creek Ent., Inc.
937 Santa Fe Drive
Denver, CO 80204

Chilstone Garden Ornaments
Sprivers Estate, Horsmonden
Kent TN12 8DR
England

City Lights
2226 Massachusetts Avenue
Cambridge, MA 02140

Clare House Ltd.
35 Elizabeth Street
London SW1
England

Clarence House
40 E. 57th Street
New York, NY 10022

The Classic Illumination
431 Grove St.
Oakland, CA 94607

Claxton Walker & Assoc.
10000 Falls Road
Potomac, MD 20854

Cohasset Colonials by Hagerty
38 Parker Avenue
Cohasset, MA 02025

Coker Creek Crafts
P.O. Box 95
Coker Creek, TN 37214

Diane Jackson Cole
9 Grove Street
Kennebunk, ME 04043

The Colefax & Fowler Chintz Shop
149 Ebury Street
London SW1W 9QN
England

Colefax & Fowler (Interior Design)
39 Brook Street
London W1
England

Colonial Casting Co.
443 South Colony Street
Meriden, CT 06450

Colonial Lamp & Supply Co.
P.O. Box 867
McMinnville, TN 37110

Colonial Lock Co.
172 Main Street
Terryville, CT 06786

Colonial Metalcrafters
5935 S. Broadway, Box 1135
Tyler, TX 75701

Colonial of Zeeland
103 N. Colonial Street
Zeeland, MI 49464

Colonial Restoration Materials
Route 123
Stoddard, NH 30464

Colonial Tin Craft
7805 Railroad Avenue
Cincinnati, OH 45243

Colonial Williamsburg
Craft House
Box CH
Williamsburg, VA 23185

Colonial Wood
16 Water Street
Clinton, NJ 08809

Conklin Tin Plate & Metal Co.
P.O. Box 2662
Atlanta, GA 30301

The Conservatory
209 W. Michigan Avenue
Marshall, MI 49068

Brian Considine
Post Mills, VT 05058

Conso Products
261 Fifth Avenue
New York, NY 10016

Albert Constantine & Son, Inc.
2050 Eastchester Road
Bronx, NY 10461

John Conti, Restoration Contractor
Box 189, Martin's Corner Road
Wagontown, PA 19376

Cook & Dunn Paint Corp.
P.O. Box 117
Newark, NJ 07101

Frederick Cooper
2545 W. Diversey Avenue
Chicago, IL 60647

Copper Antiquities
79 Adams Road
West Yarmouth, MA 02673

The Copper House
Rt. 4
Epsom, NH 03234

Coran-Sholes Industries
509 E. 2nd Street
South Boston, MA 02127

Cornucopia, Inc.
39 Main Street
Waltham, MA 02154

The Country Bed Shop
Box 222
Groton, MA 01450

Country Braid House
Clark Road
Tilton, NH 03276

Country Curtains at The Red Lion Inn
Stockridge, MA 01262

Country Floors
300 E. 61st Street
New York, NY 10021

Country Loft
South Shore Park
Hingham, MA 02043

Cowtan & Tout, Inc.
D & D Bldg., 17th Floor
979 Third Avenue
New York, NY 10022

Craftsman Lumber Co.
Main Street
Groton, MA 01450

Craftswomen
Box 715
Doylestown, PA 18901

Crowfoot's, Inc.
3831 Oracle Road
Tucson, AZ 85705

Crown of Fairhope
759 Nichols Street
Fairhope, AL 36352

Cumberland General Store
Rt. 3
Crossville, TN 38555

Cumberland Woodcraft Co.
R.D. 5, Box 452
Carlisle, PA 17013

Gerald Curry, Cabinetmaker
Box 1141
Auburn, ME 04210

Custom House
South Shore Drive
Owl's Head, ME 04854

Czech and Speake
88 Jermyn Street
London SW1Y 6JD
England

Daly's Wood Finishing Products
1121 N. 36th Street
Seattle, WA 98103

Dana-Deck, Inc.
P.O. Box 78
Orcas, WA 98280

Davis Cabinet Co.
Box 60444
Nashville, TN 37206

Donald E. Davis, Inc.
1325 Millersport Highway
Williamsville, NY 14221

R. H. Davis, Inc.
Gregg Lake Road
Antrim, NH 03440

Decorators Supply Corp.
3610-12 S. Morgan Street
Chicago, IL 60609

Decorators Walk
125 Newtown Road
Plainview, NY 11803

Deft, Inc.
17451 Von Karman Avenue
Irvine, CA 92714

Delaware Quarries, Inc.
River Road
Lumberville, PA 18933

Designer Imports
6386 College Boulevard
Leawood, KS 66211

Devoe & Raynolds Co.
1 Riverfront Place
Louisville, KY 40402

A. L. Diament & Co.
P.O. Box 7437
Philadelphia, PA 19101

Diamond K. Co., Inc.
130 Buckland Road
South Windsor, CT 06074

Dobson & Thomas Ltd.
838 9th Street
Santa Monica, CA 90403

Alan Dodd
295 Caledonian Road
London N1 1EG
England

Domestic Environmental Alternatives
495 Main Street
P.O. Box 1020
Murphys, CA 94247

Down Home Comforts
P.O. Box 281
West Brattleboro, VT 05301

Dremel Manufacturing
4915 21 Street
P.O. Box 518
Racine, WI 53406

Driwood Moulding Co.
P.O. Box 1729
Florence, SC 29503

Frederick Duckloe & Bros., Inc.
Portland, PA 18351

Duro-Lite Lamps, Inc.
17-10 Willow Street
Fair Lawn, NJ 07410

Dutch Boy Paints
c/o Tom Spencer
Glen Ellyn Sales Office
Suite 307, Bldg. 6
799 Roosevelt Road
Glen Ellyn, IL 60137

Dutch Products & Supply Co.
14 S. Main Street
Yardley, PA 19067

Early New England Restorations
Joinery and Forge Works
P.O. Box 45
Mansfield Depot, CT 06251

The 18th Century Co.
Haddam Quarter Road
Durham, CT 06422

18th Century Hardware Co.
131 East 3rd Street
Derry, PA 15627

Richard H. Eiselt, AIA
398 S. Grant Avenue
Columbus, OH 43215

Electric Glass Co.
1 E. Mellen Street
Hampton, VA 23663

Elegant Entries, Inc.
45 Walter Street
Worcester, MA 01604

Elon, Inc.
198 Saw Mill River Road
Elmsford, NY 10523

Empress Chandeliers
P.O. Drawer 2067
Mobile, AL 36601

Entwood Construction Fraternity
R.R. 1
Marshfield, VT 05658

The Essex Forge
15 Old Dennison Road
Essex, CT 06426

European Marble Works
661 Driggs Avenue
Brooklyn, NY 11211

Faire Harbour Boats
44 Captain Peirce Road
Scituate, MA 02066

Faneuil Furniture Hardware
94-100 Peterborough Street
Boston, MA 02215

Farmington Craftsmen
87-J Spring Lake Road
Farmington, CT 06032

Craig H. Farrow, Cabinetmaker
149 Cornwall Avenue
Waterbury, CT 06704

Faultless Div. BLI
1421 N. Garvin Street
Evansville, IN 47711

Felber Studios
110 Ardmore Avenue
P.O. Box 551
Ardmore, PA 19003

Felicity, Inc.
567 Terrace Hill Road
Cookeville, TN 38501

Fife's Woodworking & Mfg. Co.
Main Street
Northwood, NH 03261

Fine Metalwork
Deanne F. Nelson
Box 43
Bishop Hill, IL 61419

Finnaren & Haley, Inc.
2320 Haverford Road
Ardmore, PA 19003

Fisher Stoves International
P.O. Box 10605
Eugene, OR 97440

Fletcher's Paint Works
Rt. 101
Milford, NH 03055

Floorcloths, Inc.
P.O. Box 812
Severna Park, MD 21146

Focal Point, Inc.
2005 Marietta Road, N.W.
Atlanta, GA 30318

Folger Adam Co.
P.O. Box 688
100 Railroad Street
Joliet, IL 60434

Follansbee Steel Corp.
State Street
Follansbee, WV 26037

Henry Ford Museum & Greenfield
   Village
Oakwood between Southfield &
   Oakwood Boulevard
Dearborn, MI 48121

Formby's Refinishing Products, Inc.
P.O. Box 788
Olive Branch, MS 38654

French and Ball
Main Road
Gill, MA 01376

Frog Tool Co.
700 W. Jackson Blvd.
Chicago, IL 60606

Fuller O'Brien Corp.
450 E. Grand Avenue
South San Francisco, CA 94080

Fuller O'Brien Paints
P.O. Box 864
Brunswick, GA 31520

Fuller O'Brien Paints
The O'Brien Corp.
20001 W. Washington Avenue
South Bend, IN 46634

Fypon, Inc.
Box 365, 108 Hill Street
Stewartstown, PA 17363

Gargoyles, Ltd.
202 Sharpstown Center
Houston, TX 77036

Gaston Wood Finishes, Inc.
P.O. Box 1246
Bloomington, IN 47402

Carlo Germana
318 Hempstead Turnpike
West Hempstead, NY 11552

Giannetti's Studios
3806 38th Street
Brentwood, MD 20722

Glen-Bels Country Store
Rt. 5
Crossville, TN 38555

Glen-Gery Corp.
P.O. Box 280
Shoemakersville, PA 19555

Glidden-Durkee
900 Union Commerce Bldg.
Cleveland, OH 44115

Good Stenciling
Box 387
Dublin, NH 03444

Good Time Stove Co.
P.O. Box F
Goshen, MA 01032

Grampa's Wood Stoves
P.O. Box 492
Ware, MA 01082

Great American Salvage Co., Inc.
901 E. 2nd Street
Little Rock, AR 72203

Greeff Fabrics
150 Midland Avenue
Port Chester, NY 10573

Green Boughs Cabinet Maker's Shop
2021 Valentine Drive
Grand Rapids, MI 49505

Greene's Lighting Fixtures, Inc.
Chandelier Warehouse
40 Withers Street
Brooklyn, NY 11211

A. Greenhalgh & Sons Painting
Farwell Road
Tyngsborough, MA 01879

Grilk Interiors
220 E. 11th Street
Davenport, IA 52803

Bernard E. Gruenke, Jr.
Conrad Schmidt Studios
2405 S. 162nd Street
New Berlin, WI 53157

Guardian National House Inspection,
    Inc.
Box 115
Orleans, MA 02653

P.E. Guerin, Inc.
23 Jane Street
New York, NY 10014

Guild of Shaker Crafts
401 West Savidge Street
Spring Lake, MI 49456

Guilfoy Cornice Works
1234 Howard Street
San Fransicso, CA 94005

Jack Guinan
Box 215
Barnesville, PA 18214

Gurian's
276 Fifth Avenue
New York, NY 10001

Guyon, Inc.
65 Oak Street
Lititz, PA 17543

Haas Wood and Ivory Works
64 Clementina Street
San Francisco, CA 94105

Hallelujah Redwood Products
39500-J Comptche Road
Mendocino, CA 95460

Hampshire Pewter Co.
Rt. 28
Wolfeboro, NH 03894

Hannett-Morrow, Inc.
146 E. 5th Street
New York, NY 10022

S. Harris Co., Inc.
580 S. Douglas Street
El Segundo, CA 90245

Harris Manufacturing Co.
P.O. Box 300
Johnson City, TN 37601

David McLaren Hart & Associates
Architects
77 Washington Street, N.
Boston, MA 02114

The Harvin Co.
Waynesboro, VA 22980

Wilbert R. Hasbrouck
Historic Resources
711 S. Dearborn Street
Chicago, IL 60605

Hathernware Ltd.
Loughborough
Leicestershire LE12 5EW
England

Heads Up, Inc.
3201 W. MacArthur Boulevard
Santa Ana, CA 92704

Hearthside Mail Order
Box 24
West Newbury, VT 05468

Clovis Heimsath Associates, Architects
On The Square
Fayetteville, TX 78940

Heirloom Rugs
28 Harlem Street
Rumford, RI 02916

Charles Hemming
Flat Above
176 Deptford High Street
Deptford
London SE8
England

Hendricks Tile Mfg. Co., Inc.
P.O. Box 3573
Richmond, VA 23234

Heritage Lanterns
70A Main Street
Yarmouth, ME 04096

Heritage Rugs
P.O. Box 404
Lahaska, PA 18931

S. M. Hexter Co.
2800 Superior Avenue
Cleveland, OH 44114

Hi-Art East
6 N. Rhodes Center, N.W.
Atlanta, GA 30309

Allen Charles Hill, AIA
Historical Preservation and Architecture
25 Englewood Road
Winchester, MA 01890

Historic Boulevard Services
1520 W. Jackson Boulevard
Chicago, IL 60607

Historic Charleston Reproductions
105 Broad Street
Charleston, SC 29401

The Hitchcock Chair Co.
Riverton, CT 06065

Glen Hofecker
Rt. 1, Box 224A
Sugar Grove, NC 28679

Holland Shade Company, Inc.
306 E. 61st Street
New York, NY 10021

Homecraft Veneer
901 West Way
Latrobe, PA 15650

R. Hood and Co.
R.F.D. 3, College Rd.
Meredith, NH 03253

The Hope Co., Inc.
2052 Congressional Drive
St. Louis, MO 63141

Horton Brasses
P.O. Box 95, Nooks Hill Road
Cromwell, CT 06416

The House Carpenters
Box 217
Shutesbury, MA 01072

House of Spain & Trouvez L'Europe, Inc.
34 Gansevoort Street
New York, NY 10014

House of Webster
Rogers, AR 72756

David Howard, Inc.
P.O. Box 295
Alstead, NH 03602

Howell Construction
2700 12th Avenue, S.
Nashville, TN 37204

Hubbardton Forge and Wood Corp.
Bomoseen, VT 05732

S & C Huber, Accoutrements
82 Plants Dam Road
East Lyme, CT 06333

Wm. Hunrath Co., Inc.
153 E. 57th Street
New York, NY 10022

Hurley Patentee Lighting
R.D. 7 - Box 98A
Kingston, NY 12401

Hyde Manufacturing Co.
54 Eastford Road
Southbridge, MA 01550

Ice Nine Glass Design
6128 Oldson Memorial Hwy.
Golden Valley, MN 55422

Illinois Bronze Paint Co.
300 E. Main Street
Lake Zurich, IL 60047

International Consultants, Inc.
227 S. 9th Street
Philadelphia, PA 19107

Ironbridge Gorge Trading Co., Ltd.
Coalport China Works Museum
Coalport, Telford TF 8 7BR
England

Iron Horse Antiques, Inc.
R.D. 2
Poultney, VT 05764

Irreplaceable Artifacts
526 E. 80th Street
New York, NY 10021

William H. Jackson Co.
3 E. 47th Street
New York, NY 10017

Charles W. Jacobsen, Inc.
401 S. Salina Street
Syracuse, NY 13202

Jo-El Shop
7120 Hawkins Creamery Road
Laytonsville, MD 20760

H & R Johnson Tiles Ltd.
Highgate Tile Works
Tunstall
Stoke-on-Trent ST6 4JX
England

Jones & Erwin, Inc.
232 E. 59th Street
New York, NY 10022

Peter Jones
Sloane Street
London SW1
England

The Judson Studios
200 S. Avenue 66
Los Angeles, CA 90042

Christiane Kahrmann
7 West Eaton Place
London SW1X SLU
England

Katzenbach and Warren, Inc.
950 Third Avenue
New York, NY 10022

Steve Kayne Hand Forged Hardware
17 Harmon Place
Smithtown, NY 11787

KB Moulding, Inc.
508A Larkfield Road
East Northport, NY 11731

Stephen Kelemen
Design Associates
77 Main Road
Orient Point, NY 11957

Kenmore Carpet Corp.
979 Third Avenue
New York, NY 10022

Kensington Historical Co.
P.O. Box 87
East Kingston, NH 03827

Kentile Floors
58 Second Avenue
Brooklyn, NY 11215

Kentucky Wood Floors, Inc.
7761 National Turnpike
Louisville, KY 40214

King's Chandelier Co.
Highway 14
Eden, NC 27288

Kingsworthy Foundry Co., Ltd.
Kingsworthy
Winchester, Hants SO23 7QG
England

Kittinger Co.
1885 Elmwood Avenue
Buffalo, NY 14207

Klise Manufacturing Co.
601 Maryland Avenue
Grand Rapids, MI 49505

Parker Knoll Textiles, Ltd.
P.O. Box 30
West End Road, High Wycombe
England

Kohler Co.
Kohler, WI 53044

Koppers Co., Forest Products Div.
1900 Koppers Bldg.
Pittsburgh, PA 15219

Kristia Associates
P.O. Box 1118
Portland, ME 04104

John Kruesel
R.R. 6
Rochester, MN 55901

J. & R. Lamb Studios
151 Walnut Street
Northvale, NJ 07647

The Lamp Shop
24 Bedfordbury
Covent Garden
London WC2
England

Landis Designs
194 Governor Road
Hershey, PA 17033

David Lawrence
50 Sheep Street
Stow-On-The-Wold
Gloucestershire
England

Lead Glass Co.
14924 Beloit Snodes Road
Beloit, OH 44609

Lee/Joffa, Inc.
979 Third Avenue
New York, NY 10022

Lemee's Fireplace Equipment
815 Bedford Street
Bridgewater, MA 02324

The Lennox Shop
Rt. 179
Lambertville, NJ 08530

Levy's Gasolier Antiques
Box 627
Washington, DC 20044

Joe Ley Antiques
620-622 E. Market Street
Louisville, KY 40202

Liberty and Co., Ltd.
Regent Street
London W1R 6AH
England

Liberty of London
229 E. 60th Street
New York, NY 10022

Liberty Village Foundation
2 Church Street
Flemington, NJ 08822

Howard Lieberman, P.E.
Home Buyers Inspection Service
277 White Plains Road
Eastchester, NY 10709

The Lily Collection
1313 N. Main Street
Ann Arbor, MI 48104

Locks & Handles
8 Exhibition Road
London SW7 2HF
England

Ernest Lo Nano
S. Main Street
Sheffield, MA 01257

London Architectural Salvage & Supply
    Co., Ltd.
St. Michael's Church
Mark Street
Shoreditch
London EC2 A4ER
England

The London Venturers Company
2 Dock Square
Rockport, MA 01966

Lone Star Doors and Millwork
600 N. Wildwood Street
Irving, TX 75060

Thomas G. Loose,
    Blacksmith-Whitesmith
R.D. 2, Box 203A
Leesport, PA 19533

Ludowici-Celadon
201 N. Talman Avenue
Chicago, IL 60612

Luigi Crystal
7332 Frankford Avenue
Philadelphia, PA 19136

Kenneth Lynch & Sons, Inc.
78 Danbury Road
Wilton, CT 06897

Magnolia Hall
726 Andover Drive
Atlanta, GA 30327

Maine Line Paints
13 Hutchins Street
Auburn, ME 04210

Manor Art Glass
20 Ridge Road
Douglaston, NY 11363

Marble Modes, Inc.
15-25 130th Street
College Point, NY 11356

MarLe Company
170 Summer Street
Stamford, CT 06904

Marshalltown Trowel Co.
P.O. Box 738
Marshalltown, IA 50158

Ephraim Marsh Co.
P.O. Box 266
Concord, NC 28025

Gina Martin
359 Avery Street
South Windsor, CT 06074

The Martin-Senour Co.
1370 Ontario Avenue, N.W.
Cleveland, OH 44113

Louis Maslow and Son, Inc.
979 Third Avenue
New York, NY 10022

Master's Stained and Etched Glass Studio
729 West 16th Street, No. B-1
Costa Mesa, CA 92627

Materials Unlimited
4100 Morgan Road
Ypsilanti, MI 48197

Maurer & Shepherd, Joyners
122 Naubuc Avenue
Glastonbury, CT 06033

Mercer Museum Shop
Pine and Ashland Streets
Doylestown, PA 18901

Meredith Stained Glass Studio
231 Mill Street, N.E.
Vienna, VA 22180

Metropolitan Lighting Fixture Co., Inc.
1010 Third Avenue
New York, NY 10010

Mexico House
P.O. Box 970
Del Mar, CA 92014

Michael's Fine Colonial Products
22 Churchill Lane
Smithtown, NY 11787

D. R. Millbranth, Cabinetmaker
R.R. 2, Box 462
Hillsboro, NH 03244

Newton Millham, Blacksmith
672 Drift Road
Westport, MA 02790

The Millworks
Box 175
Paisley
Ontario, Canada NO6 2NO

Mimram Stained Glass Studio
Diswell House, Monks Rise
Welwyn Garden City, Herts
England
Welwyn Garden 26169

Minwax Company, Inc.
Box 995
Clifton, NJ 07104

Mohawk Industries, Inc.
173 Howland Avenue
Adams, MA 01220

Mrs. Monro, Ltd.
11 Montpelier Street
London SW7
England

Benjamin Moore & Co.
51 Chestnut Ridge Road
Montvale, NJ 07645

Gates Moore
River Road, Silvermine
Norwalk, CT 06850

Morgans
5 Leigh Street
London WC1H 9PT
England

R. Jesse Morley, Jr.
88 Oak Street
Westwood, MA 02090

Thomas Moser, Cabinet Maker
Cobb's Bridge Road
New Gloucester, ME 04260

Mountain Lumber Company
1327 Carlton Avenue
Charlottesville, VA 22901

Maurice J. Murphy
73 Burnside Street
Lowell, MA 01851

Lehlan Murray
Box 19
Bishop Hill, IL 61419

National Home Inspection Service of
New England, Inc.
2 Calvin Road
Watertown, MA 02172

The National House Inn
102 South Parkview Road
Marshall, MI 49068

National Products, Inc.
900 Baxter Avenue
Louisville, KY 40204

Nesle, Inc.
151 E. 57th Street
New York, NY 10022

Newbury Design, Inc.
P.O. Box 265
Wellesley, MA 02181

Simon Newby, Cabinetmaker
Shop at 670 Drift Road
Westport, MA 02790

New Hampshire Blanket
Main Street
Harrisville, NH 03450

Newstamp Lantern Co.
227 Bay Road
North Easton, MA 02356

New York Flooring
340 E. 90th Street
New York, NY 10028

Nichols & Stone Company
232 Sherman Street
Gardner, MA 01440

E. A. Nord Sales Co.
P.O. Box 1187
Everett, WA 98206

W.F. Norman Corp.
P.O. Box 323-J
Nevada, MO 64772

Norman's of Salisbury
P.O. Drawer 799
Salisbury, NC 28144

North Coast Chemical Co.
6300 17th Avenue, S.
Seattle, WA 98108

Northeast American Heritage Co.
77 Washington Street, N., Suite 502
Boston, MA 02114

Nowell's Inc.
490 Gate Five Road
Sausalito, CA 94965

NUHL
2041 Independence Street
Cape Girardeau, MO 63701

Craig Nutt Fine Wood Works
2308 Sixth Street
Tuscaloosa, AL 35401

Old Carolina Brick Co.
Rt. 9, Box 77
Majolica Road
Salisbury, NC 28144

Old Colony Curtains
P.O. Box 759
Westfield, NJ 07090

Old-Fashioned Milk Paint Co.
Box 222H
Groton, MA 01450

Old House Supplies
Pandora's Antiques
2014 Old Philadelphia Pike
Lancaster, PA 17602

Old Lamplighter Shop
Rt. 12-B
Deansboro, NY 13328

Old Mansions Co.
1305 Blue Hill Avenue
Mattapan, MA 02126

Olde New England Masonry
27 Hewitt Road
Mystic, CT 06355

Old Stone Mill Corp.
Old Stone Mill
Adams, MA 01220

Olde Theatre Architectural Salvage Co.
1309 Westport Road
Kansas City, MO 64111

Old Timey Furniture Co.
Box 1165-A
Smithfield, NC 27577

Old Town Restorations
158 Farrington Street
St. Paul, MN 55102

Old World Moulding and Finishing
  Co., Inc.
115 Allen Blvd.
Farmingdale, NY 11735

Open Pacific Graphics
43 Market Square
Victoria, B.C., Canada

Orlandini Studios, Ltd.
633 W. Virginia Street
Milwaukee, WI 53204

Orleans Carpenters Reproductions
P.O. Box 107-C
Orleans, MA 02653

J. F. Orr & Sons
Village Green, Rt. 27
Sudbury, MA 01776

Osborne & Little, Ltd.
304 Kings Road
London SW3 5UH
England

Ox-Line Paints
Lehman Bros. Corp.
115 Jackson Avenue
Jersey City, NJ 07304

Packard Lamp Co., Inc.
67 E. 11th Street
New York, NY 10003

Stephen W. Parker, Blacksmith
Box 40
Craftsbury, VT 05826

Parma Tile Mosaic & Marble Co., Inc.
14-38 Astoria Blvd.
Long Island City, NY 11102

Megan Parry/Wall Stenciling
1727 Spruce Street
Boulder, CO 80302

Pat's Antiques
P.O. Box 777
Smithville, TX 78957

Peerless Rattan & Reed Mfg. Co., Inc.
97 Washington Street
New York, NY 10006

Penco Studios
1137 Bardstown Road
Louisville, KY 40204

Period Brass, Inc.
25 E. James Street
Falconer, NY 14733

Period Furniture Hardware Co.
P.O. Box 314, Charles Street Station
123 Charles Street
Boston, MA 02114

Period Lighting Fixtures
Dpt. M3
1 W. Main Street
Chester, CT 06412

Period Pine
P.O. Box 77052
Atlanta, GA 30357

Perkowitz Window Fashions, Inc.
135 Green Bay Road
Wilmette, IL 60091

Mark F. Pfaller Associates
3112 W. Highland Blvd.
Milwaukee, WI 53208

Pfanstiel Hardware Co.
Hust Road
Jeffersonville, NY 12748

Walter Phelps
Box 76
Williamsville, VT 05362

Pilgrim's Progress, Inc.
225 Henry Street
New York, NY 10002

Pine Bough
Main Street
Northeast Harbor, ME 04662

Pinecrest, Inc.
2118 Blaisdell Avenue
Minneapolis, MN 55404

Pioneer Lamps & Stoves
75 Yesler Way
Seattle, WA 98104

Pittsburgh Paints
1 Gateway Center
Pittsburgh, PA 15222

Plain & Fancy Accents
714 E. Green Street
Pasadena, CA 91101

Pompei Studios for Stained Glass Art
455 High Street
Medford, MA 02155

Portland Franklin Stove Foundry, Inc.
57 Kennebec Street
Portland, ME 04104

Portland Willamette Company
6800 N.E. 59th Place, Box 13097
Portland, OR 97213

Potlach Corporation - Townsend Unit
P.O. Box 916
Stuttgart, AR 72160

Pratt & Lambert
625 Washington Street
Carlstadt, NJ 07072

Preservation Associates, Inc.
P.O. Box 202
Sharpsburg, MD 21782

The Preservation Partnership
70 W. Central Street
Natick, MA 01760

Preservation Resource Center
Lake Shore Road
Essex, NY 12936

Preservation Resource Group
5619 Southampton Drive
Springfield, VA 22151

Preway, Inc.
1430 Second Street, N.
Wisconsin Rapids, WI 54494

Francis J. Purcell, II
R.D. 2, Box 7
New Hope, PA 18938

Quaker City Manufacturing Co.
701 Chester Pike
Sharon Hill, PA 19079

Quaker Lace Co.
24 W. 40th Street
New York, NY 10018

Rainbow Art Glass Co.
49 Shark River Road
Neptune, NJ 07753

The Rambusch Co.
40 W. 13th Street
New York, NY 10011

Readybuilt Products Co.
Box 4306, 1701 McHenry Street
Baltimore, MD 21223

Reed Wallcoverings
P.O. Box 105293
Atlanta, GA 30348

Reid Classics
P.O. Box 8383
Mobile, AL 36608

Rejuvenation House Parts Co.
4543 N. Albina Avenue
Portland, Oregon 97217

The Renovation Source, Inc.
3512-14 N. Southport Avenue
Chicago, IL 60657

The Renovators Co.
Box 284
Patterson, NY 12563

Renovator's Supply
71 Northfield Road
Millers Falls, MA 01349

Restoration A Speciality
6127 N. E. Rodney Street
Portland, OR 97211

Restoration Center
130 W. 28th Street
New York, NY 10001

Restorations, Ltd.
Jamestown, RI 02835

Restorations Unlimited, Inc.
24 W. Main Street
Elizabethville, PA 17023

Joseph Richter, Inc.
249 E. 57th Street
New York, NY 10022

J. Ring Stained Glass Studio, Inc.
2125 E. Hennepin Avenue
Minneapolis, MN 55414

Ritter & Son Hardware
46901 Fish Rock Road
Anchor Bay (Gualala), CA 95445

Dennis Paul Robillard, Inc.
Front Street
South Berwick, MA 03908

Robinson Iron Corporation
Robinson Road
Alexander City, AL 35010

The Rocker Shop of Marietta, Georgia
1421 White Circle, N.W.
P.O. Box 12
Marietta, GA 30061

Jane Kent Rockwell
Interior Decorations
48-52 Lincoln Street
Exeter, NH 03833

Rococo Designs
417 Pennsylvania Avenue
Santa Cruz, CA 95062

Royal Windyne, Ltd.
1316 W. Main Street
Richmond, VA 23230

Roy Electric Co., Inc.
1054 Coney Island Avenue
Brooklyn, NY 11230

Saldarini & Pucci
156 Crosby Street
New York, NY 10012

The Saltbox
2229 Marietta Pike
Lancaster, PA 17603

Arthur Sanderson & Sons, Ltd.
Berners Street
London W1A 2JE
England

Richard L. Sanderson
210 Michigan Avenue
Sturgis, MI 49091

San Francisco Victoriana
2245 Palou Avenue
San Francisco, CA 94124

Santa Cruz Foundry
1113 Court Street
Hanford, CA 92230

Richard E. Sargent
Box 83
Hartland 4 Corners, VT 05049

Scalamandré Silks, Inc.
950 Third Avenue
New York, NY 10022

Schrader Wood Stoves & Fireplaces
724 Water Street
Santa Cruz, CA 95060

F. Schumacher & Co.
939 Third Avenue
New York, NY 10022

I. Schwartz Glass & Mirror Co., Inc.
412 E. 59th Street
New York, NY 10022

A. F. Schwerd Mfg. Co.
3215 McClure Avenue
Pittsburgh, PA 15212

Mrs. Eldred Scott
The Riven Oak
Birmingham, MI 48012

John L. Seekamp
472 Pennsylvania Street
San Francisco, CA 94107

Self Sufficiency Products
Environmental Manufacturing Corp.
P.O. Box 126
Essex Junction, VT 05452

Shakertown Corporation
P.O. Box 400
Winlock, WA 98596

Shaker Workshops, Inc.
14 Bradford Street
Concord, MA 01742

Shenandoah Manufacturing Co.
P.O. Box 839
Harrisburg, VA 22801

Shepherd Oak Products
Box 27
Northwood, NH 03261

Sherwin-Williams Co.
101 Prospect Avenue, N.W.
Cleveland, OH 44101

Ship 'n Out
Harmony Road
Pawling, NY 12564

Silk Surplus
223 E. 58th Street
New York, NY 10022

Silk Surplus
843 Lexington Avenue
New York, NY 10021

Silver Bridge Reproductions
Box 49
New Braintree, MA 01531

Silverton Victorian Mill Works
Box 523
Silverton, CO 81433

Simpson Timber Co.
900 Fourth Avenue
Seattle, WA 98164

Robert W. Skinner, Inc.
Rt. 117
Bolton, MA 01740

Tayssir Sleiman
423 Horsham Road
Horsham, PA 19044

Southern Highland Handicraft Guild
P.O. Box 9545
Asheville, NC 28805

Spanish Pueblo Doors, Inc.
P.O. Box 2517
Santa Fe, NM 87501

Spanish Villa
2145 Zercher Road
San Antonio, TX 78209

William Spencer
Creek Road, Rancocas Woods
Mount Holly, NJ 08060

Grep Spiess, Inc.
216 and 246 E. Washington Street
Joliet, IL 60433

Spring City Electrical Mfg. Co.
Hall & Main Streets
Spring City, PA 19475

Standard Roofings, Inc.
670 S. Clinton Avenue
Trenton, NJ 08611

Standard Trimming Corp.
1114 First Avenue
New York, NY 10021

Stansfield's Lamp Shop
P.O. Box 332
Slate Hill, NY 10973

Stark Carpet Corp.
979 Third Avenue
New York, NY 10022

Jay Thomas Stauffer, Pewterer
707 W. Brubaker Valley Road
Lititz, PA 17543

StencilArt
232 Amazon Place
Columbus, OH 43214

Stenciled Interiors
Hinman Lane
Southbury, CT 06488

Stencil Specialty Co.
377 Ocean Avenue
Jersey City, NJ 07305

Steptoe and Wife Antiques Ltd.
3626 Victoria Park Avenue
Ontario, Canada M2H 3B2

L. D. Stevens Colonial Lighting
2423 E. Norris Street
Philadelphia, PA 19125

William Stewart & Sons
708 N. Edison Street
Arlington, VA 22203

Thomas Strahan Co.
10 New England Executive Park
Burlington, MA 01803

Donald Streeter
P.O. Box 237
Franklinville, NJ 08322

Stroheim & Romann
155 E. 56th Street
New York, NY 10022

Structural Slate Co.
Pen Argyl, PA 18072

Student Craft Industries
Berea College
Berea, KY 40404

Studio Design, Inc.
49 Shark River Road
Neptune, NJ 07753

Studio Stained Glass
117 S. Main Street
Kokomo, IN 46901

Sturbridge Yankee Workshop
Old Turnpike
Sturbridge, MA 01566

Sunburst Stained Glass Co.
P.O. Box 5
New Harmony, IN 47631

Sun Designs
Rexstrom, Inc.
P.O. Box 157, Dept. 18
Delafield, WI 53018

Sunflower Studio
2851 Road B½
Grand Junction, CO 81501

Sunshine Lane
Box 262
Millersburg, OH 44654

Suntree
1871 Main Road
Westport Point, MA 02791

Superior Clay Corporation
P.O. Box 352
Uhrichsille, OH 44683

T and O Plaster Castings
80 Victoria Road
Romford, Essex
England

Tennessee Fabrication Co.
2366 Prospect Street
Memphis, TN 38106

Thermograte Enterprises, Inc.
2785 N. Fairview
St. Paul, MN 55113

Richard E. Thibaut, Inc.
P.O. Box 1541, General Post Office
New York, NY 10001

The Paul Thomas Studio
108 E. 24th Street
Minneapolis, MN 55404

Thomastown Chair Works
Box 93
Thomastown, MS 39171

Thompson & Anderson, Inc.
53 Seavey Street
Westbrook, ME 04092

John Thompson Design Group
420-A Zena Road
Woodstock, NY 12498

Thonet
491 E. Princess Street
P.O. Box 1587
York, PA 17405

Tom Thumb Nursery
South Boulevard
Nyack, NY 10960

The Toby House
517 E. Paces Ferry Road, N.E.
Atlanta, GA 30305

A Touch of Glass
1671 Newbridge Road
Long Island, NY 11710

Townshend Furniture
Rt. 30
Townshend, VT 05353

Tremont Nail Co.
P.O. Box 111
Wareham, MA 02571

Trouvailles, Inc.
P.O. Box 50
64 Grove Street
Boston, MA 02172

R. T. Trump & Co., Inc.
666 Bethlehem Pike
Flourtown, PA 19031

Turco Coatings, Inc.
Wheatland & Mellon Streets
Phoenixville, PA 19460

J. Gordon Turnbull, AIA
Architecture/Preservation/Planning
15 Vandewater Street
San Francisco, CA 94133

Twigs
76 Batterymarch Street
Boston, MA 02110

Unique Art Glass Co.
3649 Market Street
St. Louis, MO 63110

United Gilsonite Laboratories
Jefferson Avenue & New York
Scranton, PA 18501

United House Wrecking Corp.
328 Selleck Street
Stamford, CT 06902

Up Country Enterprise Corp.
Old Jaffrey Road
Peterborough, NH 03458

Urban Archeology, Ltd.
137 Spring Street
New York, NY 10012

The Valentas
2105 S. Austin Blvd.
Cicero, IL 60650

Norman Vandal, Cabinetmaker
P.O. Box 67
Roxbury, VT 05669

Albert Van Luit & Co.
4000 Chevy Chase Drive
Los Angeles, CA 90039

Vermont Castings, Inc.
Randolph, VT 05060

Vermont Marble Co.
61 Main Street
Proctor, VT 05765

Vermont Structural Slate Co., Inc.
P.O. Box 98
Fair Haven, VT 05743

Victorian Reproduction Enterprises
1601 Park Avenue South
Minneapolis, MN 55404

The Village Forge
P.O. Box 1148
Smithfield, NC 27577

Village Lantern
598 Union Street
North Marshfield, MA 02059

Villeroy + Boch
Interstate 80 at New Maple Avenue
Pine Brook, NJ 07058

Vintage Oak Furniture
23812 A-2 Via Fabricante
Mission Viego, CA 92691

Vintage Wood Works
Rt. 2, Box 68D
Quinlan, TX 75474

Virginia Metalcrafters
1010 E. Main Street
Waynesboro, VA 22980

VIRTU Artisans in Leaded Glass
P.O. Box 192
Southfield, MI 48037

Stephen von Hohen Country Furniture
P.O. Box 485
W. Broad Street
Trumbauersville, PA 18970

Garrett Wade Company
320 Fifth Avenue
New York, NY 10001

Charles Walker Mfg. Co.
189 13th Street
San Francisco, CA 94103

Denny Walker
335 Brooklands Street, Apt. 3
Akron, OH 44305

Wallin Forge
R.R. 1, Box 65
Sparta, KY 41086

Wall Stencils by Barbara
R. R. No. 2, Box 462
Hillsboro, NH 03244

Walton Stained Glass
209 Railway Street
Campbell, CA 95008

Warner & Sons Ltd.
7-11 Noel Street
London W1V 4AL
England

E. G. Washburne & Co.
83 Andover Street
Danvers, MA 01923

Washington Copper Works
South Street
Washington, CT 06793

Washington Stove Works
Box 687, 3402 Smith Street
Everett, WA 98206

Wasley Lighting Division
Plainville Industrial Park
Plainville, CT 06062

Watco-Dennis Corp.
Michigan Avenue & 22nd Street
Santa Monica, CA 90404

Watercolors, Inc.
Garrison, NY 10524

Watts & Company, Ltd.
7 Tufton St., Westminster
London, SW1P 3QB
England

Waverly Fabrics
58 W. 40th Street
New York, NY 10018

The Weather Vane
347 S. Elm Street
Greensboro, NC 27401

Halstead S. Welles & Associates
287 E. Houston Street
New York, NY 10002

H.S. Welles Fireplace Co.
209 E. 2nd Street
New York, NY 10009

Welsbach Lighting Products Co.
240 Sargent Drive
New Haven, CT 06511

Westlake Architectural Antiques
3315 Westlake Drive
Austin, TX 78746

Westmoore Pottery
Rt. 2, Box 159-A
Seagrove, NC 27341

West Rindge Baskets, Inc.
Box 24
Rindge, NH 03461

The Robert Whitley Studio
Laurel Road, Box 69
Solebury, PA 18963

Whittemore-Durgin Glass Co.
Box 2065
Hanover, MA 02339

I. M. Wiese, Antiquarian
Main Street
Southbury, CT 06488

John A. Wigen Construction
R.D. 1, Box 281
Cobleskill, NY 12043

Wikkmann House
Box 501
Chatsworth, CA 91311

Helen Williams - Rare Tiles
12643 Hortense Street
North Hollywood, CA 91604

Williamsburg Blacksmiths, Inc.
Buttonshop Road
Williamsburg, MA 01096

Wilson's Country House
P.O. Box 244
West Simsbury, CT 06092

Charles J. Winston
515 Madison Avenue
New York, NY 10022

Noel Wise Antiques
6503 St. Claude Avenue
Arabi, LA 70032

Richard W. Withington, Inc.
Hillsboro, NH 03244

Woodcraft Supply Corp.
313 Montvale Avenue
Woburn, MA 01801

Wood Mosaic
P.O. Box 21159
Louisville, KY 40221

Woodstock Soapstone Co., Inc.
Box 223
Woodstock, VT 05091

The Woodstone Co.
Westminster, VT 05158

The Woodworkers' Store
21801 Industrial Blvd.
Rogers, Minnesota 55374

World Imports
530 14th Street, N.W.
Atlanta, GA 30318

The Wrecking Bar
292 Moreland Avenue, N.E.
Atlanta, GA 30307

The Wrecking Bar
2601 McKinney Avenue
Dallas, TX 75204

Wrightsville Hardware
North Front Street
Wrightsville, PA 17368

Yankee Craftsman
357 Commonwealth Road
Wayland, MA 01778

Ye Olde Mantel Shoppe
3800 N.E. 2nd Avenue
Miami, FL 33137

York Spiral Stair
Main Street
North Vassalboro, ME 04962

Z-Brick Co.
Woodinville, WA 98072

Selected Bibliography

Primary Sources: Study of original works by past American architects, builders, designers, and architectural critics can provide more useful information than any other source. The amount of material available on Colonial-period homes is extremely limited today just as it was in the 1600s and 1700s. The design of such buildings may derive as much from English, French, German, or Spanish sources as it does from North American influences. After the early 1800s, books of house plans began to proliferate. Unfortunately, their republication has slowed in recent years after the issue of such basic volumes as Downing and Vaux. The reader is urged to consult Henry Russell Hitchcock's new expanded edition of *American Architectural Books* (Da Capo Press, 1976) which outlines in bibliographic form the wealth of material produced from the late 18th century to the year 1895. One hopes that this volume will be updated to include material through the 1930s.

Included in the following list are only volumes available in reprint form.

André, Daly fils et Cie. *American Victorian Architecture.* Reprint of the 1886 edition of *L'Architecture Américaine.* New York: Dover Publications, 1975.

Benjamin, Asher. *American Builder's Companion.* 1827 edition. New York: Dover Publications, 1969.

Bicknell, A. J. *Village Builder.* 1872 edition. Watkins Glen, N.Y.: The American Life Foundation & Study Institute, 1976.

Bicknell, A. J. and W. T. Comstock. *Victorian Architecture.* Reprints of Bicknell's *Detail, Cottage, and Constructive Architecture,* 1873, and Comstock's *Modern Architectural Designs and Details,* 1881. Watkins Glen, N.Y.: The American Life Foundation & Study Institute, 1978.

Downing, Andrew Jackson. *The Architecture of Country Houses.* 1850 edition. New York: Dover Publications, 1969.

Eastlake, Charles Lake. *Hints on Household Taste.* 4th revised edition, 1878. New York: Dover Publications, 1969.

Hussey, E. C. *Home Building.* 1876 edition. Watkins Glen, N.Y.: The American Life Foundation & Study Institute, 1976.

Moreland, Frank. *The Curtain-Maker's Handbook.* Originally published as *Practical Decorative Upholstery,* 1889. New York: E. P. Dutton, 1980.

Palliser, Palliser & Co. *Palliser's New Cottage Homes and Details.* 1887 edition. Watkins Glen, N.Y.: The American Life Foundation & Study Institute, n.d.

Scientific American. *American Victoriana.* San Francisco: Chronicle Books, 1980.

Vaux, Calvert. *Villas and Cottages.* 2nd edition, 1864. New York: Dover Publications, 1970.

Wharton, Edith and Ogden Codman, Jr. *The Decoration of Houses.* 1902 edition. New York: W. W. Norton & Co., 1978.

Woodward, George Everston. *Woodward's Architecture and Rural Art.* Volumes 1 and 2, 1867 and 1868, reprinted as one volume, 1978. Watkins Glen, N.Y.: American Life Foundation & Study Institute, 1978.

_____. *Woodward's Country Homes.* 1865 edition. Watkins Glen, N.Y.: The American Life Foundation & Study Institute, 1977.

Secondary Sources, Books: Within the past ten years more books on historic architecture and preservation have been published in North America than in any decade since the 1920s. Most are guides or histories of period styles, and some provide useful information for the home restorer seeking help with particular problems.

Blumenson, John J.-G. *Identifying American Architecture.* Nashville, Tenn.: American Association for State and Local History, 1977.

Condit, Carl. W. *American Building: Materials and Techniques from the First Colonial Settlement to the Present.* Chicago: University of Chicago Press, 1968.

Cooke, Lawrence S. *Lighting in America: From Colonial Rushlights to Victorian Chandeliers.* New York: A Main Street Press Book, Universe Books, 1976.

Early American Life Society. *The Architectural Treasures of Early America.* 8 vols. of the White Pine monographs edited and rearranged. New York: Arno Press, 1977.

Fowler, John and John Cornforth. *English Decoration in the Eighteenth Century.* London: Barrie & Jenkins, 1974.

Garrett, Elisabeth Donaghy. *American Interiors: Colonial and Federal Periods.* New York: Crown Publishers, 1980.

Grow, Lawrence. *The Old House Book of Bedrooms.* New York: Warner Books, 1980.

_____. *The Old House Book of Living Rooms and Parlors.* New York: Warner Books, 1980.

_____. *Old House Plans: Two Centuries of American Domestic Architecture.* New York: A Main Street Press Book, Universe Books, 1978.

Handlin, David P. *The American Home, Architecture and Society, 1815-1915.* Boston: Little, Brown and Co., 1979.

Harris, Cyril M., ed. *Historic Architecture Sourcebook.* New York: McGraw-Hill Book Co., 1977.

Hayward, Arthur H. *Colonial and Early American Lighting.* New York: Dover Publications, 1962.

Isham, Norman M. *Early American Houses and a Glossary of Colonial Architectural Terms.* New York: Da Capo Press, 1967.

Loth, Calder and Julius Toursdale Sadler, Jr. *The Only Proper Style: Gothic Architecture in America.* Boston: New York Graphic Society, 1975.

Maass, John. *The Victorian Home in America.* New York: Hawthorne Books, 1972.

Nylander, Jane C. *Fabrics for Historic Buildings.* Washington, D.C.: Preservation Press, 1977.

Page, Marian. *Historic Houses Restored and Preserved.* New York: Whitney Library of Design, 1976.

Peterson, Harold L. *American Interiors from Colonial Times to the Late Victorians.* New York: Charles Scribner's Sons, 1971.

Pierson, William H., Jr. *American Buildings and Their Architects: The Colonial and Neoclassical Style.* Garden City, N.Y.: Doubleday and Co., 1970.

Scully, Vincent. *American Architecture and Urbanism.* New York: Frederick Praeger, 1969.

Seale, William. *Recreating the Historic House Interior.* Nashville, Tenn.: American Association for State and Local History, 1979.

_____. *The Tasteful Interlude: American Interiors through the Camera's Eye.* New York: Praeger Publishers, 1975.

Stanford, Deirdre and Louis Reens. *Restored America.* New York: Praeger Publishers, 1975.

Stephen, George. *Remodeling Old Houses Without Destroying Their Character.* New York: Alfred A. Knopf, 1972.

Time-Life Books. *The Old House.* Alexandria, Va.: Time-Life Books, 1979.

Waring, Janet. *Early American Stencils on Walls and Furniture.* New York: Dover Publications, n.d.

Whiffen, Marcus. *American Architecture Since 1780.* Cambridge, Mass.: The M.I.T. Press, 1969.

Pamphlets, Leaflets, Brochures, and Other Specialized Literature:
There are three primary sources for this kind of material which is often directed to very specific problem areas. The office of Technical Preservation Services of the Heritage, Conservation, and Recreation Service (HCRS), Department of the Interior, Washington, DC 20243, is responsible for a continuing series of "Preservation Briefs," some of which are listed below. These may be obtained from the Information Exchange at HCRS. A second source is the American Association for State and Local History, 1315 Eighth Avenue, South, Nashville, TN 37203. The third is the Association for Preservation Technology. For a list of the titles available, one should write to the organization at Box 2487, Station D, Ottawa, Ontario K1P 5W6, Canada.

Brightman, Anna. "Window Treatments for Historic Houses, 1700-1850." Technical Leaflet No. 17. Washington, D.C.: National Trust for Historic Preservation, n.d.

Cummings, Abbott Lowell. *Bed Hangings: A Treatise on Fabrics and Styles in the Curtaining of Beds, 1650-1850.* Boston: The Society for the Preservation of New England Antiquities, 1961.

_____. *Rural Household Inventories Establishing the Names, Uses, and Furnishing of Rooms in the Colonial New England Home.* Boston: The Society for the Preservation of New England Antiquities, 1964.

Curtis, John Obed. "Moving Historic Buildings." Washington, D.C.: Heritage, Conservation, and Recreation Service, 1979.

Frangiamore, Catherine Lynn. "Wallpapers in Historic Preservation." Publication No. 185. Washington, D.C.: Office of Archeology and Historic Preservation, 1977.

_____. "Rescuing Historic Wallpaper: Identification, Preservation, Restoration." Technical Leaflet No. 76. Nashville, Tenn.: American Association for State and Local History, 1974.

Judd, Henry A. "Before Restoration Begins—Keeping Your Historic House Intact." Technical Leaflet No. 67. Nashville, Tenn.: American Association for State and Local History, 1973.

Little, Nina Fletcher. "Historic Houses: An Approach to Furnishing." Technical Leaflet No. 17. Nashville, Tenn.: American Association for State and Local History, 1970.

Mack, Robert G. "The Cleaning and Waterproof Coating of Masonry Buildings." Washington, D.C.: Heritage, Conservation, and Recreation Service, 1975.

_____. "Repointing Mortar Joints in Historic Brick Buildings." Washington, D.C.: Heritage, Conservation, and Recreation Service, 1976.

McKee, Harley J. *Introduction to Early American Masonry, Stone, Brick, Mortar, and Plaster.* Washington, D.C.: National Trust for Historic Preservation, 1973.

Myers, Denys Peter. "Gaslighting in America: A Guide for Historic Preservationists." Washington, D.C.: Heritage, Conservation, and Recreation Service, 1978.

Myers, John H. "Aluminum and Vinyl Sidings on Historic Buildings." Washington, D.C.: Heritage, Conservation, and Recreation Service, 1980.

Neblett, Nathaniel P. "Energy Conservation in Historic Homes." Washington, D.C.: Historic House Association of America, 1980.

Nielsen, Salley E. "Insulating the Old House." Portland, Maine: Greater Portland Landmarks, Inc., 1977.

"The Preservation of Historic Adobe Buildings." Washington, D.C.: Heritage, Conservation, and Recreation Service, 1978.

Smith, Baird M. "Conserving Energy in Historic Buildings." Washington, D.C.: Heritage, Conservation, and Recreation Service, 1978.

Sweetser, Sarah M. "Roofing for Historic Buildings." Washington, D.C.: Heritage, Conservation, and Recreation Service, 1978.

Weiss, Norman R. "Exterior Cleaning of Historic Masonry Buildings." Washington, D.C.: Heritage, Conservation, and Recreation Service, 1975.

Periodicals: A handful of magazines, almost all published on a bimonthly basis, devote much space to preservation topics. One of two monthlies, *The Magazine Antiques,* concentrates primarily on the decorative arts. Four of the publications are available only to members of two respective organizations: The National Trust for Historic Preservation (*Historic Preservation* and *Preservation News*) and The Victorian Society in America (*19th Century* and the Society's *Bulletin*). Membership fees are extremely reasonable and the publications are a bargain.

American Preservation (bimonthly)
P.O. Box 589
Martinsville, NJ 08836

Americana (bimonthly)
Americana Subscription Office
381 W. Center Street
Marion, OH 43302

Bulletin (monthly) and *19th Century* (bimonthly)
The Victorian Society in America
East Washington Square
Philadelphia, PA 19106

Colonial Homes (bimonthly)
P.O. Box 10159
Des Moines, IA 50350

Home Restoration (bimonthly)
P.O. Box 327
Gettysburg, PA 17325

The Magazine Antiques
551 Fifth Avenue
New York, NY 10017

Old-House Journal (monthly)
69A Seventh Avenue
Brooklyn, NY 11217

Preservation News (monthly) and *Historic Preservation* (bimonthly)
The National Trust for Historic Preservation
1785 Massachusetts Ave., N.W.
Washington, DC 20036

Standards for Rehabilitation & Guidelines for Rehabilitating Historic Buildings

While every old structure presents special problems to the restorer, there are general rules of an environmental nature, design, and construction which should be followed in any project. These have been most usefully codified by the United States Department of the Interior for the purpose of determining whether a particular restoration or rehabilitation project qualifies as a "certified rehabilitation" as called for by the Tax Reform Act of 1976 and the Revenue Act of 1978. Rehabilitation, itself, is defined as the "process of returning a property to a state of utility, through repair or alteration, which makes possible an efficient contemporary use while preserving those portions and features of the property which are significant to its historic, architectural, and cultural values." A better definition of the restoration/preservation/rehabilitation process would be difficult to articulate. The official "standards" and "guidelines" are similarly free of bureaucratic jargon and nonsense which render many government publications less than useful. Copies of this document may be secured from the Office of Archeology and Historic Preservation, Heritage Conservation and Recreation Service, U.S. Department of the Interior, Washington, D.C. 20240.

Standards for Rehabilitation

1. Every reasonable effort shall be made to provide a compatible use for a property which requires minimal alteration of the building, structure, or site and its environment, or to use a property for its originally intended purpose.

2. The distinguishing original qualities or character of a building, structure, or site and its environment shall not be destroyed. The removal or alteration of any historic material or distinctive architectural features should be avoided when possible.

3. All buildings, structures, and sites shall be recognized as products of their own time. Alterations that have no historical basis and which seek to create an earlier appearance shall be discouraged.

4. Changes which may have taken place in the course of time are evidence of the history and development of a building, structure, or site and its environment. These changes may have acquired significance in their own right, and this significance shall be recognized and respected.

5. Distinctive stylistic features or examples of skilled craftsmanship which characterize a building, structure, or site shall be treated with sensitivity.

6. Deteriorated architectural features shall be repaired rather than replaced, wherever possible. In the event replacement is necessary, the new material should match the material being replaced in composition, design, color, texture, and other visual qualities. Repair or replacement of missing architectural features should be based on accurate duplications of features, substantiated by historic, physical, or pictorial evidence rather than on conjectural designs or the availability of different architectural elements from other buildings or structures.

7. The surface cleaning of structures shall be undertaken with the gentlest means possible. Sandblasting and other cleaning methods that will damage the historic building materials shall not be undertaken.

8. Every reasonable effort shall be made to protect and preserve archeological resources affected by, or adjacent to any project.

9. Contemporary design for alterations and additions to existing properties shall not be discouraged when such alterations and additions do not destroy significant historical, architectural or cultural material, and such design is compatible with the size, scale, color, material, and character of the property, neighborhood or environment.

10. Wherever possible, new additions or alterations to structures shall be done in such a manner that if such additions or alterations were to be removed in the future, the essential form and integrity of the structure would be unimpaired.

Guidelines for Rehabilitating Historic Buildings

THE ENVIRONMENT

Recommended	*Not Recommended*
Retaining distinctive features such as the size, scale, mass, color, and materials of buildings, including roofs, porches, and stairways that give a neighborhood its distinguishing character.	Introducing new construction into neighborhoods that is incompatible with the character of the district because of size, scale, color, and materials.
Retaining landscape features such as parks, gardens, street lights, signs, benches, walkways, streets, alleys, and building set-backs that have traditionally linked buildings to their environment.	Destroying the relationship of buildings and their environment by widening existing streets, changing paving material, or by introducing inappropriately located new streets and parking lots that are incompatible with the character of the neighborhood.
Using new plant materials, fencing, walkways, street lights, signs, and benches that are compatible with the character of the neighborhood in size, scale, material and color.	Introducing signs, street lighting, benches, new plant materials, fencing, walkways and paving materials that are out of scale or inappropriate to the neighborhood.

BUILDING SITE

Recommended	*Not Recommended*
Identifying plants, trees, fencing, walkways, outbuildings, and other elements that might be an important part of the property's history and development.	
Retaining plants, trees, fencing, walkways, street lights, signs, and benches that reflect the property's history and development.	Making changes to the appearance of the site by removing old plants, trees, fencing, walkways, outbuildings, and other elements before evaluating their importance in the property's history and development.
Basing decisions for new site work on actual knowledge of the past appearance of the property found in photographs, drawings, newspapers, and tax records. If changes are made they should be carefully evaluated in light of the past appearance of the site.	Leaving plant materials and trees in close proximity to the building that may be causing deterioration of the historic fabric.
Providing proper site and roof drainage to assure that water does not splash against building or foundation walls, nor drain toward the building.	

Archeological features

Recommended	*Not Recommended*
Leaving known archeological resources intact.	Installing underground utilities, pavements, and other modern features that disturb archeological resources.
Minimizing disturbance of terrain around the structure, thus reducing the possibility of destroying unknown archeological resources.	Introducing heavy machinery or equipment into areas where their presence may disturb archeological resources.
Arranging for an archeological survey of all terrain that must be disturbed during the rehabilitation program. The survey should be conducted by a professional archeologist.	

BUILDING: STRUCTURAL SYSTEMS

Recommended	*Not Recommended*
Recognizing the special problems inherent in the structural systems of historic buildings, especially where there are visible signs of cracking, deflection, or failure.	Disturbing existing foundations with new excavations that undermine the structural stability of the building.
Undertaking stabilization and repair of weakened structural members and systems.	Leaving known structural problems untreated that will cause continuing deterioration and will shorten the life of the structure.
Replacing historically important structural members only when necessary. Supplementing existing structural systems when damaged or inadequate.	

BUILDING: EXTERIOR FEATURES

Masonry: Adobe, brick, stone, terra cotta, concrete, stucco and mortar

Recommended	*Not Recommended*
Retaining original masonry and mortar, whenever possible, without the application of any surface treatment.	Applying waterproof or water repellent coatings or surface consolidation treatments unless required to solve a specific technical problem that has been studied and identified. Coatings are frequently unnecessary, expensive, and can accelerate deterioration of the masonry.
Repointing only those mortar joints where there is evidence of moisture problems or when sufficient mortar is missing to allow water to stand in the mortar joint.	Repointing mortar joints that do not need repointing. Using electric saws and hammers to remove mortar can seriously damage the adjacent brick.
Duplicating old mortar in composition, color, and texture.	Repointing with mortar of high Portland cement content can often create a bond that is stronger than the building material. This can cause deterioration as a result of the differing coefficient of expansion and the differing porosity of the material and the mortar.
Duplicating old mortar in joint size, method of application, and joint profile.	Repointing with mortar joints of a differing size or joint profile, texture or color.
Repairing stucco with a stucco mixture that duplicates the original as closely as possible in appearance and texture.	
Cleaning masonry only when necessary to halt deterioration or to remove graffiti and stains and always with the gentlest method possible, such as low pressure water and soft natural bristle brushes.	Sandblasting, including dry and wet grit and other abrasives, brick or stone surfaces; this method of cleaning erodes the surface of the material and accelerates deterioration. Using chemical cleaning products that would have an adverse chemical reaction with the masonry materials, i.e., acid on limestone or marble.
Repairing or replacing, where necessary, deteriorated material with new material that duplicates the old as closely as possible.	Applying new material which is inappropriate or was unavailable when the building was constructed, such as artificial brick siding, artificial cast stone or brick veneer.
Replacing missing significant architectural features, such as cornices, brackets, railings, and shutters.	Removing architectural features such as cornices, brackets, railings, shutters, window architraves, and doorway pediments.
Retaining the original or early color and texture of masonry surfaces, including early signage wherever possible. Brick or stone surfaces may have been painted or whitewashed for practical and aesthetic reasons.	Removing paint from masonry surfaces indiscriminately. This may subject the building to damage and change its appearance.

Wood: Clapboard, weatherboard, shingles and other wooden siding

Recommended	*Not Recommended*
Retaining and preserving significant architectural features, whenever possible.	Removing architectural features such as siding, cornices, brackets, window architraves, and doorway pediments. These are, in most cases, an essential part of a building's character and appearance that illustrate the continuity of growth and change.
Repairing or replacing, where necessary, deteriorated material that duplicates in size, shape and texture the old as closely as possible.	Resurfacing frame buildings with new material that is inappropriate or was unavailable when the building was constructed such as artificial stone, brick veneer, asbestos or asphalt shingles, and plastic or aluminum siding. Such material can also contribute to the deterioration of the structure from moisture and insects.

Architectural Metals: Cast iron, steel, pressed tin, aluminum, zinc

Recommended	*Not Recommended*
Retaining original material, whenever possible.	Removing architectural features that are an essential part of a building's character and appearance, illustrating the continuity of growth and change.
Cleaning when necessary with the appropriate method. Metals should be cleaned by methods that do not abrade the surface.	Exposing metals which were intended to be protected from the environment. Do not use cleaning methods which alter the color, texture, and tone of the metal.

Roofs and Roofing

Recommended	*Not Recommended*
Preserving the original roof shape.	Changing the essential character of the roof by adding inappropriate features such as dormer windows, vents, or skylights.
Retaining the original roofing material, whenever possible.	Applying new roofing material that is inappropriate to the style and period of the building and neighborhood.
Providing adequate roof drainage and insuring that the roofing materials provide a weathertight covering for the structure.	
Replacing deteriorated roof coverings with new material that matches the old in composition, size, shape, color, and texture.	Replacing deteriorated roof coverings with new materials that differ to such an extent from the old in composition, size, shape, color, and texture that the appearance of the building is altered.
Preserving or replacing, where necessary, all architectural features that give the roof its essential character, such as dormer windows, cupolas, cornices, brackets, chimneys, cresting, and weather vanes.	Stripping the roof of architectural features important to its character.

Windows and Doors

Recommended	*Not Recommended*
Retaining and replacing existing window and door openings including window sash, glass, lintels, sills, architraves, shutters, doors, pediments, hoods, steps, and all hardware.	Introducing new window and door openings into the principal elevations, or enlarging or reducing window or door openings to fit new stock window sash or new stock door sizes.
	Altering the size of window panes or sash. Such changes destroy the scale and proportion of the building.
Duplicating the material, design, and the hardware of the older window sash and doors if new sash and doors are used.	Installing inappropriate new window or door features such as aluminum storm and screen window insulating glass combinations that require the removal of original windows and doors.
Installing visually unobtrusive storm windows and doors, where needed, that do not damage existing frames and that can be removed in the future.	Installing plastic, canvas, or metal strip awnings or fake shutters that detract from the character and appearance of the building.
Using original doors and door hardware when they can be repaired and reused in place.	Discarding original doors and door hardware when they can be repaired and reused in place.

Entrances, porches, and steps

Recommended	*Not Recommended*
Retaining porches and steps that are appropriate to the building and its development. Porches or additions reflecting later architectural styles are often important to the building's historical integrity and, wherever possible, should be retained.	Removing or altering porches and steps that are appropriate to the building's development and style.
Repairing or replacing, where necessary, deteriorated architectural features of wood, iron, cast iron, terra cotta, tile, and brick.	Stripping porches and steps of original material and architectural features, such as hand rails, balusters, columns, brackets, and roof decoration of wood, iron, cast iron, terra cotta, tile, and brick.
	Enclosing porches and steps in a manner that destroys their intended appearance.

Exterior Finishes

Recommended	*Not Recommended*
Discovering the historic paint colors and finishes of the structure and repainting with those colors to illustrate the distinctive character of the property.	Removing paint and finishes down to the bare surface; strong paint strippers whether chemical or mechanical can permanently damage the surface. Also, stripping obliterates evidence of the historical paint finishes.
	Repainting with colors that cannot be documented through research and investigation to be appropriate to the building and neighborhood.

BUILDING: INTERIOR FEATURES

Recommended	*Not Recommended*
Retaining original material, architectural features, and hardware, whenever possible, such as stairs, elevators, hand rails, balusters, ornamental columns, cornices, baseboards, doors, doorways, windows, mantel pieces, paneling, lighting fixtures, parquet or mosaic flooring.	Removing original material, architectural features, and hardware, except where essential for safety or efficiency.
	Replacing interior doors and transoms without investigating alternative fire protection measures or possible code variances.
Repairing or replacing, where necessary, deteriorated material with new material that duplicates the old as closely as possible.	Installing new decorative material and paneling which destroys significant architectural features or was unavailable when the building was constructed, such as vinyl plastic or imitation wood wall and floor coverings, except in utility areas such as bathrooms and kitchens.
Retaining original plaster, whenever possible.	Removing plaster to expose brick to give the wall an appearance it never had.
Discovering and retaining original paint colors, wallpapers and other decorative motifs or, where necessary, replacing them with colors, wallpapers or decorative motifs based on the original.	Changing the texture and patina of exposed wooden architectural features (including structural members) and masonry surfaces through sandblasting or use of other abrasive techniques to remove paint, discoloration and plaster, except in certain industrial or warehouse buildings where the interior masonry or plaster surfaces do not have significant design, detailing, tooling, or finish; and where wooden architectural features are not finished, molded, beaded, or worked by hand.
Where required by code, enclosing an important interior stairway in such a way as to retain its character. In many cases glazed fire rated walls may be used.	Enclosing important stairways with ordinary fire rated construction which destroys the architectural character of the stair and the space.
Retaining the basic plan of a building, the relationship and size of rooms, corridors, and other spaces.	Altering the basic plan of a building by demolishing principal walls, partitions, and stairways.

NEW CONSTRUCTION

Recommended	*Not Recommended*
Keeping new additions and adjacent new construction to a minimum, making them compatible in scale, building materials, and texture.	
Designing new work to be compatible in materials, size, scale, color, and texture with the earlier building and the neighborhood.	Designing new work which is incompatible with the earlier building and the neighborhood in materials, size, scale, and texture.
Using contemporary designs compatible with the character and mood of the building or the neighborhood.	Imitating an earlier style or period of architecture in new additions, except in rare cases where a contemporary design would detract from the architectural unity of an ensemble or group. Especially avoid imitating an earlier style of architecture in new additions that have a completely contemporary function such as a drive-in bank or garage.
	Adding new height to the building that changes the scale and character of the building. Additions in height should not be visible when viewing the principal facades.
	Adding new floors or removing existing floors that destroy important architectural details, features and spaces of the building.
Protecting architectural details and features that contribute to the character of the building.	
Placing television antennae and mechanical equipment, such as air conditioners, in an inconspicuous location.	Placing television antennae and mechanical equipment, such as air conditioners, where they can be seen from the street.

MECHANICAL SYSTEMS: HEATING, AIR CONDITIONING, ELECTRICAL, PLUMBING, FIRE PROTECTION

Recommended	*Not Recommended*
Installing necessary mechanical systems in areas and spaces that will require the least possible alteration to the structural integrity and physical appearance of the building.	Causing unncessary damage to the plan, materials, and appearance of the building when installing mechanical systems.
Utilizing early mechanical systems, including plumbing and early lighting fixtures, where possible.	Attaching exterior electrical and telephone cables to the principal elevations of the building.
Installing the vertical runs of ducts, pipes, and cables in closets, service rooms, and wall cavities.	Installing the vertical runs of ducts, pipes, and cables in places where they will be a visual intrusion.
	Concealing or "making invisible" mechanical equipment in historic walls or ceilings. Frequently this concealment requires the removal of historic fabric.
	Installing "dropped" acoustical ceilings to hide mechanical equipment. This destroys the proportions and character of the rooms.
Insuring adequate ventilation of attics, crawlspaces, and cellars to prevent moisture problems.	
Installing thermal insulation in attics and in unheated cellars and crawlspaces to conserve energy.	Installing foam, glass fiber, or cellulose insulation into wall cavities of either wooden or masonry construction. This has been found to cause moisture problems when there is no adequate moisture barrier.

SAFETY AND CODE REQUIREMENTS

Recommended	*Not Recommended*
Complying with code requirements in such a manner that the essential character of a building is preserved intact.	
Working with local code officials to investigate alternative life safety measures that preserve the architectural integrity of the building.	
Investigating variances for historic properties allowed under some local codes.	
Installing adequate fire prevention equipment in a manner that does minimal damage to the appearance or fabric of a property.	
Adding new stairways and elevators that do not alter existing exit facilities or other important architectural features and spaces of the building.	Adding new stairways and elevators that alter existing exit facilities or important architectural features and spaces of the building.

Index

People who live in and love old houses (or new houses in a traditional style) are constantly searching for ideas, products, and services to improve their homes.

In our effort to bring you the best possible information on old houses, we hope you will share your expertise with us. We would like to know what products or services you would recommend that we might consider for inclusion in the next edition of THE BRAND NEW OLD HOUSE CATALOGUE. And we hope you will let us know what titles would be helpful additions to our OLD HOUSE series.

Please send your recommendations to: Lawrence Grow, c/o Special Sales Department, Warner Books, 75 Rockefeller Plaza, New York, N.Y. 10019.

THE OLD HOUSE BOOKS
Edited by Lawrence Grow

THE BRAND NEW OLD HOUSE CATALOGUE
3,000 Completely New and Useful Products, Services, and Suppliers for Restoring, Decorating, and Furnishing the Period House—From Early American to 1930s Modern
#97-557   224 pages $9.95 in quality paperback; $17.95 in hardcover

THE OLD HOUSE BOOK OF BEDROOMS
96 pages, including 32 color pages
#97-553 $7.95 in quality paperback; $15.00 in hardcover

THE OLD HOUSE BOOK OF LIVING ROOMS AND PARLORS
96 pages, including 32 color pages
#97-552 $7.95 in quality paperback; $15.00 in hardcover

Forthcoming:
THE OLD HOUSE BOOK OF OUTDOOR LIVING SPACES
THE OLD HOUSE BOOK OF DINING ROOMS AND KITCHENS
THE OLD HOUSE BOOK OF HALLS AND STAIRCASES

Look for these books in your favorite bookstore. If you can't find them, you may order directly by sending your check or money order for the retail price of the book plus 50¢ per order and 50¢ per book to cover postage and handling to: Warner Books, P.O. Box 690, New York, N.Y. 10019. N.Y. State and California residents, please add sales tax.